MEDIUMS, MYSTICS & THE OCCULT

BOOKS BY MILBOURNE CHRISTOPHER

ESP, Seers & Psychics
Houdini: The Untold Story
The Illustrated History of Magic
Mediums, Mystics & the Occult

MILBOURNE CHRISTOPHER

MEDIUMS, MYSTICS & THE OCCULT

THOMAS Y. CROWELL COMPANY
New York   Established 1834

The illustrations used in this book are from the author's collection.

Designed by Abigail Moseley

Manufactured in the United States of America

ISBN 0-690-00476-1

1 2 3 4 5 6 7 8 9 10

Library of Congress Cataloging in Publication Data

Christopher, Milbourne.
  Mediums, mystics & the occult.

  Bibliography: p.
  Includes index.
  1. Psychical research. 2. Occult sciences.
3. Mysticism—East (Far East) I. Title.
BF1031.C53   133.8   74-26812
ISBN 0-690-00476-1

For Ding

who for more than half a century has tried to convince credulous investigators that a knowledge of conjuring is essential for their probes of unexplained psychical phenomena

CONTENTS

ILLUSTRATIONS

Following page 161

Photographing the dead—Abraham Lincoln appears with Houdini

William Stead and a ghostly visitor

Beatrice Houdini's letter of February 9, 1928, to Arthur Ford

The statement Mrs. Houdini signed for Ford's friends in 1929, and evidence of her physical condition at the time of the Ford séance

Houdini and Argamasilla, the man who could "see" through metal

John Mulholland, demonstrating how mediums can switch slates

Two views of a sword penetrating the body of Mirin Dajo

Self-impalement exhibited by Yogi Rayo, an Austrian fakir

Following page 233

Margery, the Boston medium, ringing a bell box and lifting a table with her head

How, according to Houdini, Margery caused a megaphone to "fly" and upset a threefold screen

Satirical handbill found among Houdini's papers after his death in 1926

Two views of alleged psychic hand produced by Margery

Two types of "ectoplasm" produced by Margery

One of Margery's early "spirit" gloves, a cast of a bare "spirit" foot made years before by a British medium, and proof that the "spirit" thumbprints of Margery's dead brother were those of a living man

Der Spiegel cover of Uri Geller

Advertisement for a Geller show in Washington, D.C.; the psychic and Dr. Andrija Puharich, his American sponsor

MEDIUMS, MYSTICS & THE OCCULT

A NEW AGE OF MIRACLES

Apartment keys bend and spoons sometimes break when Uri Geller, an intense young mystic from Tel Aviv, stares at them and strokes them. Psychic surgeons in Brazil and the Philippines make incisions without scalpels, remove tumors in seconds, and cause the skin to heal instantly. An astronaut who has made headlines with an ESP test en route to the moon endorses Geller and mental healing. Blindfolded psychics in the Soviet Union and the United States identify colors and read with their fingertips.

Has the world gone mad, or are we on the threshold of an age of miracles? Academic interest mounts in subjects once scoffed at on the campus. More than a hundred American colleges now offer courses in parapsychology, and readers of the British journal *New Scientist* said in answer to a query that they believe by a preponderance of more than 70 percent that ESP is possible, even if not yet proved conclusively.

Books on mediums, mystics, and psychics who claim supernormal powers are read avidly by a confused public seeking to learn more about phenomena that seem contrary to the laws of nature and bewilder scientists.

Time's cover story for March 4, 1974, heralded "Boom Times on the Psychic Frontier." *Newsweek*'s issue of the same date, in a feature article on "Parapsychology: The Science of the Uncanny," said advocates of mind-over-mind and mind-over-matter theories "seem to be making steady progress in their battle to convince the scientific establishment that there is at least something in their research that is worth investigating."

The saga of the earliest "scientific" examinations of mediums is a depressing one; honest investigators were frequently taken in by the tricks of skilled deceptionists.

The spread of modern spiritualism can be dated to the night of March 31, 1848, when two little girls, Margaret and Kate Fox (their exact age is still a matter of controversy), who lived with their parents in a small Hydesville, New York, farmhouse called on an invisible "Mr. Splitfoot" to answer their questions after they went to bed. The mysterious raps they received in reply created a sensation.

When Margaret went to stay with Leah Fox Fish, her much older married sister in Rochester, New York, Leah discovered that she, too, could communicate with the spirits and conduct séances that the public could attend for a fee.

Interest in the new "spiritual telegraph" reached such a pitch that the citizens of Rochester investigated the phenomena at Corinthian Hall on the evening of November 14, 1849. A conscientious committee reported they could find no explanation for the strange sounds. A second Rochester group, made up of Frederick Whittlesey, vice-chancellor of the state of New York; H. H. Langworthy, a physician; William Fisher, an attorney; A. P. Haskell, a judge; and D. C. McCallum, a businessman, tested the sisters the following day. Whittlesey resigned while the tests were in progress, but the other investigators agreed that they had been completely mystified.

A third committee, which included Leonard Kenyon, a skeptic who asserted he would leap into the rapids just above Niagara Falls if he did not detect the secret, was as perplexed as the first two had been. There is no record, however, of Kenyon jumping into the rapids.

Margaret and Leah capitalized on the publicity they had received and went on tour. Three University of Buffalo physicians—Austin Flint, Charles A. Lee, and C. B. Coventry—visited the room at the Phelps House hotel where the mediums were holding séances in February 1851. Believing a public statement might "serve to prevent further waste of time, money and credulity, to say nothing of sentiment and philosophy, in connection with this so long successful imposition," the doctors sent a report of their investigation to the *Commercial Advertiser*.

They said they had followed a system that had proven practical in diagnosing diseases. It was obvious to them the knocking noises were not caused by special equipment or machinery; the raps were heard in any room in which the mediums were present.

> On carefully observing the countenances of the two females, it was evident that the sounds were due to the agency of the younger sister, and that they involved an effort of will. She evidently attempted to conceal an indication of voluntary effort, but in this she did not succeed. A voluntary effort was manifest, and it was plain that it could not be continued very long without fatigue.

Having decided the sounds were not vocal, the investigators centered their attention on muscular contractions; they concluded the noises came from one of the bodily joints. The doctors had examined another woman who produced similar raps by clicking two bones in her knee; they reasoned Margaret Fox used the same technique. They were not right, but they were close.

By 1857, so many fantastic accounts had been printed about the marvels of American mediums that the *Boston Courier* offered a prize of five hundred dollars to anyone able to produce authentic phenomena. Three Harvard professors—Benjamin Peirce, Louis Agassiz, Eben Horsford—and Benjamin A. Gould, an astronomer who lived in Cambridge, served as judges. The contestants were Catherine (Kate) Fox and her sister Leah; the Davenport Brothers, two young men from Buffalo, who caused spirit hands to materialize and musical instruments to play while they were tied in a wardrobe-like cabinet; a Mrs. Kendrick and J. V. Mansfield, two specialists in producing written spirit messages; and George Redmond, a versatile psychic, who was reputed to be adept in several phases of spiritualist phenomena.

For three days in June the investigating committee studied the contestants; then they reported in the *Courier* that no one had "communicated a word imparted to the spirits in an adjoining room . . . read a word in English written inside a book or folded sheet of paper . . . answered any question 'which the superior intelligence must be able to answer' . . . tilted a piano without touching it or caused a chair to move a foot."

Having failed to demonstrate any "force which technically could be denominated 'spiritual' or which was hitherto unknown to science, or a phenomenon of which the cause was not palpable to the committee," the judges said none of the participants in the contest merited the award.

The committee further stated, "Any connection with spiritualistic circles, so called, corrupts the morals and degrades the intellect. They therefore deem it their solemn duty to warn the community against this contaminating influence which surely tends to lessen the truth of men and the purity of women."

Although this pronouncement infuriated mediums, it markedly increased their business. Contrary to the hopes of the committee, droves of sensation-seekers attended séances to find out for themselves what really happened during a sitting.

The first sizable sum of money for psychical research given to a center of advanced learning in the United States came from Henry Seybert, a Philadelphia philanthropist and a firm believer in communication with the dead. Shortly before he died in 1883, Seybert offered the University of Pennsylvania sixty thousand dollars with the proviso that it establish a chair of moral and intellectual philosophy and arrange for a faculty committee "to make a thorough and impartial investigation of all systems of Morals, Religion or Philosophy which assume to represent the Truth, and particularly of Modern Spiritualism."

The Seybert Commission began its work in March 1884 with Dr. William Pepper, the university provost, as ex officio chairman. Dr. Horace Howard Furness, the acting chairman, and Professor George S. Fullerton, the secretary, consulted with Thomas H. Hazard, a close friend of the late benefactor and himself a spiritualist.

Hazard recommended Mrs. S. E. Patterson, a prominent Philadelphia medium, as the first subject. Her specialty—spirit messages on slates. Hazard said he had recently received several messages from Seybert through her mediumship. The investigators had been told that the communications were written on the inner surfaces of two blank slates after they had been tied or otherwise fastened together, so they offered Mrs. Patterson a pair of hinged slates. The medium bit off a small piece of her soapstone pencil, assuring the committee that this gave it more spiritual power, then put the fragment between the two slates. She did not object when members of the committee screwed the two free sides of the slates together. According to the *Preliminary Report* of the Seybert Commission, published in 1887, the medium held the slates under a table, as was her custom, and waited for the spirits to write. After an hour and a half with no response from the dead, the first session ended. Hazard was chagrined. Not only had the medium never failed before, but she generally produced many messages each day for her regular clients.

When a second Patterson sitting, lasting eighty minutes, proved to be as unproductive as the first, the committee arranged for the most famous "slate" medium on record—"Dr." Henry Slade to come from New York for their observation.

Slade, an American, had performed in Australia, Great Britain, and on the European continent. While in St. Petersburg, he amazed Grand Duke Constantine. Slade held a single slate beneath a table. Rasping sounds indicated that two messages were being written down simultaneously. Sure enough, when the slate was brought into the light, there were two inscriptions: one reading from left to right, the other in the reverse direction.

Slade's staunchest supporter, Johann K. F. Zöllner, professor of physics and astronomy at the University of Leipzig, told of even more incredible feats by Slade in his book *Transcendental Physics*—surely the strangest work ever written on the subject. (The English translation by Charles Charlton Massey was published in 1881.) In addition to producing written messages from the dead, Zöllner said, Slade was able to pass a solid wooden ring onto the solid wooden leg of a table and to tie knots in a cord after the ends had been tied and fastened with sealing wax. Zöllner's theory: the medium took the objects into the fourth dimension.

The Seybert Commission did not share this opinion. They said Slade's Philadelphia séances were "fraudulent throughout." No elaborate laboratory devices were needed for them to reach this decision: "close observation was all that was required."

Slade used several methods. It was apparent almost at once that when a long message was produced, the words were carefully inscribed and the sentences were properly punctuated, while replies to questions asked during the sitting were terse, scrawled, and "scarcely legible." Slade switched a prepared slate (one on which he had written earlier) for an examined one in the first instance; in the second, he wrote with a small concealed bit of soapstone as he held the slate with his hand under a table.

When a prepared slate was brought into play, Slade counterfeited the noise of invisible forces writing by scratching the slate with his fingernail.

Harry Kellar, the great American magician of his time, was playing in Philadelphia during the investigation. At the request of a committee member, he gave the group a private show. The illusionist materialized words in Spanish, English, French, Chinese, Gujerti, and Japanese on slates brought by the investigators without anyone detecting trickery. The purpose of this demonstration, Kellar said later, was to prove that men who were experts in academic fields could be deceived if they didn't know the secrets of conjuring.

One of the founders of modern spiritualism came to Philadelphia at the committee's request: Margaret Fox who now called herself Margaret Fox Kane had married the Arctic explorer Elisha Kent Kane in their own ceremony without benefit of civil or church authority. Kane died in 1857. Nine years later she told of their romance in her book, *Memoir and the Love-Life of Doctor Kane: Containing the Correspondence, and a History of the Acquaintance, Engagement and Secret Marriage between Elisha K. Kane and Margaret Fox*. In one of Kane's letters, he had pleaded: "Do avoid the 'spirits.' I cannot bear to think of you as engaged in this course of wickedness and deception. . . . I can't bear the idea of your sitting in the dark, squeezing other people's hands."

Undeterred by her dead spouse's wish, Margaret sat motionless behind a table or stood by the door of a bookcase in Philadelphia as raps sounded. When she balanced herself on four heavy glass tumblers that had been placed mouth down on the floor, there was silence. Another evening she again stood on the

glasses, and faint knocks were heard. She permitted committeeman Furness to touch her feet as the raps came. He reported,
"I distinctly feel them in your feet. There is not a particle of mo-
tion in your foot, but there is an unusual pulsation."

Alleged messages transmitted from the dead by Margaret
Fox Kane, Henry Slade, and other psychics tested by the
members of the Seybert Commission were found lacking in substance. In their *Preliminary Report* the committeemen said they
"had not been cheered . . . by the discovery of a single novel
fact." Though it was their announced intention to continue the
investigation, this was the only report ever issued.

Margaret herself explained the pulsations noted in her feet a
year after the Seybert-sponsored study was published. A sensational story appeared on September 24, 1888, in the *New York
Herald* under the following heading:

"GOD HAS NOT ORDERED IT."

A Celebrated Medium Says
the Spirits Never Return.

CAPTAIN KANE'S WIDOW,
*One of the Fox Sisters,
Promises an Interesting
Exposure of Fraud.*

A reporter had visited the "small, magnetic" middle-aged
medium in her rooms on West 44 Street in New York City. Emo-
tionally overwrought, Margaret told the story of her tragic life,
breaking off occasionally to sit at a piano "and pour forth fitful
floods of wild, incoherent melody."

Margaret called Leah, her older sister, "her damnable
enemy." She said she hated her: "My God, I'd poison her! No, I
wouldn't, but I'll lash her with my tongue. She was twenty-three
years old the day I was born. . . . Ha! Ha!" Trying to explain
why she was so furious, the medium continued:

When Spiritualism first began Kate and I were little children, and
this old woman, my older sister, made us her tools. Mother was a
silly woman. She was a fanatic. I call her that because she was
honest. She believed in these things. . . . We were but innocent
little children. What did we know? Ah, we grew to know too much!

Our sister used us in her exhibitions and we made money for her. Now she turns on us because she's the wife of a rich man. . . . Oh, I am after her! You can kill sometimes without using weapons, you know.

In this article and subsequent ones Margaret recalled how she and her younger sister had tied a string to an apple and bumped the apple on the floor by their bed to make the first spirit raps. Then, when members of the community came to their house, the girls discovered a new way to produce noises—by snapping their toes against the lower end of their wooden bed. She said she would show the public how they had been cheating at the New York Academy of Music on Sunday evening, October twenty-first.

"Is it all a trick?" the *Herald* reporter asked as Margaret took him to the door. "Absolutely," she replied, and gazing into space, she posed her own question: "Spirits, is he not easily fooled?" Three raps of confirmation sounded on the door.

Newsmen who attempted to get Margaret's older sister's side of the story were told by her maid that Leah had suddenly left town; no one knew when she would return.

The Academy of Music was jammed for the much-publicized exposure. If there were not more believers than skeptics in the audience, there were at least as many. When Dr. C. M. Richmond, a dentist and an amateur conjurer, and Frank W. Stechan, a theatre manager, demonstrated and explained how messages appeared on blank slates and how tables tilted, the *Evening Post* reported the following day that the believers "gave vent to their disapproval by hisses and groans."

A murmur swept through the auditorium as Margaret, dressed in black, came onstage from the wings. Too nervous to speak distinctly enough to be heard, she soon slipped off her right shoe and put her foot on a wooden stool.

"The entire house became breathlessly still," the *World* reported, "and was rewarded by a number of little, short, sharp raps—those mysterious sounds which have for forty years frightened and bewildered hundreds of thousands of people in this country and in Europe." Three doctors had volunteered to study the movements of Margaret's foot. They agreed that the sounds were made by the snapping "action of the first joint of her large toe."

Margaret's sister Kate sat in a box adjacent to the stage that night. Less than two weeks before, she too had stated in print: "Spiritualism is a humbug from beginning to end. It is the greatest humbug of the century."

On one of my first trips to New York I met the man who had gone on tour with Margaret after her appearance at the Academy of Music. Elmer P. Ransom, then a young magician, had presented the show, comprised for the most part of his duplication of current spiritualistic feats. The climax came when Margaret put her foot on a sounding board and demonstrated how she made the raps. Ransom's wife, whom I met later, could snap her big toe in exactly the same way.

I asked Ransom how Margaret had caused the raps to sound on walls and doors. "Women wore floor-length dresses in those days," he explained. "She pulled her right foot from her shoe under the cover of the dress, then bent her leg so her foot touched the wall or door as she stood before it, facing the sitters."

The tour had been shorter than planned, Ransom added, since believers created disturbances in most of the halls where they played. Moreover, Mrs. Kane, while sober on stage, drank so heavily at other times he was relieved when they went their separate ways.

While Margaret Fox Kane's theatrical career had been brief, that of the Davenport Brothers—the most successful stage mediums of their era—spanned more than half a century. Ira Erastus Davenport and his younger brother, William Henry Harrison Davenport, as boys had learned how to release their hands after their wrists had been tied together with ropes. Upon freeing their hands, they played guitars and other musical instruments, then replaced their hands in the original knotted loops.

They performed first in the dark parlor of their Buffalo, New York, home. When they went on the road, they carried with them a large wooden box, similar to a three-door clothes' cabinet. Sitting facing one another on planks that had been firmly nailed in place inside this structure at the opposite ends, they permitted volunteers to tie their hands together behind their backs, then to run the ends of the ropes through holes in the planks and bind their ankles in the same way.

Yet almost as soon as the three front doors had been closed, "spirit" hands waved out through the diamond-shaped apertures in the doors, and bells, tambourines, and stringed instruments, which had been placed inside the cabinet with the brothers, began to sound.

According to a letter written years later by Ira Davenport to Houdini, the brothers became professionals in 1855. This and other Davenport correspondence in my collection enables me to fill in hitherto unpublished facts about their travels. A strong attraction from the start, they added William M. Fay, another Buffalo medium, to their staff, and after establishing their reputation in the United States, sailed for England in 1864. Their "Startling Wonders" stirred up controversy in London; in Liverpool an angry mob stormed the stage. This outburst, Ira said, was provoked by "professional jealousy, religious prejudice and anti-American feelings." There were also disturbances in Huddersfield and Leeds, and they were taunted on the streets by such cries as "Yankee Doodle, Barnum's Humbug and Yankee Swindle."

Magicians Tolmaque, Sutton, Redmond, Iawaka, and John Henry Anderson—one of the greatest British showmen—added cabinet séances to their routines. Though none of these performers could equal the Davenports in their specialty, the brothers crossed the channel to Paris. Again there was opposition, this time from Henri Robin, a popular conjurer who also had a cabinet built so he could present their marvels. Despite an attempt by antagonists to sabotage their opening at the Salle Hertz, the French emperor summoned the Americans to the palace at Saint Cloud for a command performance, and during the four years they were abroad, they appeared for the Russian czar, the Prussian king, and other monarchs.

Fay left the troupe after their return to the United States to tour in South America with magician Harry Kellar, who had joined the brothers as a ticket taker and then became their advance agent.

Rather than compete with Kellar and Fay in South America, the Davenports performed in the principal islands of the Caribbean in the spring of 1874, then returned to France that November. After touring Spain, Portugal, Belgium, Switzerland, and Italy, they traveled around the world, amazing audiences in Egypt, India, New Zealand, Tasmania, and Australia. This venture, Ira Davenport said, took about three years and seven months.

William Davenport died in Australia in 1877; Ira came back to his home in Mayville, New York. Occasionally, with another partner, he appeared in Boston, Washington, and various cities of Pennsylvania, as well as in nearby Buffalo. He toured Jamaica and Cuba in 1906, and gave his last public show on November 19, 1906, for "a regiment of Uncle Sam's boys four miles from Santiago de Cuba."

Houdini visited the old showman at Mayville in July 1911. Ira explained to the young escapologist the rope tie he had used in his cabinet. Houdini tells about this in his book *A Magician Among the Spirits,* published in 1924.

For many years Kellar, the magician who had worked with the Davenport Brothers and Fay, featured their cabinet séance. John Nevil Maskelyne, who later became one of Britain's greatest illusionists, started in show business as an "Anti-Spiritualist," offering a near facsimile of the Davenport act.

Maskelyne, Kellar, and Houdini crusaded in their day against psychic fraud. As a professional magician and as the chairman of the Society of American Magicians Occult Investigation Committee, during my travels in North and South America and in the British Isles, Europe, and Asia, I have seen many of the marvels that parapsychologists say "need further study."

As a youngster, I read books on black magic and occultism in addition to those on conjuring—legitimate deception presented as entertainment. Reginald Scot's epic *Discovery of Witchcraft,* published in London in 1584, included descriptions of the methods of sleight-of-hand performers, who claimed no supernormal powers.

I tried the tricks Scot explained with cups and balls, coins, cords, and cards; they worked. When I recited the witches' charms and incantations quoted by Scot and other writers, nothing happened. I avidly read newspaper accounts of Harry Price's black magic ritual on Mount Brocken in Germany in 1932. Price, the most prominent investigator of psychical phenomena in Britain, followed the instructions given in an ancient manual to learn if he, with the assistance of a virgin girl, could change a goat into a handsome young man. The goat was covered with a cloth as the incantation was pronounced. The cloth was pulled away. Under it was . . . the goat! I noted Price had not conformed strictly to the mystical formula. The rite should be carried out while a full moon illuminates the mountain; that night dark clouds obscured it.

I visited the city editor of the Baltimore *Evening Sun* and said I would like to try a similar experiment in the city's Druid Hill Park. He was intrigued by the notion. If I would supply the virgin girl and the goat, he would arrange for three professors from Johns Hopkins University to act as an observing committee. The professors agreed to participate. I found a goat and was looking for a girl "pure in heart" when I remembered that the ancient formula Price had used was taken from a manual in his collection in England. I searched for a similar incantation in old books at the Enoch Pratt Free Library, at the Peabody Institute, and at Johns Hopkins. No luck.

I called the Library of Congress in Washington and was referred to V. Valta Parma, the curator of rare books. Yes, he said, there were several ancient volumes of black magic in the rare book collection. I took the early train to Washington the next morning. Parma, a short man with swarthy skin, wearing an open-neck sports shirt and a dark tie, greeted me cordially. He was less receptive when I told him the use I planned to make of the goat-to-man incantation.

Black magic, he solemnly assured me, was a viable force in the modern world. We had lunch in the library restaurant, then returned to his book-lined office.

For four hours the custodian of a trove of exceedingly hard-to-find volumes told me of his experiences in the occult. As a young man, Parma had made contact with the spirit world by means of a Ouija board. After arduous study, he became proficient in summoning demons. Once, when he lived in a cottage in the Black Forest of Germany, he had foolishly called on a fire demon when the leaves he had raked on the lawn were burning slowly. Instantly mighty flames leaped up and almost destroyed the cottage.

It was eerie, sitting in one of the great libraries of the world, a monument to mankind's quest for learning, listening to an apparently intelligent man tell stories more fantastic than those printed in the pages of *Weird Tales,* a then popular pulp magazine.

It was clear that Parma was serious. He was trying to convince me that occultism was not to be taken lightly. He began to talk of elemental spirits, invisible but powerful forces from another world. A few years before, Parma said, he had dropped a gold collar button as he tried to fit it into his starched dress shirt before a dinner party. When he reached for it, a prankish spirit swept it under the bed. Evil spirits, he continued, were responsible for what many people thought were suicides. Parma leaned across his desk. Had I read about the wave of recent suicides? I had. He smiled. In many instances, he asserted, those accounted suicides had not jumped from the windows of tall buildings. They had been pushed from behind by invisible, malignant forces.

When I reminded him of the purpose of my visit, my wish to find a goat-to-man incantation and ritual, Parma was quiet for several long seconds. It would take time, he said, to find the proper spell. He took my address and said he would write to me.

Many months went by before an envelope from the Library of Congress turned up in my mail. I ripped it open. The letter inside was dated February 9, 1933.

Dear Mr. Christopher:
You probably have been wondering why you have not heard from me, but the fact is I have been unable to outline any program that would be at all constructive. . . . From your conversation with me, you will understand why I would not wish to have any part in such an experiment as you are contemplating and hope you will plan to give it up. Probably you noticed in this morning's Washington *Post* and probably Baltimore papers the account of the murder of an elderly woman resulting from such dabbling in medieval superstitions, as that which you are proposing. Some such tragedy is

the inevitable result of dabbling in matters, the laws of which are unknown.

Sincerely,

V. Valta Parma
Curator, Rare Book Collection

By the time I received this letter there was no longer a news peg for a goat-to-man witchcraft experiment in Baltimore. Though I have since read the spell Price used on Mount Brocken, I have never put the words to test.

My own viewpoint on the occult is not that of V. Valta Parma. I believe every area of mysticism should be investigated. The more we know about "medieval superstitions," the better. That is the purpose of this book; to give those not familiar with deceptive techniques a better understanding of what too often are called "unexplained phenomena."

LLER —
ER METAL

An ep   ending broke out in Britain in November 197   twenty-six-year-old guest on "Talk-
In," a popula   w, stared fixedly at a fork, rubbed
it—and it bent.   ers jammed the BBC switchboard
with fantastic tal   handsome young Israeli with black
shoulder-length h   rcing brown eyes looked out from
the video screen, h   used the cutlery in their homes to
warp.

The epidemic spr   with extensive coverage in the national newspapers. Rep   ters interviewed women, girls, and
small boys who professed to have the same metal-disturbing
power. Geller himself demonstrated to the press that he could
flatten wedding rings, bend keys, and break bracelets—while the
objects were held by their owners.

The virus traveled with Uri when he appeared on television
in Europe. The epidemic reached a crescendo in Sweden. A distraught woman claimed that Geller's strange power was so irre-
sistible that, as she watched him, the metal birth-control device
in her uterus suddenly straightened, and she became pregnant.

Uri, however, is his own most appreciative audience. His
eyes light up, his eyebrows rise in amazement, as he displays a
spoon and shouts: "Look, it's bending!" or takes up a broken
watch and exclaims: "Listen, now you can hear it ticking!" Some

scientists think that once Geller's mysterious power is understood, it will alter accepted concepts of matter, time, and space. Investigators at the Stanford Research Institute in Menlo Park, California (not a part of the university, but a respected organization which runs scientific tests for the government, industries, and other groups) did not see Geller bend metal under controlled laboratory conditions, but they were baffled by his ESP feats, and said these warranted "further testing."

Geller is not the conventional psychic. He dresses casually in tight trousers, colorful sports shirts, and odd jackets. More interested in sports than theology, he tells audiences and reporters that his power comes from outer space. Andrija Puharich, the neurologist-parapsychologist who brought Geller to America and arranged for the tests at the Stanford Research Institute, is more specific. In his book *Uri*, published in 1974, Puharich reveals that Geller and himself have been chosen by the computerized denizens of Hoova, a mysterious planet millions of light-years away, to act as their intermediaries on earth. Voices from *Spectra*, a Hoova spaceship, speak to Puharich in rooms where Geller is entranced; they also communicate through tape recorders. From Hoova, Puharich says, emanates the invisible force that enables Geller to bend metal, change lead into gold, read minds, and drive an automobile while blindfold. From Hoova come radiations that dematerialize dogs, move the hands of watches when Geller holds them, and lift heavy objects (such as movie cameras) when he stares at them. Geller then is Hoova's human outlet; Puharich is his prophet.

The young man through whom this mighty extraterrestrial power pours was born in Tel Aviv on December 20, 1946. Itzhaak (Isaac) Geller, his father, had fled from Hungary when Hitler's armies swarmed across Europe. Settling with his wife in Palestine, he volunteered for the British tank corps and fought in North Africa against Rommel. Later, as a sergeant major in the Israeli army, Itzhaak and his armored unit staved off Arab raids and participated in the ensuing wars.

Uri was three years old when his father fell in love with another woman. His mother moved out and struggled to support Uri and herself. Six years later she, too, began a new romance, and Geller was sent to live in a kibbutz. He was eleven when she took him to the island of Cyprus, where her second husband, Ladislav Gera, ran a small hotel. Uri studied at a Catholic school in Nicosia. Talented at languages, he became fluent in English; he also learned Greek and a little Turkish to go with the Hebrew he had acquired in Israel and the Hungarian used for conversation at home.

Among the residents at Gera's hotel was an agent of the Shin Beth, the Israeli army intelligence corps. Uri told Puharich that at sixteen he, too, became a spy, picking up mail for the agent and learning how to do such things as opening envelopes and reading their contents without tearing the glued flaps. (Puharich mentions this only in passing in his book; it is, of course, one of many ruses used by professed psychics to get information secretly.)

After Uri's stepfather died, his mother sold the hotel, and they returned to Tel Aviv, where he began the required three years of service in the armed forces. As a paratrooper officer candidate, he completed the course but did not receive a commission. Sergeant Geller was on leave in Tel Aviv when the Six-Day War erupted in June 1967. He joined his company and traveled by truck to Jerusalem. During his first night in action, bullets from an Arab machine gun pierced his arms. Recuperating, as a member of the staff of a boys' summer camp, Geller strengthened his muscles by weight lifting and practiced squeezing techniques to limber his fingers. He still works out every day, and has developed a viselike grip. It was at camp that he met two of his future collaborators—Shipi (Shimson) Strang, a tall, quiet, twelve-year-old camper, and his sixteen-year-old sister, Hannah, who came to visit him.

Completing his term of military service late the following year, Geller worked for a Tel Aviv textile company and picked up money on the side by posing for a photographer. Neither of these occupations satisfied him; he yearned for wealth and fame.

As a boy Uri had learned an effective watch trick. Calling attention to the time, he would place a watch facedown on someone's palm; then, seemingly by thought alone, he would alter the positions of the hour and minute hands. After years of practice, he could pull out the stem and twist it so deftly that only a magician who knew the technique could detect the movement.

On All Fools' Eve, March 31, 1848, Margaret and Kate Fox, then small girls, heard the mysterious rapping sounds in the family farmhouse in Hydesville, New York, that heralded the birth of modern spiritualism. *Opposite page (from top)*: Margaret, Kate, and their older sister, Leah, in later years. In 1888, Margaret revealed how the raps were made in a stage demonstration at the New York Academy of Music.

Ira Erastus Davenport and his brother, William Henry Harrison Davenport, of Buffalo, New York, were the first successful stage mediums. After a long American tour, they sailed to Europe in 1864, where they repeated their triumphs.

While the Davenport Brothers were bound hand and foot in a large wooden cabinet, bells rang, musical instruments played, and pale hands materialized.

Credulous observers of the Davenports proposed theories that were more wonderful than the phenomena they sought to explain. Some people believed that gigantic "spirit" arms lifted the brothers into the air during their dark-room demonstrations.

Another theory dispensed with "spirit" hands in favor of "invisible forces," which were said to be capable of playing instruments as they soared through the air.

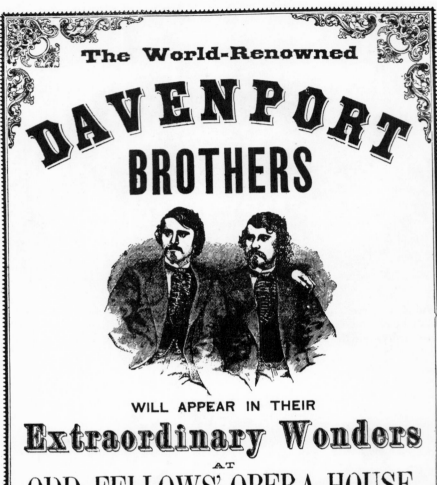

The World-Renowned

DAVENPORT
BROTHERS

WILL APPEAR IN THEIR

Extraordinary Wonders

AT

ODD FELLOWS' OPERA HOUSE,

LEXINGTON, KY

TWO DAYS ONLY,

FRIDAY, OCTOBER 15, SATURDAY, OCTOBER 16.

Admission Fifty Cents.

Reserved Seats 25 Cents extra.

Cleverly worded posters publicized the Davenport show. William Fay, another medium, helped perplex audiences with "Startling Wonders."

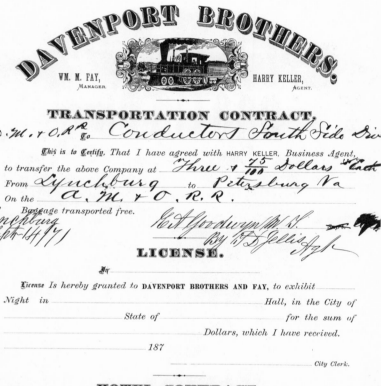

DAVENPORT BROTHERS.

WM. M. FAY, MANAGER.

HARRY KELLER, AGENT.

TRANSPORTATION CONTRACT.

A. M. & O. R. R. To Conductors South Side Div

This is to Certify, That I have agreed with HARRY KELLER, Business Agent,
to transfer the above Company at Three & 75/100 Dollars Each
From Lynchburg to Petersburg Va
On the A. M. & O. R. R.
Baggage transported free.

Lynchburg
Sept 14/71

E A Goodwyn M S.
By W D Jellis Agt

LICENSE.

In

License Is hereby granted to DAVENPORT BROTHERS AND FAY, to exhibit

Night in _____ Hall, in the City of

_____ State of _____ for the sum of

_____ Dollars, which I have received.

_____ 187

_____ City Clerk.

HOTEL CONTRACT.

I promise and agree with HARRY KELLER, Agent DAVENPORT BROTHERS, to Board
and Lodge the Troupe of Seven persons, more or less, at the rate of
Two Dollars per day each person. It
is also agreed and understood that if the above Troupe, or any part thereof,
wish to remain for a longer or shorter period than one day, the price shall be
the same in proportion for a day or parts of a day; one Meal or Loding considered one-fourth of a day. Mr. I. E. Davenport and Lady to have Room
_____ Mr. W. H. H. Davenport and Lady to have Room
_____ Prof. Wm. M. Fay and Lady to have Room
_____ If, from any unforseen event, the Troupe should
fail to arrive, no charge to be made, and this Contract to be null and void.

Mr Fay's Boy 1/2 Rate

H. Keller, Agent.

Holt & Bro Landlords'
Howell House.

Davenport contracts carried data about where the troupe would stay, the halls in
which they would play, and transportation for their next appearance.

Elizabeth Tomson, an American medium, though sewn in a coverall, stitched at the neck, wrists, and feet, nevertheless produced fresh flowers and a live snake during a test séance in England. However, Sir Hiram Maxim proved she was a fraud.

Mrs. Tomson and Sir Hiram posed for a picture after she confessed to the deceptions that she had practiced in the U.S. and Great Britain.

Geller had seen a number of conjurers perform; he realized that their most effective feats were those where the mind, not the hand, apparently created the mystery. Late in 1969, with Shipi, his young friend from the summer camp, he worked out a mental routine and, after trying it at parties and other social gatherings, became a full-time professional psychic. As Geller frankly admitted to Puharich, his primary assets were his "naïve appearance" and his showmanship.

The account published in *Haolam Haze,* an Israeli periodical, on February 20, 1974, of Uri's initial successes in his native land is far more intriguing than the story Geller tells today. Baruch Katoni, proprietor of the Zarkor Theatre, had been bewildered by Uri's telepathic feats. It seemed impossible for the performer to see the words written by volunteers behind his back on a blackboard, yet he seldom made a mistake. Katoni knew that Shipi, who had been introduced to him as Geller's younger brother, was in the audience, but he never gave the boy a second thought, until the night he noticed him signaling the performer. Katoni voiced his objection to this, and Shipi did not attend the next show. His place was taken by Shipi's sister, Hannah. When a *Haolam Haze* reporter questioned her, Hannah admitted she had cued Uri, but added that despite this he possessed powers she was unable to understand. The paper also noted that Isaac Savan, another confederate, confessed that he, too, had secretly conveyed information from his seat to the stage. Enthusiastic reviews and word-of-mouth praise for Geller's psychic marvels led him, Katoni said, to demand so much money for his appearances that the Zarkor Theatre could no longer afford him. He went to play instead at the Solan Theatre for impresario Micky Feld. Eager to provide an attraction as competition for his former star, Katoni hired a conjurer named Ayalon, who until then had performed only for small groups, but who professed to have the same phenomenal powers.

After convincing audiences he was indeed as gifted as Geller, Ayalon called in the press and announced he had posed as a psychic to prove that Geller was a charlatan. He then exposed the tricks that had made Geller's reputation and his own. Whether Ayalon intended to do this originally or whether circumstances provoked this disclosure is still a matter of conjecture in Israel.

Geller's performance raised doubts in the mind of others. Four computer technicians from Jerusalem formed the vanguard of the skeptics. They attended Uri's shows, took seats in various parts of the theatre, and followed his moves with binoculars night after night. Discovering his ruses, they would shout aloud the secrets. They were in the studio audience when Geller taped a show for television. They insisted he perform his blackboard feature with the words written by spectators on the far side of the board, so that no one could see them from the front. Uri, understandably furious, ignored this demand; the program was scrapped.

After a trip to Italy, Geller made the mistake of exhibiting a photograph of himself with Sophia Loren. Members of the press, examining it closely, pronounced it a paste-up hoax, and Uri's credibility suffered another blow.

More damaging was criticism from Isaac Kelzon, professor of physics at the University of Tel Aviv and an amateur conjurer. Had Geller not claimed to possess supernormal powers, Kelzon would have joined audiences in applauding him. Alarmed because of Uri's appeal to the superstitious and his influence on the credulous, Kelzon denounced him. He himself could—and did—perform many of the same incredible feats without the aid of the "power" Geller insisted he possessed.

When Andrija Puharich came to Israel in 1971 to test Uri, he was already preconditioned to regard Geller's work favorably. A Chicagoan of Yugoslavian ancestry, Puharich had received his medical degree from Northwestern University in 1947. A year later, at the age of thirty, he set up the Round Table Foundation to sponsor research in extrasensory perception and opened a laboratory in Glen Cove, Maine.

In "Can Telepathy Penetrate the Iron Curtain?" an article Puharich contributed to the 1957 winter issue of *Tomorrow*, he expressed his conviction that it could. Five years earlier he and other experimenters in parapsychology had been called to the Pentagon in Washington to discuss the possibility of ESP's being used by army intelligence. Puharich had said even then that it

could be employed effectively, along with more traditional systems for gathering information and gauging its worth.

Puharich experimented in Maine with Eileen Garrett, Peter
Hurkos, and other psychics, and proved to his own satisfaction
the existence of clairvoyance and telepathy. However, those who
possessed these gifts were not always in control of them, and
they were not as specific as he had thought they would be.

In *The Sacred Mushroom*, published in 1959, and *Beyond
Telepathy*, published three years later, Puharich explored the effects of *Amanita muscaria* and ways to increase the ESP potential. John G. Fuller's book *Arigó: Surgeon of the Rusty Knife*,
published in 1974, tells of Puharich's belief in the late Brazilian
psychic surgeon and his attempt to bring Arigó to the United
States for study under laboratory conditions.

Shocked to learn of Arigó's death in January 1971, Puharich
fasted for two weeks as he pondered the relative importance of
developing electronic hearing devices for his Intelectron Corporation versus a full-time, dedicated exploration of ESP and the
power of the psyche. The latter, he decided, far outweighed the
former. On the first of April, he was ready to undertake an in-
depth, comprehensive investigation. All he needed was a great
subject.

When he heard about Geller, Puharich packed his still and
movie cameras, his notebooks and scientific equipment, and flew
to Tel Aviv. Geller was headlining at the Zorba, a nightclub in
the adjacent city of Jaffa, when the parapsychologist arrived in
August 1971. An hour before midnight Uri donned a blindfold
and, without a miss, identified the words written on the blackboard behind his back by volunteers from the audience. Puharich was not too impressed by this or by the climax to Uri's
act—breaking a ring held by the owner in her hand as he concentrated. Possibly stooges could account for these crowd-pleasing
stunts. After the show, Uri performed in Puharich's room for an
hour, and the American and two Israeli friends came to the unan-
imous conclusion that Geller definitely sent and received
thoughts without trickery. Later Uri convinced Puharich that the
ring-breaking feat also was genuine. At long last the investigator
had found the super-psychic of his dreams!

On this trip abroad Puharich witnessed another strange psychic occurrence. At Bad Krozingen, in Germany, he sat in a room with Dr. Konstantin Raudive, a Latvian who used an unusual technique to communicate with the dead. Puharich switched on his tape recorder; Raudive asked for messages. When the tape was played back, Raudive's words were followed by faint noises. The American strained to make sense of them. Soon he recognized the voice of his dead mother speaking two words in Croatian. Anxious to get on with his scientific investigation of Geller, Puharich spent only a few days with Raudive, but the spirit voices he heard in Raudive's presence were to echo in his mind long afterward.

The daily testing sessions with Uri, which began in Tel Aviv in November 1971, are described in Puharich's book. The Israeli's talents proved to be far more formidable and diversified than the investigator had dared imagine. By concentration alone Geller was able to do the following: move compass needles ninety degrees; cause matches to slide along a glass surface; dematerialize a marked steel ring enclosed in a wooden box and make the ring reappear in the empty wooden box; dematerialize the ink cartridge of a ball-point pen while the pen was in a cigar box, then produce the same cartridge three days later; and cause a leather camera case, which Puharich said was locked in a closet at his house in Ossining, New York, to materialize in Tel Aviv.

Ingeniously staged tricks? Mediumistic phenomena? Not according to Puharich. He hypnotized Geller, and a voice, the source of which the investigator could not detect, was heard in the room. Later the same voice spoke from tapes on his recording machine. It answered questions; then the cassettes *dematerialized.*

Geller was controlled by a superior intelligence on the far-off planet Hoova, the voice said. The force that enabled Uri to circumvent the laws of nature beamed down on him from *Spectra,* a spaceship as large as a city. Sometime in the future a craft from Hoova would land on the Earth. From time to time Uri and Puharich would receive further instructions.

The American—selected, he was told, because of his remarkable thought processes—immediately took command of the terrestrial situation. The mysterious voice had suggested that a movie be made about Uri; Puharich assigned a friend to the task of preparing the script. Geller needed a business manager; Puharich found him one in Israel—Yasha Katz. The voice had said Geller and Katz should go to Germany; they went.

Puharich's friends raised the thousands of dollars needed to pay for an investigation of Uri's phenomena at the Stanford Research Institute. This seemed a master stroke. The American public would learn of the young Israeli's importance after he had stunned the parapsychologists at Menlo Park, California. But as the time approached for Geller to fly to the West Coast, he became increasingly apprehensive, and the voice from Hoova expressed doubts to Puharich as to the wisdom of this venture. At length, however, permission was given for Uri to meet the researchers.

The welcome in California could not have been more cordial. Former astronaut Edgar D. Mitchell was to supervise the experiments; physicists Harold Puthoff and Russell Targ were tremendously impressed by Geller's impromptu feats. One of several brass rings that Puthoff brought with him bent after Uri had examined it and told the physicist to cover it with his hand. Another vanished from Uri's clenched fist; hours later, it fell from the air in front of Puthoff while Uri was walking behind him.

After visiting the laboratory and seeing the equipment on November 12, 1972, Uri announced he would be ready to be tested the following morning. He was not an easy subject. He made it clear that he might walk out at any time and not return.

The researchers made two interesting discoveries. They had heard, as have many people before and since, that Uri could bend metal *without touching it*. Spoons did indeed bend in the laboratory, but Uri had always handled them before the curvature appeared. Rings became misshapen, but only after they had been in his powerful hands. Not a single object dematerialized while he was being filmed or video-taped.

Geller scored his greatest successes indicating which one of ten closed aluminum film cans held a concealed steel ball or was partially filled with water; guessing the number that would be uppermost after a die had been shaken in a closed box; and sketching a near facsimile of a design, which had been selected at random from several in another room by an investigator, then enclosed in one envelope and sealed in a second before he came to the laboratory.

The voice-over on a Stanford film report of these tests stresses that the design duplication feat is not to be considered "a laboratory experiment, since the activity is totally under Geller's control." This and the feats with film cans and dice are part of Uri's stock in trade: he performs them in parlors and on television.

Three interested observers came to spend a day at the Stanford Research Institute while Geller was there: Ray Hyman, a University of Oregon professor of psychology, who has often been consulted by the Defense Department; George Lawrence, an official of the Pentagon's Advanced Research Projects Agency; and Robert Van de Castle, a parapsychologist from the University of Virginia.

Uri told the visitors that before the 1972 Olympic Games opened in Munich, he and his friends had visited the grounds. The blaze of lights irked him; with a single snap of his fingers, he doused every bulb and neon tube on the site. Later while riding in a cable car with witnesses, he concentrated and stopped the car halfway between the starting point and mountaintop.

He gave an exhibition of his skill for the guests. Lawrence wrote down a number between one and ten on a pad while Uri covered his eyes with his hands and turned away his head. Hyman, a proficient magician and mentalist himself, noted, though no one else did, that Uri was peeking through his fingers. The professor, who could not see the face of the pad from his seat beside Geller, knew the number as soon as Uri did. Watching the arm of a writer or following the movements of the upper end of a pen or pencil is a dodge mediums have used for years.

Geller did not attempt any feat as spectacular as the outdoor exploits he had described, but he made the needle of a compass move slightly while he was staring at it. Lawrence, shifting his weight as Uri had done and exerting pressure on the floor, caused the needle to swing far more. Uri then charged him with practicing deception; he said Lawrence had used a concealed magnet or some other device. This was untrue.

Time magazine received favorable reports from a correspondent about Geller's work in the laboratory. The editors mulled over a possible cover story on the psychic. The mere fact that a nightclub performer was the subject of expensive scientific scrutiny at a prestigious research center intrigued them. Was Geller a medium or a trickster? Someone recalled that Charles Reynolds, a member of the Society of American Magicians Occult Investigation Committee, and David B. Eisendrath, Jr., had written a devastating article for *Popular Photography* on Ted Serios, who claimed to be able to project mental images on Polaroid film. Reynolds was hired as a consultant.

He and James Randi, a professional magician from Canada who is an avid crusader against psychic fraud, were present when Geller gave a demonstration for *Time* in February 1973. Reynolds had decided that two pairs of eyes familiar with deceptive techniques were better than one. While he observed from one angle, Randi watched from another. After Geller left, Randi duplicated Uri's telepathy tricks and metal-bending stunts for the editors, and Reynolds summed up the data he had gathered on Geller's background.

Friday, March 2, was Occult Night at the Society of American Magicians. Before Reynolds and I went onstage to comment as films of Russian mediums were projected, he told me that *Time*'s article on Geller was scheduled for the next issue, and added that he had invited Yasha Katz, Geller's manager, to see the show. When the performance was over, Reynolds introduced me to Katz. A few moments later Katz challenged me—his one hundred thousand dollars to my ten thousand dollars—that I could not duplicate or explain Uri's marvels. I accepted immediately before twenty witnesses. I gave Katz my address, asked him to put the challenge into writing, and said that as soon as I received his letter, we could meet, set the time and place, and select the judges.

Katz's letter never came. That Monday the March twelfth issue of *Time* carried their article on Geller. He was not the subject of the cover story. Professor Hyman had "caught Geller in some outright deceptions" during his brief visit to the Stanford Research Institute, the magazine said, and Randi had duplicated the psychic's feats at their office. This was not the sort of nationwide publicity that Puharich, Geller, and Katz appreciated. It did, however, lead to Uri's first appearance on network television in America. A slight bend appeared in a "spike" held by Jack Paar on his late-night ABC talk show. Uri drew designs that had been sealed in envelopes before the program began, and he called the number on the surface of a die that had been shaken in a box. Edgar Mitchell, another guest, assured Paar Uri had materialized a metal tie ornament that the astronaut had lost long before he met Geller.

When CBS-TV's "Sixty Minutes" planned in August to run a segment on scientific research in the field of parapsychology, James Jackson, the producer, called me before his unit flew to California to ask what precautions they should take to rule out trickery. In essence, I told him not to let Uri touch any forks, spoons, watches, or sealed cans before he went onstage and to keep close tabs on his hands. No metal bent while Uri was on camera with Mike Wallace; nor did any of the broken watches provided by CBS start ticking as Uri gazed at them. I was filmed in New York after having seen the footage shot on the West Coast. Mike asked if I thought Uri was a fraud. I replied I had seen nothing that indicated he had psychic powers.

Randi performed a similar service for the "Johnny Carson Show." On the Carson program, Geller sat by the table on which the requested props rested for more than twenty minutes—and nothing happened. Some people thought this was evidence that Uri was a genuine psychic. They reasoned that if he were a trickster, he would have done something—anything! Believers say that sensitives often are unable to produce marvels when skeptics are present, but I have as yet to hear of a skeptical reporter who didn't get a demonstration from Uri, or an auditorium audience, a show, once he walked out on the stage. All of Uri's tricks worked on Merv Griffin's television show. Merv was not interested in testing. Merv wanted a performance, and Geller delivered.

I was in the seventh row when Uri appeared at Town Hall in New York on September 25, 1973. "This is a phenomenon," a program note stated, "that might blow apart the reigning Orthodox Scientific Values."

Andrija Puharich welcomed the audience. Since I had last seen him, his hair had grown longer and shaggier. He talked of Geller's work for parapsychologists here and abroad, said it was raising serious questions in philosophical and religious circles. Uri entered from the side of the stage. Tall, graceful, his hair neatly coiffed, he wore a short-sleeved, open-at-the-neck red shirt and sleek, black, clinging slacks. Though nervous, he said he would try to do his best but the audience must be with him.

He needed several volunteers. No men! Women were more open-minded than men. He would start with simple things, "Not tricks, not magic." Uri invited those who wished to participate to raise their hands. Perhaps sixty pairs of hands shot up in the air. He pointed, "You, you, you," until six were chosen. One woman he led to the blackboard; the other five sat in chairs to the audience's right.

Standing at the front of the stage, holding a portable microphone in his right hand, Uri asked the woman at the blackboard behind him to write a color. She wrote rose. He did not get it. She wrote down another color—green. "Green," he called out confidently, and the audience applauded heartily. I wondered where Shipi, who was still traveling with Uri, was sitting.

Geller sat down in a chair on one side of the stage; grasping the microphone and holding an opaque shield to cut off his view of the blackboard, he asked that the name of a capital city, "Not Rome, not Paris," be written. The woman wrote Denver. He hesitated, wrinkled his brow, looked strained. "It's a city in America." He asked the audience to repeat the name of the city silently in their minds. "Denver!" Tumultuous applause. He also asked the woman to draw a simple object, "Not a house, not a flower." She drew a round face with lines for eyes and mouth. On his board Uri drew a circle. Again a warm response from out front.

One woman selected a color and wrote the word on the blackboard; another stood by his side at the front of the stage and tried to get the mental impression Uri said he would receive from the color and convey to her. This took some time, but eventually she said purple. Purple it was.

Then Geller chatted informally with the audience. He told them he had been born in Tel Aviv twenty-six years ago, said that at seven he realized he had a gift. His mother liked to play cards. When she came home, he could always tell her how much money she had won.

Yes, he said in answer to a question, he believed in God. He described an experience with a flying saucer. He said Israel would never lose a war; it was protected by an invisible field of energy. Its source, the Great Pyramid in Egypt! Long, long ago travelers from a distant planet had landed there. In two or three years he would have a message of great importance for the world. When he felt strange, he knew something momentous was about to happen. Several times in the past he had felt that way, and "something big" had occurred.

Now he was ready for broken watches. Were there any in the audience? Several women rushed forward. Choosing a time-piece, he put it in the hand of a volunteer who had been sitting onstage. He held his hand over her hand. He strained, listened, and shook his head. "Try winding it!" someone at the rear of the hall shouted. "Try it with Beverly." (Beverly was the name of the woman who has received his "purple" thought.)

None of the broken watches started. He shrugged and asked for a finger ring. Forty women hurried down the aisles with rings of all sorts. He picked out one and told the owner to hold it in her closed fist while she stood by his side. He strained to concen-trate, then asked her to open her hand. He picked up the ring and shook his head. He replaced it, concentrated again, and he re-peated this several times, then became disgusted. He said he would try one last time. When the woman opened her hand, he took the ring and held it up triumphantly to show the audience it had developed a crack. I myself could not see the break from the seventh row, but the woman agreed that the ring was broken. Uri said the crack would widen. By the time members of the audi-ence had surged onstage around him, the ring had opened wide.

Almost fifteen hundred people had paid either four or six dollars for their tickets. Those who believed in Geller before the show believed in him when it was over; those who were dubious remained dubious; and those few who thought him a fraud had also not changed their view.

In October Ted Kavanau, news director of Metromedia's ten-o'clock New York report phoned and asked me to come to the studio to look at some film they had shot at Geller's apartment. I watched as the reel was being edited. So did Yasha Katz, Geller's manager. This was the first time I had seen him since "Occult

Night" at the Society of American Magicians. "Whatever happened to your hundred thousand to ten thousand dollar challenge?" I asked. He raised his eyebrows. "That was just a joke," he insisted.

Kavanau wanted my opinion of Geller. I gave it, but the reporter and the camera crew who had filmed Uri assured him there had been no deception. "Send me with your reporter and the crew to Geller," I suggested. "Have him repeat any of his marvels." The producer phoned Geller. Uri said he would welcome anyone from the station except me.

If someone really had the power that Geller claims he has, I'm sure such a person would delight in astonishing magicians. With nothing to hide, what great fun it would be to see the expressions on the faces of those who present mere tricks.

Most reporters who write about Geller do not know how mentalists and magicians perform their feats. Some, however, try to find an explanation that will satisfy both themselves and their readers. Andrew Tobias, for instance, whose "Okay, He Averted World War III, But Can He Bend a Nail?" appeared in the September 10, 1973, issue of New York magazine. After talking with Randi and visiting Louis Tannen's magic shop, he changed his initial views on Geller. When Tobias met him in the apartment of Judith Skutch, who heads her own Foundation for Parasensory Investigation, Geller concentrated and drew a heart pierced by an arrow. This was the same design that Tobias had earlier sealed in two envelopes and brought with him. A later session had far different results. Having seen the Stanford Research Institute film of Geller successfully guessing eight times the top spots on a die, the writer bought his own box and his own die, and they never left his sight for even an instant. Eight times Uri tried; and eight times he failed. Tobias had another design sealed in an extra-heavy envelope. He watched Uri like a hawk, never giving him the opportunity to get at the package unobserved. Result: Uri again failed.

New York Daily News reporter Donald Singleton phoned me in October, the night before I left on a tour to the West Coast. He had been with Geller in Philadelphia. Backstage at the KYW-TV studio, where Uri taped a "Mike Douglas Show," Geller had bent the key to Hugh Downs's hotel room and several others belonging to the station's staff. At a party given by the sponsors of Geller's public show, Singleton had been present when rings warped and an amulet bent. The following night, while Singleton stood with the psychic in a theatre lobby, a soft-drink machine began acting up, sending crushed ice cascading down long after the flow should have stopped. Uri said things like this happened wherever he went; at the Stanford Research Institute, on three occasions, candy-vending machines had poured forth their wares.

These were amusing bits for the story Singleton was writing, but what really perplexed him was how Uri was able to duplicate the drawing sealed in two opaque envelopes and to bend borrowed keys. Singleton had taken a photographer to Geller's apartment in New York; the photographer swore Uri bent his key while he was watching closely. Singleton had not been in the room at the time. How, he wanted to know, could he guard against trickery at his next visit? I suggested that after he drew a design at home, he wrap aluminum foil around it before he sealed it in the envelopes, that he take a thick key, and that he never let the envelopes or the key out of his sight.

I was in Hollywood when the second of Singleton's two-part series appeared in the November 8, 1973, *Daily News.* Geller tried for thirty minutes to duplicate the design; then he gave up. He put Singleton's key aside, while he diverted the reporter with bending a spoon. Later he again called attention to the key. There was an "ever so slight" bend in it, but Singleton admitted he had been unable to watch it as closely as he had planned.

It is extremely difficult for an observer not to be distracted. Charles Reynolds told me that when Uri worked in the *Time* office in New York, Geller had taken a key (Reynolds's), stroked it gently a number of times, then put it down, suggesting that some other piece of metal might respond to his thoughts more quickly. While a search was being made for something suitable, Reynolds and Randi *saw* Uri casually pick up the key, and gripping it firmly, press the tip down on a table to force a slight bend in the key. As this was being done, Uri's eyes followed the activity in the office and never once looked down.

The *Time* people did not see this move. Why should they? Geller was not performing then. In key bending, as in many other feats of deception, the vital move is made before the trick (as the audience sees it) begins.

Picking up the key so that his fingers concealed the bend, Uri asked a *Time* staffer to hold it, then after due concentration, he announced it was beginning to bend. Having been alerted, and with their attention focused on the volunteer's hand, the on-lookers saw the slight distortion after Geller lifted his fingers which had been rubbing the key. Uri often puts a key on a table after his first slight bend and rocks it back and forth with a finger-tip. As the key is no longer flat, this rocking emphasizes the bend.

Later, after the key has been passed from one spectator to another so they can examine it, Geller puts the key aside, and goes on with his other tricks until the right opportunity comes for him to pick it up again. Then, unobserved, he increases the extent of the curve.

When a bent key or spoon is displayed, Geller promises that the bend will become more pronounced; it does—after he has seized the opportunity to increase it.

Often a photographer will take a picture after the first bending of a spoon. While he is busy changing plates, or advancing the film, Geller bends the spoon more. Thus a series of pictures can be taken showing the metal "in the process of bending." Another of Uri's effective dodges is to show a key with its flat side facing the TV camera, then to turn the key so that the bend (which is already there) seems to take place as the viewer watches.

With war raging between the Israeli and Arabic armies in 1973, reporters naturally asked Uri why he wasn't there bending hostile tanks and cannon. The question annoyed him. If he could do that, he replied, he would be in the front lines, but, as yet, his power had not developed to that extent.

Judy Bacarach, whose interview with the mind-over-metal expert appeared on October 12, 1973, in the *Washington Post,* was having lunch with Geller when he announced that his knife had warped and held it up to show her. She had not been looking at the knife, nor had she been watching the spoon that Uri later held up to display its unusual curve. Geller stated no one could possibly do this with manual pressure. A skeptic, she reached for a spoon and bent it in two herself.

"You must be very strong," Uri marveled, and he turned the conversation from cutlery to his career. He talked about the intelligence in outer space that had manifested itself through Jesus and Muhammad and was now supplying him with power. He talked about his American mentor, Andrija Puharich, who was writing a book about his incredible experiences with Uri. This inspired Judy Bacarach to call Puharich's wife and ask how the advent of Geller had affected their life.

Anna Puharich said she was no longer living with her husband. Bored with his talk of flying saucers, voices that spoke from tape machines, and his championship of Uri's mystical cause, she had moved out.

The *Washington Post* photographer who took pictures of Geller that day had a strange experience. Uri, who has learned quite a bit about photography since he met Puharich, asked the cameraman to cover the lens with a leather bag, then snap a rubber band around it to hold the improvised cap in place. Proclaiming he could take pictures of himself under these conditions, Uri tried several times. All the exposures except two came out black . . . but these two were close-up shots of Uri's face! This new addition to his repertoire brought him extensive publicity several weeks later.

Uri complained to several American interviewers that, although he had appeared on many television programs and been featured in stories in magazines and newspapers, few people were aware that he existed. In Israel, he said, crowds followed him through the streets.

Unhappy with his impact on the United States, Uri had cause for jubilation in Britain. England, like Israel, is a relatively small country. Literally overnight, he achieved fame there.

Announcer Jimmy Young described what was happening during his daytime Radio 2 show in London on Friday, November 23, 1973. Uri bent a key with his mental power; then he held a paper knife, stroked it, and the letter opener broke in two. Phone calls to the station reported stranger occurrences miles away. A watchmaker's tweezers twisted out of shape as he listened; the ladle a housewife in Harrow had been using to stir soup in her kitchen warped; a gold bracelet contorted on the wrist of a woman in Goldalming, Surrey.

That evening most TV viewers watched the "Miss World" competition on Channel 1; Geller was David Dimbleby's guest on the 10:30 "Talk-In" that followed. "Can Thoughts Bend Metal?" the listing asked. Apparently they could. While Uri was amazing Dimbleby in the studio, knives, forks, and spoons were bending in homes throughout England.

Not since P. C. Sorcar, the Indian illusionist, had sliced through a girl with a buzz saw on Dimbleby's father's program in 1956 had a telecast created such a stir. That show ran overtime; only the studio audience witnessed the restoration. To still the furor, Richard Dimbleby had to explain the next day that the magician's assistant had not been murdered.

Front-page stories in Saturday's papers carried such headlines as "URI CATCHES BRITAIN BENDING" and "URI PUTS BRITAIN IN A TWIST." At a hastily arranged press conference, the Israeli psychic demonstrated his unusual talent and told reporters, "I don't know how I do it."

No mention was made of the planet Hoova or the spacecraft *Spectra*. En route to the airport in a taxi with Bryan Silcock of the *Sunday Times*, Uri bent the key to Silcock's desk, then put a curve in a KLM metal paper knife while waiting for the announcement of his Paris flight. During the day he had found time to make arrangements for a future concert-hall tour and a cross-channel psychic experiment for the *Sunday People*, a national weekly.

At half past twelve the next day in France, Uri turned west toward England. A front-page story in the newspaper had alerted its readers to be ready with their old cutlery and broken watches. "Bend!" cried Uri, and, according to the account in the *Sunday People* published a week later, the command mysteriously started 856 broken watches to ticking. On one, the hands began moving *backward,* and a twelve-year-old Brighton boy reported his bent knife had straightened.

Then Clifford Davis, television editor of the *Daily Mirror*, set up one of the most unusual luncheon parties ever held at the London Hilton. The guests were women and girls who claimed metal had bent in their homes during Geller's "Talk-In" telecast. Davis, a showman, wanted an interesting story. He suggested everyone shut their eyes and concentrate. While all eyes were shut, a silver-plated Hilton coffee spoon "curled itself around a saucer."

There were heated discussions in academic circles about Uri's powers. The *New Scientist* in its issue of November 29 commented: "Something more than a good story for journalists is at issue here." Geller had convinced many scientists, including those at the Stanford Research Institute, that what he did was worthy of investigation.

The *New Scientist* invited Geller to appear before a committee made up of specialists: a representative of the Society for Psychical Research, a psychologist, a biologist, one of their own reporters, a reporter from a national newspaper and—"a professional magician of international standing." Though Uri has been in England since, he has not accepted the invitation.

Following a brief visit to Paris, Geller flew to the United States; a *News of the World* reporter went with him. Roy Stockdill's "My Fantastic Week with Uri" appeared in the December second issue of the British weekly. Elated by his television triumph in London, Geller boasted of his success with women. He said he won them over with his "power." No preliminary dates were necessary. He read their minds, he said, and bent them to his will.

Geller tried his new camera trick for a *News of the World* photographer in Miami Beach. Michael Brennan fastened an opaque cap on the lens of his Nikon F camera. Holding the camera at arm's length with his extended hands, Uri aimed the covered lens at his face and began clicking away. Occasionally he brought the lens cap to his forehead, explaining he was photographing his mind. When the film was developed, the shots of his mind were blank. Two frames, however, carried images of his face. These were published under a front-page double streamer: "URI'S MIRACLE PICTURES. WITNESSES SAY: NO SIGNS OF TRICKERY."

A day later the *Daily Mail* quoted two experts. Dennis Constantine, president of the Council of Professional Photographers of Europe, said it was impossible to produce an exposure on film when a metal cap covered the camera lens. Reginald Mason, editor of *Amateur Photographer,* thought infrared light might have penetrated the opaque cover or possibly an exposed film had been in the camera.

Though Uri was then in Europe, he continued to be a subject of great interest to British readers. David Berglas, Ali Bongo, Romark, and other conjurers duplicated his metal bending for the press. Robert Harbin, who had at first accepted Geller as a psychic, changed his mind and joined the skeptics.

There were rumors that when Geller returned to England, he would move the hands on Big Ben, stop an escalator in the Piccadilly Circus underground station, and warp one of the royal crowns on display in a glass case at the Tower of London.

He was featured on Thames TV's "Is Seeing Believing?" on January 15, 1974. Geller said he had stalled the French liner *Renaissance* with his mind. Then, as before, spoons bent when he rubbed them. Clifford Davis headed his *Daily Mirror* story the next day: "URI DOES IT AGAIN." Davis, an associate member of the Magic Circle, said, "I'm convinced that Uri does have a strange psychic power." Tim Ewbank said in the *Daily Mail* that once again metal had behaved peculiarly in British homes while Geller was on the screen. What made this especially noteworthy was that Uri was not even in England at the time; the show had been taped before his November "Talk-In" debut.

On January twenty-fourth Dan Coolican began a series of articles on Uri in the *Daily Express;* a front-page headline said the writer knew how Geller bent metals. An Israeli army officer had revealed the secret. A chemical rubbed on spoons and forks made them as brittle as crackers. Coolican also demonstrated the trick on television. Five days later, however, he admitted he was again baffled. He had gone to Copenhagen where Geller had disproved the chemical theory by washing his hands thoroughly before he bent a key. John Rhodes commented on Coolican's experience in Denmark in *The Budget,* the monthly journal of the British Ring of the International Brotherhood of Magicians: "Pity some of our professional magicians weren't present."

Geller had flown to West Germany from the United States to appear on "Drei am Neun" ("Three Times Nine"), a prime-time television panel show on January seventeenth. Front-page stories told of his astounding feats. The next day, *Der Spiegel,* the largest-selling news weekly in Europe, sent Herman Schreiber to interview him. When Uri rubbed Schreiber's fork, it broke in half. But Uri refused to repeat this demonstration for Werner Geissler-Werry, the specialist in close-up magic *Der Spiegel* had called in as a consultant.

Analyzed by the Federal Institute for Material-Testing in Berlin, Schreiber's fork showed traces of a chemical at the breakage point. The official report said if the fork had been forcibly bent back and forth five times, this stress would have fatigued the metal. A diluted nitrate of mercury rubbed on the fatigued portion would then cause the fork to break when a slight pressure was applied. This procedure was tried with another fork of the same metallic composition. The resulting fracture, compared under a 200-power microscope with the break in the reporter's fork, proved to be identical.

Aqua regia and other corrosives have been used by entertainers for many years. The technique was discussed as long ago as 1895 in the "Tricks of Strong Men," a chapter of Samri S. Baldwin's book *The Secrets of Mahatma Land Explained.*

Geissler-Werry, the editor and publisher of *Magische Welt* (*Magic World*), described Geller's subtle TV presentation in the January 28 issue of *Der Spiegel.* Uri first passed a fork to a guest on the panel for inspection. Then he picked up three more; he gave one to the host, one to a girl panelist with instructions to grip the prongs, and put the remaining fork on the table. Afterward viewers had the erroneous impression that every fork had been examined. Uri's fingers had masked the slight bulge created by the fatiguing process before the program began. As he rubbed this with his thumb and fingers, the fork broke in two. Geller's picture had made the cover, but the text of the story must have caused him considerable anguish.

By varying his methods, Uri succeeded in baffling those like the *Daily Express* writer who knew one of his techniques but not the others. In Germany, as in Britain, viewers of the TV show had reported that while they watched Geller's performance, cutlery warped in their homes. Once the idea has been implanted that such things can occur, autosuggestion often produces "miracles." Some were undoubtedly unaware that they themselves had bent the objects; others yearned to see their names in the papers.

Late in January Uri flew to England to capitalize on the publicity he had received during his absence. In London he talked with a British publisher about an autobiography, considered offers from national newspapers to write articles, and avoided confrontation with the *New Scientist* investigating committee.

Geller was to open in Birmingham early in February. Then he read that members of The Magic Circle had booked front-row seats. Panicking, he canceled this date and others to follow, telling reporters before he left the country that he had received a phone call threatening his life. Uri had been terrified, not by an Arab assassin, but by the horrifying thought of public exposure.

A spoon-bending psychosis swept Scandinavia when Geller toured there. My friend Finn Jon, a Norwegian conjurer, was interviewed by an Oslo journalist an hour after Uri had completed a press conference. She showed the magician a bent spoon "as proof of Geller's power." Finn Jon asked her to place the spoon on the table, behind which they were sitting, then to take both of his hands in hers. The spoon quivered and turned over! "The people who saw this," Finn said, "were so baffled that later if someone said the spoon had been dancing, they would have agreed."

Some Danish TV viewers believed Geller had amazing curative powers. As they gazed at him on the television screen, scratches healed, coughing children quieted, and old women reported their arthritic pains ceased.

DN (*Dagens Nyheter*), the influential Stockholm daily, warned readers that there was more to Geller's feats than met the eye. Helmut Fischmeister, a professor at Chalmers Institute of Technology in Gothenburg, had told their reporter that he had not had the opportunity to say he had discovered a corrosive additive on the spoon that Uri had snapped in two during his television appearance. The professor and other scientists had discussed the seemingly inexplicable marvel following Geller's demonstration, but time ran out before Fischmeister could announce his find. He was not the only scientist to report a chemical had secretly been employed, the professor added; academic friends in Austria and Norway had reached the same conclusion after they, too, had subjected Geller-broken tableware to close scrutiny.

Magician Alexander Adrion had written disparagingly of Uri in *Die Zeit*, a German periodical, in February; then the publisher offered a hundred thousand marks to Geller, or anyone else, who under controlled conditions was able to prove they could disturb metal with their minds.

Bjørn Sørum, president of the Norwegian Magic Circle, announced an award of fifty thousand krone for an authentic mind-over-matter performance in the March twenty-sixth issue of *VG*, an Oslo paper. Felix Greenfield, a member of the Society of American Magicians Occult Committee, had personally offered Geller ten thousand dollars on Metromedia's "Midday" television program in New York City if he could reveal what was in Greenfield's sealed envelope as he had in the case of an envelope sealed by the program host. Geller said he would perform this feat later, but he has never done so. Nor has he accepted the other challenges. Why should he? He can make more money from personal appearances—without running the risk of public embarrassment.

Charles Reynolds showed me evidence of Uri's duplicity in Geller's "impossible photograph" stunt before the psychic made the cover on the June issue of *Popular Photography*. Two articles shattered the Geller legend. The first, by Reynolds, explained the tricks the self-professed mystic had performed for *Time*. The second, by Yale Joel, a former *Life* photographer who is now a free lance, said Uri had attempted to take photographs of his mind through the sealed lens cap on Joel's Pentax camera. After clicking away, Geller had lost interest in the camera and said he would like to try a telepathy test. The photographer and his son were sent into another room to draw a picture and seal it in two envelopes. When they returned, Uri duplicated their chair design, and Joel, who was busy taking photographs of this and of Geller's spoon bending, forgot about the episode with the Pentax. Later when the Tri-X film was developed, there was a surprise near the end of the reel. Joel enlarged the image, and—lo and behold—there in the upper right-hand corner was Geller. But something else was also there, something far more fascinating. In the center of the frame was a round black object, held at the sides by a thumb and fingers. The lens cap had been removed!

The "impossible photograph" mystery was solved. While the photographer and his son were in the other room making the sketch for the telepathy experiment, the lens cap, which had been fastened with black tape, had been taken off, and the shutter had been triggered. Had Uri done this himself, or had one of his friends assisted him? Joel found the picture could have been snapped either way. The Geller photograph and two similar photographs—one taken by one person who held the camera at arm's length, and the other taken by a second person—illustrated the article. Joel had not been present, so he couldn't be sure which procedure had been used, but he had the conclusive proof of fraud.

Yet Geller still draws standing-room-only audiences. The majority of his patrons have not read about the various exposures. They prefer to believe affirmative stories, such as those in the June 1973 issue of *Psychic* and the December 1973 and January and February 1974 issues of *Fate*.

I have gathered data on Uri in many cities during my travels. In San Francisco, for instance, I talked with Jim Dunbar. He had been the host of ABC-TV's "A.M." show in New York when Geller was a guest. Jim cautioned the young lady who worked as a production assistant not to let Uri near the props he had requested for the program. Just before the show went on the air, Jim entered a side room. Geller, with one of the ten film cans in his hands, was there, talking with the girl. In Toronto a magician was in the studio control booth before a Geller show was taped. He saw Geller pick up a bunch of keys from a table on the set and carry them behind the scenes; later Uri replaced them. During the program one of these keys bent as Geller stroked it.

Dr. Joyce Brothers was prepared when she welcomed Uri to her syndicated TV show in New York. Uri said he was in the mood to bend spikes. (The "spikes" Geller and some writers refer to are long nails.) Uri started unwrapping the nails, which had been bound together with black tape. She stopped him, opened her purse, and took from it her own nail. "Bend this," she challenged. Geller's power left him!

On the "Mike Douglas Show" in Philadelphia one of the nails had been previously bent. When Geller stripped away the tape, he held this nail, concealing the bend (an inch or so above the pointed end) with the fingers of one hand. With the other hand he picked up a straight nail, which he banged on the table to show its solidity, but it was the first nail that a panel guest grasped by the head, as Uri, still masking the bend with his fingers, stroked the metal. After due concentration and gentle rubbing, Uri slid his fingers away to reveal that the nail had bent.

One of the two nails Geller displayed on the Jack Paar television program had been previously bent in the middle. This bend was slight. Unless attention had been called to it, it might have gone unnoticed. Paar held the nail, with ends extending above and below his fist, and Uri rubbed the upper portion. When the ebullient Geller proclaimed that the nail had distorted, and the camera came in for a tight close-up view, this slight bend could be seen.

Geller might have caused this nail to "bend" visibly. Anyone can do it. Hold a bent nail between your thumb and index finger. From one angle the nail appears to be straight. A slight, slow roll then brings the bend into view.

As studios supply the nails for Geller's use, he must have access to them before the program goes on the air. Unless he bends one backstage, the nail feat will not be performed. In his television shows, there are almost always more props supplied than he will use. Those he has not handled secretly are not used.

Uri bends or breaks borrowed rings onstage, or during his impromptu exhibitions, by the pressure of his unusually strong fingers. He puts a ring on a woman's palm and tells her to close her hand. She sees the ring several times as he tries to bend it with his "power." Before the final attempt, he bends the ring manually. The spectator afterward remembers having seen the unbent ring in her hand; she will frequently say she felt it bend, because he has told her that it will do just that while she holds it.

If the ring breaks this heightens the effect. Once a crack has been displayed, Uri will later force the ends apart. Occasionally the rings offered by spectators are too substantial for him to bend. In these instances he shrugs after several tries and gives up. Should a magician dare to do this, the audience would hiss, but Geller is a "psychic," and the audience sympathizes with him. He has tried so hard, been so "honest," that he gets applause for his failures, as well as his successes.

Some scientists and even a few laymen who have read modern conjuring books are flabbergasted when Uri holds a watch, stares at it—and it stops. William Hooper described the feat in Volume Three of his *Rational Recreations*, published in London in 1774. Even then it was old. A concealed magnet halts the movement of the balance. The magnet can be hidden in a table-top or, as in Uri's case, palmed. However, readers are advised not to try this stunt with their own watches—at least not if they value them. Once a watch has been magnetized, it will run erratically after the magnet has been removed.

Watchmakers are not as awed by Uri's trick of starting broken watches as less knowledgeable spectators; they know that watches often start running again when they are handled, but there are few watchmakers in Geller's audiences. Uri specifies that no parts must be missing from the watches. Sometimes none of the timepieces given to him react to his power. When one does, there is loud applause.

Geller is quick to take advantage of any situation. Often there is trouble with the studio equipment during a television-taping session. If he is present, he suggests this was caused by his mysterious power. While performing in Israel, he wavered on the stage and seemed to lose consciousness. He asked for a doctor. One came up from the audience. Uri said he was ill because something important had occurred in Egypt. He was sure Nasser had died. After the show the spectators learned of the Egyptian president's death. The word spread that Uri had known of this the moment it happened. Not until *Haolam Haze* investigated the story in 1974 did the public learn the facts. Danny Peletz, who was backstage at the Solan Theatre that night, said someone had heard the news-flash on a radio. The word was passed to Uri, and he staged the fainting act to convince those out front that he had received this information psychically.

While Geller was at the Stanford Research Institute, he left one day and then came back saying that he had a feeling there would be a terrible airplane crash. There was a crash, but the news had been broadcast before Uri made his prediction.

The tales Geller tells to TV audiences and newspaper reporters are more fantastic than his tricks. Once, he said, he projected himself astrally to Brazil. He was living in New York with Andrija Puharich at the time. Puharich asked him to go there again and bring back evidence of his visit. Shortly afterward, Geller produced a Brazilian coin. Other "evidence" of Geller's astral projections is equally ridiculous. Uri once claimed he had transported himself to a distant beach; as proof, he removed his shoes and poured out some sand.

Uri assured James Crenshaw who wrote a three-part series on him for *Fate* magazine that while with a Greek Orthodox archbishop in New York, a waiter poured white wine in Geller's glass and the liquid changed to red. Had he been trying to convince the churchman he had Christlike powers? Geller did not say. Why else would he perform that old chemical trick?

In his book on Uri, Puharich says Wellington, the parapsychologist's dog, vanished from a room and reappeared outside the house. This he accepts as proof of the mighty force from another planet. Martin Gardner in the May 16, 1974, issue of *New York Review of Books* offered another solution to this "mystery." Did Geller toss Wellington out through a window or door, Gardner asked? This seemed likely, for not long afterward the dog, who until then had been friendly, bit Uri.

Puharich described another miracle that he said occurred in Uri's presence. Nine pens suddenly appeared on a desk spelling out the word "WHY." Then, as Uri and his sponsor watched, the pens "flipped simultaneously in the air." Six came down, side by side, in a row; the other three formed a triangle.

You won't be seeing Uri Geller perform this on stage or on television. As a perceptive British editor remarked when he heard about the parapsychologist's book: "With friends like Puharich, Geller doesn't need enemies."

One wonders how long dedicated researchers, trying desperately to validate any phase of psychic phenomena, will continue to search for the true source of Uri's power. The frustrated son of a famous Israeli soldier candidly admitted to his biographer that his prime assets were his "naïve appearance" and his showmanship. These, plus his strong agile fingers, his alert eyes, and cleverly contrived ruses, enable him to present his tricks effectively.

Geller is supremely confident; he firmly believes he can deceive anyone who does not know his methods. He confessed during a television segment, taped in another country and transmitted in Israel in April 1974, that he cheated when he first attracted attention in Tel Aviv. Since then, he stressed, he has relied solely on his mysterious power. Uri made a similar statement to Francine du Plessix Gray, whose article, "Parapsychology and beyond" appeared in the August 11, 1974, issue of *The New York Times Magazine*. He said his aides in Israel had jotted down the numbers on the license plates of the automobiles that brought members of the audience to his shows, then added notes on the cards of the facial features, sex, and clothing of the people who got out of the cars, and conveyed this information to him. In this way he could ask a person he had never seen before to write down the license number of his car, and then astound him by dramatically revealing the number.

Though Francine du Plessix Gray saw Randi duplicate Uri's metal-bending and watch tricks, she reported that she still thinks there is the "possibility" that Geller's "telepathic feats are genuine."

Uri is more tense than he has been in the past; he has gained weight, and in recent television conversations, he has attributed the fantastic tales about the planet Hoova and the spaceship *Spectra* to Puharich. Geller says magicians try to duplicate his authentic mind-over-metal demonstrations by switching keys, but he still refuses to appear on television programs with conjurers who are critical of his performance.

Only once, to my knowledge, has Geller been challenged in court. Before Puharich brought him to the United States, an irate Israeli spectator sued Geller in magistrates' court in Beersheba for breach of contract, charging that he had failed to perform the supernormal feats of telepathy, parapsychology, and telekinesis he advertised. Instead, complained Uri Goldstein, a mechanical-engineering student at the University of the Negev, Geller's act consisted merely of sleight-of-hand and stage tricks. The judge agreed; he ordered Geller not only to refund the money Goldstein had paid for admission but to foot court costs of the case.

Geller is at his ingenious best in laboratories where he is being observed by scientists who believe he has extraordinary ESP ability and think—without justification—that they have ruled out every possibility of fraud. Unless an expert in deception is present while such tests are being conducted, these experiments are as valid as a four-dollar bill.

PSYCHIC SURGERY

Thousands of sufferers, some with serious or terminal illnesses, have been treated in recent years by psychic surgeons in the Philippines and in Brazil. The painless operations in the Philippines are performed rapidly: a cyst is extracted in less than two minutes; an ovary is removed in ten.

"Dr." Antonio Agpaoa, the most famous of the many spiritual healers in and around Manila, wears a short-sleeved, open-necked sports shirt rather than traditional operating-room garb. His patient stretches out on a table, which has been covered by a sheet. The short, amiable mystic kneads the skin over the infected area; then, suddenly—using the edge of his open hand as a scalpel—he slashes into the flesh.

Wiping away quickly the spurting blood, Agpaoa inserts his fingers into the wound and removes a blob of red tissue. This he snips off with a pair of scissors; then he sloshes alcohol over the incision and holds the flesh firmly together. When he releases his grip, the skin heals instantly.

According to an article by Lois Borkan in the January 1966 issue of *Fate* magazine, Meyer Kronenberg, a Miami Beach businessman, and Nelson C. Decker, a San Clemente, California, chiropractor, spent a day the previous March watching Agpaoa at work. The twenty-six-year-old psychic surgeon then used a second-floor room in Manila as a clinic. He completed an abdominal operation on an old woman in five minutes. Later a growth was swiftly removed from the shoulder of a teen-age girl. When the miracle man cut another patient's nose and the blood began to flow, "Dr. Tony" squeezed the skin between his fingers, and asked the startled Kronenberg to reach over and pull out the growth that seemed to emerge from the small incision.

Decker also assisted Agpaoa and obviously thought psychic surgery would prove more profitable than chiropractics. He later advertised in *Fate* that copies of the 8-millimeter color film he had made of the procedures and of his booklet, *Bare Hand Psychic Surgery*, an account of his studies with Eleuterio Terte, another Philippine practitioner, and "Dr. Tony," were available for seventy-five dollars.

A "scientific" theory explaining why the incisions made by psychics leave no scars has been advanced by Harold Sherman, author of *"Wonder" Healers of the Philippines,* published in 1967. Sherman, president of ESP Research Associates Foundation of Little Rock, Arkansas, admits he is neither a scientist nor a physician, but he has told in other books of his successes in sending telepathic messages and projecting his astral body to distant places. He quotes the opinion of an anonymous Swiss friend who, Sherman says, holds degrees in medicine, chemistry, physics, and electronics.

According to this unnamed authority, the human body is made up of atomic cells held "properly spaced from each other and in proper place by an invisible force called electronic flux." The cells adhere because "unequal polar forces" act upon them. When "Dr. Tony's" right hand strikes the flesh, the sharp impact "unpolarizes" the cells beneath it. As they are driven apart, the skin opens. Once the disturbing hand is lifted, the cells resume their normal position.

Agpaoa himself does not attempt to explain his operations; he simply states he has a God-given power. He does not enter a trance like Eleuterio Terte, the most noted of his competitors in the Philippines, nor does "Dr. Tony" perform a religious ritual prior to his surgery, though he has said he gained his power after he prayed and fasted on the side of a secluded mountain.

Reportedly he performed his first psychic operation at the age of nine. No set fees were charged for his early cures: Agpaoa accepted donations from grateful patients. The poor flocked to him for treatment, then affluent government officials, judges, and military leaders sought his aid. By the mid-1960's clients from Europe, America, and the Orient were arriving in ever-increasing numbers. He often operated eight or ten times a day. Even so, allowing for the maximum time of ten minutes to an operation, he had ample free time left to spend with his wife and family.

William Henry Belk, director of the foundation he set up for the study of psychic phenomena, received so many enthusiastic reports of "Dr. Tony's" marvels that he flew from Miami to Manila in 1965 to see for himself the fantastic operations.

Intrigued by medical techniques that might possibly open up a new era in surgery, Belk financed a series of laboratory tests at the Tokyo Institute of Religious Psychology. In Elizabeth Read's "Science Measures Psychic Healer's Force," an article published in the January 1967 issue of *Fate*, she said that Dr. Hiroshi Motoyama supervised the investigation in February 1966. The previous month he had expressed astonishment at the psychic's being able to plunge his hands into bodies and remove growths without first administering anesthetics or hypnotizing his patients. Motoyama was equally amazed to find these operations left no scars and to see the patients afterward walking without assistance from the operating table to the door. But for some reason it apparently never occurred to the researcher to start his scientific investigation in the operating room. His February experiments were designed solely to ascertain if the psychic could "influence the mind and body of a subject without the use of any physical means or sensory clues."

The monitoring instruments employed were (1) an electroencephalograph (to chart brain waves via electrodes fastened to the scalp); (2) a plethysmograph (to indicate expansion or dilation of blood vessels in the fingers); (3) a galvanic graph (to measure variations in skin response caused by excitation); and (4) a pneumatograph (to record the pattern of respiration).

"Dr. Tony" and one of his targets (either Miyoko Tojo, a youth, or Kinue Motoyama, the psychologist's mother) rested on beds, separated by an opaque screen, in one room; the instruments to which they were attached were housed behind a concrete wall in another.

Each day for five days the mystic from the Philippines participated in five tests. During each he concentrated for sixty seconds, relaxed for three minutes, then tried to exert an invisible influence again. A weak electric shock signaled him when to start and stop his concentration.

Analyzing the twenty-five sets of graph patterns, Dr. Motoyama concluded that when "Dr. Tony" concentrated, measurable changes occurred in both his and his target's minds and bodies. "We can find a fixed direction (becoming quiet or active) caused by the concentration in the sender or the receiver." Between the changes, the psychologist reported, there were often indications as to "the direction of the changes." Not enough tests were made to be statistically conclusive, Motoyama cautioned, but he thought the results warranted further scientific study.

"Dr. Tony" returned from his trip to Japan to find business better than ever. Not all his clients were satisfied, however. Some Americans flew home from the Philippines convinced they had been cured; most returned to the United States still suffering from their various ailments. The late Joe Pyne, a caustic radio and television host in California, delighted in exposing frauds and phonies on his popular programs. After interviewing several writers who gave eye-witness accounts of the marvels they had seen across the Pacific and learning that more and more Americans, hoping for instantaneous recoveries, were departing for the Philippines each day, Pyne decided to go to Manila himself. He phoned Harold Sherman, the author of *"Wonder" Healers of the Philippines,* for the addresses of "Dr. Tony" and his competitors. Sherman complied, warning Pyne that he might encounter fraud as well as "genuine phenomena."

Pyne came back with material for the most exciting television program of his career. He ran a film of a "psychic operation," then staged a facsimile of the feat with a man playing the surgeon's role and a woman enacting the part of the patient. The "surgeon" kneaded the prone patient's abdomen, made a slashing move with his right hand, and blood oozed up from the "cut." The "surgeon" reached in and extracted an ugly red mass; after massaging the skin with his open hand, he lifted his hand to show the "incision" had healed.

Then the trickery was explained. During the kneading of the abdomen, the left hand squeezed and formed a fold in the flesh. When the "cut" was made, the "surgeon" filled the cavity with red liquid from a sponge concealed in his right hand. The wiping away of the "blood" gave the "surgeon" the opportunity to palm a bit of animal tissue and force it into the cavity as he reached down "into the body" with his fingers. Then he dramatically pulled the gory mass from the "cut." Throughout this maneuver his left fingers exerted pressure to maintain the illusion that an incision had been made in the flesh. Finally he covered the "cut" with the palm of his right hand and released the fold of skin which had been held by his left fingers. The flesh returned to its normal tautness before his right hand was lifted. Since there had been no incision, there was no scar.

Harold Sherman objected to this exposure. In the August 1967 issue of *Fate* magazine, he said Pyne had admitted real blood was used during the operations in the Philippines. The red liquid squeezed into the artificial skin cavity during the TV show was not blood. Blood would clot in the sponge the "surgeon" had palmed before it could be forced out, Sherman stated. (Sherman was right about the clotting, but the "surgeon" could have used real blood, if he had wished, by palming it, too, in a small stoppered vial.)

Sherman continued to stress in his lectures, which were illustrated with films of psychic surgery, that he did not recommend anyone going to the Philippines until the sensational healings had been authenticated by qualified authorities. Still, he insisted, he had seen genuine phenomena there.

In 1973, three West Coast travel agencies were booking psychic-surgery tours to the Philippines. Accounts of miraculous instant cures in books, magazines, and on radio and television programs, plus effective newspaper advertisements, colorful brochures printed for the travel firms by Northwest Airlines and Pan-American World Airways, and free showings of convincing films drummed up trade.

Early in 1974 the Federal Trade Commission sought and gained an injunction banning the promotion and scheduling of these flights by Gem Travel Services, Inc., of Seattle; Travel King, Inc., of San Francisco; and Phil-Am Travel Agency, which operates in both cities.

During the federal court hearing in Seattle, Richard M. Douglass testified that he had flown with his wife to Manila in November 1973. American doctors had told them that a tumor in Mrs. Douglass's throat could not be removed, even by the most skillful surgeon. They invested their lifetime savings, hoping for a miracle cure. Douglass said that after the operation he had put the allegedly "cancerous" growth in a bottle with a preservative fluid and brought it back to the States. Sworn statements by E. G. Burwalk and Arnold D. Hoekzema, the physician and the pathologist who analyzed the "cancerous tissue," were presented to the court. What had been termed a "tumor" by the psychic surgeon was, in their expert opinion, "a small bowel . . . of a small animal."

The Federal Trade Commission was instructed by the court to inform the thousand or so people who had signed up for the canceled tours that psychic surgery was a deception. "No incision is made, and diseased tissue is not removed from the human body."

The technique employed by Philippine charlatans is a variation of an ancient practice. Sorcerers of primitive tribes in many parts of the world have "cured" fellow tribesmen by applying their lips to sore areas of the body, then spitting out the stones or small bones they earlier had concealed in their mouths.

American Indian medicine men staged their healing sessions with maximum dramatic effect. Alexander Henry in his book, *Travels in Canada and the Indian Territories between the Years 1760 and 1776*, published in New York in 1809, described a typical ritual. He had been present when an Ojibwa shaman treated a young patient. She was feverish, had difficulty in breathing, and appeared to be "in the last stage of consumption." The medicine man chanted, shook a rattle, then put one end of a short, hollow bone to her skin. He sucked through it, then apparently forced the bone down his own throat, and swallowed it. This action was repeated two more times. Each time the Indian acted as if some of the pain had been transferred to his own body. With appropriate contortions, he eventually disgorged two of the bones. Embedded in a groove of one of them was "a small white substance resembling a piece of the quill of a feather." This substance, the medicine man claimed, had caused his patient's agony. The conjuring feat strengthened the impact of his appeal for help from the invisible spirits.

Wonder-workers are reported to have healed at one time or another practically every disease or ailment known to man. Down through the ages the most popular healers have been those who offered quick cures or could display some tangible evidence of their powers. Until recent times, however, few of the miracle-mongers have claimed to practice divine dentistry.

The Reverend Willard Fuller, a lively, bespectacled Louisianan, professes to be God's chosen instrument for repairing defective molars. Ordained as a Southern Baptist preacher, he spent the first ten years of his ministry without realizing that one day God would choose him for a special mission.

Until the spring of 1960 Fuller's healings were of a general nature: stomach ailments, skin disfigurements, and respiratory troubles. That March he attended a meeting held by another revivalist, the Reverend A. C. McKaig. A specialist in curing tooth decay, McKaig prayed that Fuller would be enabled to share this gift; apparently his prayer was answered. Thereafter Fuller caused fillings and inlays to materialize, and when he touched discolored incisors, they glowed with sudden whiteness.

In his book *Probing the Unexplained*, Allen Spraggett, religion editor of the Toronto *Daily Star*, tells of seeing Fuller in action at a suburban United Apostolic Faith church.

"If God can put silver or gold in a mountain, He can put it in your mouth!" the fiery evangelist shouted. Fifty or so listeners came forward; Fuller examined their teeth with the aid of a handled dental mirror. He also carried a bottle of antiseptic solution to make this task more pleasant.

Saying he had spotted two small cavities in the mouth of a volunteer, Fuller held the sides of the man's jaw and roared: "Lord, heal these teeth! For Jesus' sake!"

Those near the man on the platform peered in his mouth after this plea and reported that two fillings made of a substance that appeared to be gold were firmly fixed in place. Spraggett later questioned the volunteer. Hugo Mittendorf said he had traveled twenty-five miles to attend the service; he had not known he had any cavities, but now two gleaming new fillings sparkled in two lower molars. Others who participated in the ritual had similar experiences.

Skeptical dentists have suggested that Willard could have pressed the "fillings" on the teeth when he originally examined the mouths of the volunteers. Spraggett, however, did not observe any suspicious moves on the part of the healer. I lost interest in holy dentistry when I learned that Willard Fuller, who is credited with causing new teeth to grow as well as producing mysterious fillings, wears a set of dentures.

Perhaps the best-publicized psychic surgeon of recent times was the late Brazilian, José Arigó. A plump muscular man with dark hair and a moustache, he apparently became entranced when the spirit of a "Dr. Adolpho Fritz" possessed him. Though this spirit physician said he had been born in Munich, practiced medicine in Poland, and died in Estonia in 1918, no one has found a shred of evidence that a man with this name and background ever existed—except in Arigó's imagination. The prescriptions Arigó scrawled so swiftly that only his versatile assistant, a man known as Altimiro, could fully decipher and type, were written in Portuguese, but when Arigó assumed his Dr. Fritz role, he spoke with a heavy German accent and at times conversed in this language.

World travelers who thought the psychic surgeons of the Philippines were fast workers were stunned by the Brazilian's pace. He saw up to sixty patients in as many minutes and rarely took more than ninety seconds for even the most complex operation. Arigó shocked medical observers by borrowing their pocketknives and making incisions with the dull side of the blade. The knives were not sterilized; occasionally they were rusty. Yet, it is said, none of his clients became infected.

One of Arigó's favorite diagnostical tactics was to shove a paring knife between a patient's eyeball and the socket, then scrape. Sometimes he left the knife hanging there as he turned away. The residue he found on the blade after removing it seemingly gave him a clue to the sufferer's ailment. Following Arigó's operations, the flesh healed immediately—except for a small gash.

When I read of this, it recalled to my mind a trick I had learned as a boy. With a sharp knife I slashed my left thumb, just below the knuckle, from side to side. The bloody cut extended almost an inch. Rubbing the wound with the fingertips of my right hand, I then healed the incision in seconds, or so it appeared.

Actually I made only a small nick on the left side of my thumb. As I seemed to cut across the skin, I forced a drop of blood up through the nick and spread it with the end of the knife along the deepest wrinkle from left to right. This thin crimson line looked exactly like an open wound. I "healed" it by wiping away the blood with the secretly moistened fingertips of my right hand.

Brazil's most famous psychic surgeon was born José Pedro de Freitas in Congonhas do Campo, a city north of Rio de Janeiro in the state of Minas Gerais, on October 18, 1918. He worked on his father's farm even during the three years he went to school. His friends called him Arigó, a Portuguese term for a good-natured but not especially bright country bumpkin. Later he labored as a miner and, for a short time, with money borrowed from his father, ran a bar and restaurant. Along with other members of his family, he was keenly interested in local politics. Lamartine de Freitas, an uncle, defeated Arigó by a slim margin when he contended for the office of mayor in 1954. By then the first of the fabulous stories about his psychic operations had spread through the country.

Pedro McGregor, one of the healer's friends, tells of the incident in *The Moon and Two Mountains*, published in London in 1966. Arigó had gone to Belo Horizonte, the state capital, in 1950 with a group of Congonhas do Campo miners to attend a political rally for Senator Lucio Bittencourt. At five the following morning, having attended the rally and a barbecue at which there was heavy drinking, the senator awoke Arigó by banging on the door of his room. He asked Arigó to walk with him to a drugstore, explaining that he needed to buy a razor blade, so he could shave before boarding an early plane. On the way to the drugstore Bittencourt collapsed in the street. A policeman stayed with him while Arigó went to get him a cup of coffee. Bittencourt regained consciousness when Arigó returned and told the officer that he was still weak because his friend had performed an operation on his lungs only a few hours before. Arigó denied this; he said the senator had had too much to drink.

Later, at the hotel, Bittencourt gave Arigó his version of what he thought had happened. He said that Arigó had entered his room at two o'clock that morning, then slowly evaporated as a bald, obese foreign doctor and three aides, dressed in surgical white, materialized. The stout physician announced he was going to operate. At that moment, Bittencourt confessed, he himself fainted. The senator picked up the pajamas he had worn and showed them to Arigó. There was a slash of the sort a knife would make down the back of the jacket. Argió's comment when Bittencourt insisted he had not been dreaming was, "You should have your head examined."

According to McGregor, surgery had been on the politician's mind. Suffering from a lung tumor, Bittencourt had flown to the United States before the Belo Horizonte rally only to be told by specialists that an operation to remove the tumor was too dangerous. After the senator returned to Rio de Janeiro from Belo Horizonte, an X ray of his chest showed that the tumor had disappeared. This convinced him that Arigó had operated upon him psychically.

John G. Fuller, whose book *Arigo: Surgeon of the Rusty Knife* was published in New York in 1974, gives another version of this episode. Bittencourt, he says, went to the pharmacy to get a cup of tea—not a razor blade—and collapsed there, not in the street. Further, there was blood on the pajama top and a fresh wound on the senator's back.

The Bittencourt tale drew the sick, the halt, the lame, and the blind from Rio, São Paulo, and Bahia, as well as the neighboring villages, to the house of the psychic healer in Congonhas do Campo. Arigó worked from noon to six o'clock as a government clerk, and saw his patients in the morning and after he completed his daily chores.

The senator's story was the genesis of "Dr. Fritz" and the belief that Arigó took on the personality of a German physician when entranced; Arigó claimed that other spirits controlled his hands under "Dr. Fritz's" direction, among them, "Gilbert Pierre," a French ophthalmologist, and "Takahaski," a Japanese specialist in tumor removal.

Soon Arigó opened his own consulting rooms, the Jesus Nazarene Spiritist Center. Though he did not disavow Roman Catholicism and refused payment for his treatments, the Church censured him and the Brazilian Medical Association attacked him for practicing as a physician and as a surgeon without a license.

In the summer of 1963 two visitors from the United States arrived in Congonhas do Campo to study Arigó's miraculous cures: William Henry Belk, who later sponsored the experiments made with the Philippine healer "Dr. Tony" in Tokyo, and Andrija Puharich, neurologist-parapsychologist and publicist-to-be of Uri Geller.

Films were made of Arigó in action, and Puharich volunteered as a subject for a piece of minor surgery. A small growth had annoyed him for some time. It was in his right arm, close to the nerve that activated his little finger; it was not malignant.

Arigó borrowed a pocketknife. With characteristic impulsiveness he grasped Puharich's arm with one hand as he cut with the knife held in the other. Before he made this incision, however, he instructed Puharich to turn his head away, which the American did. Why Puharich averted his eyes at the crucial moment is hard to understand. He had gone to South America to investigate Arigó's methods. When the opportunity came to get a close-up view as the psychic surgeon went to work on Puharich's own arm, he looked in the opposite direction.

Fuller says in his book on Arigó that when Puharich saw the film of this operation he almost thought trickery had been used in the same way it had been used in the Philippines. The lipoma squeezed by the psychic surgeon from the small incision was quickly removed. However, Puharich said, there was no longer a growth in his arm, and he had the tumor preserved in a bottle.

The operation itself was over in a few seconds. No X ray had been taken of the American's arm immediately before the operation. Did the growth dissolve as growths sometimes do? Did Arigó have a lipoma concealed in his fingers and bring it into view when he pressed them to the cut? X rays taken before and after might have solved this riddle.

Puharich brought a team of American investigators that included several physicians as well as photographers, a New York University professor of Portuguese, two psychic healers from Baltimore, and a Maryland psychiatrist, to Brazil in May 1968. Along with other medical equipment, he carried a small X-ray machine, but no conclusive before-and-after operation plates have since been released.

While Arigó used a knife, a pair of nail scissors, or some other form of sharp instrument for almost all his mindboggling surgery, Fuller reported one case where he operated with his bare hands. A man named Juvenal, who worked as a chauffeur for Jacques Riffaud, a supervisor of Brazilian mining projects for a European firm, told his employer and Comtesse Pamela de Maigret, a geologist, the story of his encounter with the psychic surgeon. Convinced that he would die unless a cancerous growth in his stomach was removed, Juvenal went to Congonhas do Campo. Discouraged by the throng waiting in line to see Arigó, he had given up hope of entering the clinic that day. As Arigó left the Spiritist Center, he singled out Juvenal in the crowd, prescribed a medicine for him, and told him to return the following day.

The next morning Arigó put his patient on a makeshift table in a room at the back of the clinic, bared his midsection, and began manipulating his skin. A sharp popping sound signaled the opening of the flesh. Arigó inserted his bare hands in Juvenal's body and yanked out the cancerous material. The skin closed immediately, leaving only a tiny blemish on its surface.

When Juvenal told his employer, Riffaud, and the geologist about this incredible operation, Fuller says they were dubious; however, an X ray revealed the growth was gone.

The reader will note the procedure described for this "operation" parallels that employed by the psychic surgeons of the Philippines. No affidavits signed by those who took X rays before and after the "operation" were offered to validate the cure.

Understandably the Brazilian Medical Association sided

with legal authorities who held that "the surgeon with the rusty knife" was a charlatan. Arigó had many brushes with the law. Once while he was in custody awaiting trial, according to Pedro McGregor, "Dr. Fritz" proclaimed that if Arigó were jailed, "Fritz" and his ghostly associates would "materialize in public squares in full daylight and operate upon the needy for all to see, so long as Arigó remains in his cell." Arigó was found guilty of illegally practicing medicine. The state court of appeals sustained the verdict of the lower court, and the psychic healer was incarcerated. Those who expected the spectral surgeons to take human form and treat the poor in the open air were sorely disappointed.

In March 1957 Arigó received his first sentence: fifteen months in jail, a fine of five thousand cruzeiros, and court costs. The court of appeals modified this verdict to eight months in jail and a smaller fine. Before he started to serve this term, the President of Brazil, Juscelino Kubitschek, interceded and pardoned the psychic healer. Kubitschek had met Arigó and visited him at his home in Congonhas do Campo while campaigning for the presidency in 1955. After the election, when a pair of large kidney stones troubled his ailing daughter, the President telephoned him for help. Arigó came to Rio de Janeiro and wrote a prescription. This medicine, Kubitschek said later, caused the stones to dissolve.

Nevertheless, seven years later, in 1964, Arigó was tried and found guilty of practicing witchcraft as well as illegal medicine. Sentenced to a sixteen-month term, he was in a prison cell at Lafaiete when Andrija Puharich wrote Judge Filippe Immesi, identifying himself as an espouser of authentic psychics and an exposer of fraudulent mediums. He said he could attest to the curative effects of Arigó's surgery and prescriptions, and hoped the judge would be compassionate "in the interests of humanity."

The case was reviewed in June 1965. The conviction was upheld, but so much pressure had been exerted by Arigó's supporters that he was released from prison. Judge Immesi ruled in August that the controversial healer must return to the cell in Lafaiete, but only for a short time. Arigó was a free man again early in November 1965.

En route to Lafaiete on January 11, 1971, his Opala sedan crashed into a truck coming from the opposite direction, and Arigó was killed.

The following year, while addressing the Academy of Parapsychology and Medicine, a group formed in California to study unorthodox healing practices, Puharich said he could not prove a spirit doctor directed Arigó, but it seemed to him that the scales tipped in favor of the spirit concept. How could an untrained man outstrip any diagnostician Puharich had ever met and perform such incredible surgery unless he was guided by another greater intelligence?

Puharich abandoned the spirit theory in his 1974 book on Uri Geller. The powerful directing force of psychics, he said, came from Hoova, a hitherto undiscovered planet. The super intelligence there even arranged for him to receive by telephone the news of Arigó's tragic accident in Brazil a full hour before it happened.

Psychic surgery, as practiced in Brazil, the Philippines, and other places, is quite simply one of the cruelest hoaxes ever perpetrated on a credulous public. Writers who offer dramatic "documented" accounts of supernormal surgery without indicating how trickery can be used to create the illusion share the guilt of the modern witch doctors.

A drowning man grasps at a straw, and so do those with incurable illnesses. But a straw has more substance than the claims of the unscrupulous who pretend to cut deep into human bodies with bare hands or rusty knives and remove diseased tissue without anesthetics or sutures and without causing pain. The instant healing of severed flesh is, as I have shown, a trick, nothing more.

PETER HURKOS—
PSYCHIC SLEUTH

Peter Hurkos, a tall, restless man with dark eyes, dark hair, and an expressive face, grasps a wedding ring, a snapshot, or a necktie. He grimaces, grits his teeth, bites his lip, then reels off data about the object and the owner's history. The Dutch psychometrist (the ability to gain verifiable data from an object is known as psychometry) has been called the world's most successful psychic sleuth.

"That Hurkos ranges from 87% to 99% accuracy in his psychic projections is irrefutable," the jacket of Norma Lee Browning's *The Psychic World of Peter Hurkos*, a biography published in 1970, proclaims. Yet many incidents cited in the book belie this assertion. For instance, the suspect Hurkos identified as "the Boston Strangler" was not the person charged with the crimes.

Again, he named a thirty-four-year-old trashman as the vicious slayer of a Falls Church, Virginia, couple and their two small children. Ten days later the FBI arrested a musician, who was later tried and found guilty by a jury. Asked by his biographer to comment on this, the psychic admitted: "Oh, I picked the wrong man."

In his book *The Door to the Future*, published in 1963, Jess Stearn tells of Hurkos's attempt to predict the outcome of the 1959 baseball season. In the pages of *This Week*, a syndicated newspaper supplement, he correctly named the Los

Angeles Dodgers as the National League pennant winner but missed out when he selected the New York Yankees in the American League. Furthermore, it was the Chicago White Sox, not the Yankees, who won the world championship.

The psychometrist credited with solving murders in seventeen countries was born Pieter Van der Hurk in Dordrecht, Holland, on May 21, 1911. The son of a house painter, he worked at this trade in the summer. In the winter he went to sea, first as a messboy, then as an engine-room stoker and as an oiler, on ships bound for Java and other exotic ports in the Pacific. He was hired as a dockside cargo and passenger checker in Shanghai. When Japanese troops invaded China, he returned to the Netherlands, but, of course, this was no escape from World War II, as German forces occupied Holland in 1940.

In June 1943, Peter and his father were ordered to paint Nazi barracks in The Hague green and yellow, so they would be less visible to Allied planes. As Peter reached with his brush to daub a window, he slipped and fell headfirst from the ladder on which he was standing to the asphalt street some thirty feet below.

Three days later he regained consciousness in a hospital. There at the age of thirty-two, Hurkos says in his autobiography *Psychic,* published by Bobbs-Merrill in 1961, "I discovered the strange gift that God had given me." Almost immediately he began astounding the medical staff and the other patients with his uncanny revelations.

Before and after this injury, Hurkos stole ammunition and carried out secret missions for the Dutch resistance. Arrested when a Gestapo official seized his counterfeit passport, he was sent to the notorious Buchenwald concentration camp in Germany. Spared from the gas chamber because he was not a Jew, he suffered with other inmates until they were liberated by the advancing Canadian and American armies. Billed as Peter Hurkos, the name he had used in the underground, he made his theatrical debut in 1946 in a variety show at the *Kaas Lange* in The Hague. The following year, according to his autobiography, Hurkos took his first case as a psychic detective. Called in by the police of Limburg, another city in the Netherlands, he concentrated while clutching a coat. It had been worn by a young miner before an unknown assailant shot him. The killer, Peter proclaimed, had been a much older man; he wore glasses, had a moustache, and hobbled along on a wooden leg.

This description fitted Bernard van Tossing, the victim's stepfather; he had been taken into custody before the psychic arrived. The murder weapon, however, had not been found. Hurkos again wrinkled his brow in concentration. The weapon was on the roof of the victim's house, he told the police. On the rooftop, searchers found a pistol with two spent shells in the barrel and the old man's fingerprints. Bernard van Tossing was tried and convicted.

Hurkos said in his book the Limburg police department might deny the part he played in solving this mystery. Since then, other law-enforcement officials have stated that the psychic sleuth has exaggerated his role in widely publicized cases.

Scotland Yard, for example, informed the press on January 24, 1950, when the theft of the Stone of Scone was a major news topic in Great Britain: "We are not seeing Mr. Hurkos. We did not ask him to come to London. We have not sought his assistance. He is only one of the many telepathists, clairvoyants and water-diviners, etc., who have offered us information, all of which has been tested and sifted."

Hearing that the massive slab had been stolen from under the coronation chair in Westminster Abbey, Hurkos crossed the Channel and hurried to the scene of the theft. British papers had voiced the opinion that the historic symbol, on which the early Scottish kings were crowned, had been carted away by Scottish nationalists. This was a reasonable assumption. What better way to dramatize Scottish discontent than to recover the 400-pound stone which had remained in Westminster Abbey ever since Edward I brought it there in 1296?

After due concentration, the psychic drew a sketch, tracing the route the stonenappers had taken as they hauled their prize out of the city. The accuracy of this map has never been confirmed or denied, but Hurkos succeeded in his mission; his name appeared in many British papers, along with accounts of his triumphs on the Continent. Returning to England from Europe a week later, Hurkos drove to Glasgow. He said in his book: "I knew the stone was there. . . . but I did not find the stone."

Official investigators, through routine, painstaking police

procedures, learned the missing slab was in a ruined abbey in Arbroath, Angus County, far to the northeast of Glasgow. The Scots returned the Stone of Scone a hundred and nine days after they had taken it; no charges were pressed.

Hurkos, who was billed in the theatres as "The Man with the Radar Brain," says law-enforcement officials in Belgium, France, and Spain were more appreciative of his talent than the "cold and unbelieving" men at Scotland Yard.

Generalissimo Francisco Franco attended a performance featuring the Dutch mystic at a Madrid theatre in 1952; he also was present when Hurkos entertained at a party given in the palace by the royal physician. The Spanish dictator "did not seem to be the least bit interested," the psychic admitted later, so he gave a much shorter exhibition than usual. Despite this, here as elsewhere, Hurkos garnered considerable space in the national press. He told reporters Adolf Hitler had fled to Spain from Germany; the German leader was no longer in Spain, but he was still alive: "I'll stake my life and reputation on it." At the time of this sensational statement in 1952, there were rumors that Hitler had been seen in Argentina. Since then, evidence has been produced to prove that the Nazi führer perished in his Berlin bunker in April 1945.

Andrija Puharich, the American neurologist-parapsychologist, brought the Dutch mystic to the United States in 1956 to be tested in his Round Table Foundation laboratory at Glen Cove, Maine. Dr. Puharich has called Hurkos "one of the greatest telepathic talents of modern times," which poses a question: Is Hurkos (if he has any psychic powers at all) a psychometrist or a telepathist? The first, by definition, receives psychic impressions as he concentrates on objects; the second intercepts thoughts. His admirers believe Peter is unusually talented in both areas; his readings are not always accurate because the thoughts he receives telepathically sometimes dominate the psychic impressions, they say.

American retail tycoon William Henry Belk contributed generously to Puharich's Round Table Foundation; he thought Hurkos's psychic skill could be put to effective use in the service of the Belk department stores. Later Jess Stearn's The Door to the Future would report that Hurkos's advice was anything but helpful. Stearn quotes Belk as saying that he lost twenty thousand dollars in Utah on a Hurkos-recommended search for uranium. The psychic also predicted the new Belk stores in Atlanta and Miami would be profitable investments; they were not.

The psychometrist was living in Miami in June 1957 when Belk's ten-year-old daughter vanished without a trace from the grounds of her father's North Carolina estate. Remembering that Peter had found missing children in Europe, Belk put in a call to Miami. Hurkos advised his patron not to worry; the girl would return.

Then, according to the Browning biography, a mental picture of the child lying dead under deep water near the Belk boathouse flashed through Hurkos's mind. He called back with this tragic revelation. Amazingly, the child's body was found where he said it would be.

The Dutch mystic had visited the Belk home; he had seen the boathouse on the river. Belk in his telephone call had told him that the grounds had been searched. Was it a psychic inspiration or logic that brought the scene of the girl's death to Peter's mind?

Whatever it was, his relationship with Belk would never be the same again. If Hurkos could see into the future, Belk asked after recovering from the shock of his loss, why hadn't he been warned in time to save the girl's life?

In Miami, Hurkos starred in a series of television shows and impressed radio fans by appearing with Alan Courtney, a popular late night host; Peter gave information about listeners without hearing the voices of those who called in to question him. As Hurkos described the technique, he had merely to hold the telephone cord and data about the caller flowed from it.

Late in 1958 he performed in a Curaçao theatre and entertained Dutch troops stationed nearby. A film made the following year, with an actor playing the Hurkos role, dramatized the psychic's life and was shown on network television in 1961.

Though Hurkos recounted his adventures as a psychic detective in his 1961 autobiography, there was not even a passing reference to his work in the Jackson murder case in June of the previous year when he had gone to Falls Church, Virginia, and after considerable investigation and cogitation, picked the wrong man as the slayer. He did note, however, that he was in a new business. He had discovered a gold mine in Colorado. "The mine," he said, "is going to produce all the money I will need for my livelihood and to pursue my personal goal, the furtherance of psychic research through my foundation."

This was one of his most embarrassing predictions. The foundation, which Hurkos set up in Milwaukee, disintegrated when his wife, whom he had married in Europe, left him for the administrator. The wealth from the Colorado mine never materialized. Hurkos went back to work as an entertainer and psychic sleuth.

I watched him perform on the Steve Allen television show on July 19, 1963. Allen announced the famous Dutch psychic had recently become an American citizen. Holding and squeezing one of the opaque envelopes in which members of the studio audience had earlier sealed one of their personal possessions, Hurkos told the owner of one of these objects that there was nothing wrong with his stomach. The man agreed. The psychic then asked him why he had changed the date set for his marriage; the man replied that he hadn't.

Hurkos told a girl she had been in a ballet at school. She denied this. He asked her why she quit school. She said she hadn't; she was still attending. He stated three people lived in her house. She replied she lived by herself. He said she had a picture of her boyfriend. This was true. "Who is Tom?" he asked. She didn't know. Her boyfriend was six feet tall, Hurkos stated. She said that was right. Hurkos said she went with her boyfriend to a lake where there were trees. She disagreed. She said he took her to Disneyland.

Hurkos returned to the Steve Allen show on August twentieth. This time the objects had been placed in paper bags by their owners. He squeezed a bag and said something round was inside—"like a lipstick." It was not a lipstick, he continued, but a medicine bottle; it was brown. He asked the owner to stand. An elderly woman, with gray hair, glasses, and a Spanish accent, rose.

Hurkos said there were two people in her family. She replied that she lived alone. He said he saw an operation. She denied having had one. He said her mother had been dead many years. She said, "Yes." "You were six," he said. "No," she answered, "I was ten."

This viewer switched to another channel.

Hurkos was called in on his most famous case, that of "the Boston Strangler," in January 1964. For eighteen months a rapist-murderer had terrorized the city and nearby towns. Eleven women had been found dead, with nylon stockings or other apparel knotted around their necks. A prominent citizen offered to pay the psychic a thousand dollars and all expenses if he would use his remarkable gift to identify the killer. Peter and a friend, Jim Crane, flew in from California. Crane, six foot eight inches tall, wearing a broad-brimmed cowboy hat and carrying a pistol on his hip, served as Hurkos's bodyguard and tape-recorder operator. Unless someone taped the torrent of words that poured from the psychic's lips when he became inspired, vital clues might be missed.

The Massachusetts assistant attorney general, John S. Bottomly, had not informed the press of the psychic's arrival; his staff arranged for the acccumulated data on the killings to be brought to Hurkos's room the following day. Ever the showman, Hurkos astonished detectives and other officials by apparently only glancing at the backs of the police photographs of the crimes, then sprawling on the floor to reproduce the photographed positions of the victims. On a stage his virtuoso performance would have brought rounds of applause.

This was just the beginning. Holding the nylon stockings and undergarments with which the murderer had strangled his victims, Hurkos concentrated on the identity of the killer.

In his best-selling book *The Boston Strangler*, published in 1967, Gerold Frank quoted the psychic as saying, "I see him . . . he is not too big, five feet seven or eight— he weigh a hundred and thirty or forty pounds." The murderer had a sharp nose; his left arm bore a scar from an accident; one of his thumbs had lost its normal sensitivity; he talked French and English in a high-pitched voice; and, Hurkos continued, he was a pervert.

Then, with a map of the city of Boston before him, the psychic pointed to the area where, he said, the murderer lived. The next day an official handed Hurkos a letter a suspect had written and asked for his reaction to it. The psychic wadded the paper, gripped it, and after concentrating, blurted out that the writer of the letter was indeed the strangler!

There was only one flaw in Hurkos's brilliant performance: the letter writer was not Albert DeSalvo. DeSalvo later confessed to the crimes and gave an accurate, blood-chilling account of how, when, and where he had strangled each woman.

Hurkos himself, "the Man with the X-Ray Mind," was arrested in New York a few days after he left Boston. The headline in the February 11, 1964, issue of the *Daily News* read: "PSYCHIC SLEUTH FAILED TO SEE FBI ON HIS TRAIL."

The previous December a gas-station attendant in Wauwautosa, Wisconsin, who was filling the tank of Hurkos's car noticed two rifles and two pistols in the trunk. When asked about these weapons, Hurkos had identified himself as an FBI agent, the attendant said when he reported the incident. After Hurkos was jailed in Manhattan, Andrija Puharich posted the $2,500 bond needed for his release.

"Did you have any premonition of bad luck before they arrested you here Sunday?" the *News* reporter asked. "Not a glimmer. My powers never seem to work when I try to use them on my own behalf," Hurkos answered.

The psychic carried various badges with him: chief deputy coroner, Lake County, Illinois; special officer, Miami, Florida; deputy sheriff, Maricopa County, Arizona; honorable special assistant to the attorney general of Massachusetts. He testified in court that the Wisconsin gas-station attendant had misunderstood him; he had referred to himself as "more than the FBI." The judge who tried the case accepted this explanation.

An opportunity came in the spring of 1967 to counteract the adverse publicity he had received following "the Boston Strangler" episode and his arrest by the FBI. Hurkos was hired to track down a wealthy American businessman who had disappeared in northern Malaysia.

James H. W. Thompson had made a fortune in Bangkok, exporting Thai silk. En route to sales meetings in Singapore, he stopped off to visit friends in the Cameron Highlands. On the afternoon of Easter Sunday, March twenty-sixth, he left his friends in their mountaintop house, saying he planned to sit in the sun on the veranda. No one ever saw him again.

A former army colonel, Thompson had worked with the Office of Strategic Services in Southeast Asia. Some people thought he still gathered information for a military intelligence unit; possibly he had been kidnapped or murdered. An intensive search of the Cameron Highlands area provided no clues to the strange disappearance.

Sent by James H. Douglas and his wife of Chicago to search for the missing American—Mrs. Douglas was a sister of Thompson's—Hurkos on April nineteenth boarded a plane. Upon his arrival in Hong Kong, he went to the Chinese border. There, staring at a photograph of Thompson, he tried to sense if the missing man had been spirited off to the mainland. The vibrations were negative. Hurkos then flew on, not to Malaysia where Thompson had vanished, but to Thailand.

After walking through the rooms of Thompson's beautifully decorated house in Bangkok, and occasionally stopping to touch an Oriental art object or feel a colorful fabric, the psychic decided he was ready to move on to Malaysia.

Five days after he left California, Hurkos arrived at the cottage in the Cameron Highlands where the silk merchant had last been seen. His psychic impressions told him Thompson had been abducted by fourteen men. One walked up the driveway and awoke Thompson, who had fallen asleep in his chair. This man, whose name was Bebe, Predie, or Pridi, was a friend of Thompson's. They walked down the hill together until they were out of sight of the house; the American was seized, doped or blindfolded, then carried off in a truck. A plane flew Thompson to Cambodia, as Hurkos reconstructed the events.

Hurkos was as certain that Thompson was in Cambodia as he had been that Hilter was alive. Permission for the psychic to continue his search in Cambodia was denied. William Warren, whose "Is Jim Thompson Alive and Well in Asia?" appeared in the April 21, 1968, issue of *The New York Times Magazine,* said Pridi Phanamyong, a former prime minister of Thailand, had known Thompson. Phanamyong had been banished from Thailand in 1949, and when last heard of, was in China. Possibly this was the Pridi the psychic had named as the American's abductor.

Mrs. Katherine Thompson Wood, the missing exporter's eldest sister, was killed by an unknown intruder in her Pennsylvania home in late August 1967, five months after her brother's disappearance. Hurkos was not asked to solve this mystery, but his biographer says the psychic feels her death was in some way related to her brother's abduction. As Thompson has not been found, and as the identity of his sister's slayer has never been established, this nebulous link is still a matter of conjecture.

Hurkos appeared on television again, along with other specialists in various fields of the occult, on the July 28, 1969, syndicated "David Frost Show." He asked a young woman in the audience why she hadn't finished college; she said she was still a student. He told her she could swim but could not dive because of an ear infection. She denied ever having had any trouble with her ears. What about her throat? She admitted that her tonsils had been removed.

Putting his hand in a paper bag to touch a personal possession put there earlier by a spectator, Hurkos said, "He is clean but loves to sleep." The owner of the object turned out to be a female. The mystic said there were four people in her family; she said there were three. Later Hurkos told a young man he had almost been killed. The man denied this. "Almost drowned?" Another denial. "Who's Max?" Hurkos asked. The spectator didn't know. "Did you fall off a boat as a young kid?" "No."

Hurkos was given a box to hold containing, Frost said, an object that had been given to Leonard Lyons, the New York columnist. The psychic gave his impressions: the former owner of the object had been "great as a genius"; the object was not a statue. He had mental pictures of fire, the psychic said, and a strong wire "like a phone."

The box was opened: inside was an ornate telephone; it had been taken from Adolf Hitler's retreat in Berchtesgaden. Hurkos then amended one of his earlier statements; he said "tried to be a genius" was what he had intended to say. The impact of this reading was blunted when Frost told viewers that the box had been opened earlier backstage so that he could be sure the telephone inside would televise properly.

Most people who see Hurkos at work remember his hits and

forget his misses; his accuracy score is not impressive. A report on "Two Token Object Studies with Peter Hurkos" by Charles T. Tart, a University of California psychologist, and Jeffrey Smith, a Stanford University investigator, appeared in the April 1968 issue of the *Journal of the American Society for Psychical Research*. They said, "We believed that Mr. Hurkos did possess significant psychic abilities and we wished to demonstrate them under rigorously controlled conditions."

Fifty-three sealed opaque envelopes containing locks of hair from fifty-three people were used in the first series of experiments. One day Hurkos gave readings on fifteen envelopes in the morning and ten in the afternoon. Another day he gave seventeen impressions in one session and eleven in another. Then he presented two readings directed to the people who had helped collect the hair samples. Evaluating Hurkos's taped comments for the first three sessions, the investigators said his hits were "almost exactly at chance expectation and obviously not significant." He did slightly better in the fourth series, but only to "a nonsignificant value." "We find no evidence of extrasensory perception" was the researchers' conclusion.

Another series of experiments along the same lines was conducted later. This, too, was a disappointment. "As in the first study," the investigators said, "the results give no evidence for any parapsychological factor."

Nevertheless, for more than thirty years—ever since Hurkos fell on his head in Holland—people have insisted that he could foresee the future as well as probe the past. He is a persuasive performer; he speaks emphatically and with great conviction.

While gathering material for *The Door to the Future*, Jess Stearn listened to the taped voice of the psychic as he dramatically foretold the exact date of his own death—November 17, 1961. When the book was published in 1963, Hurkos was still alive, and he is still plying his trade in California as I write these words.

EYELESS VISION

Press reports from the Soviet Union early in 1963 informed the world that Russian scientists had made a mind-boggling discovery—Rosa Kuleshova, a young woman from Nizhni Tagil, could "see" with her fingers! While securely blindfolded in tests at the Biophysics Institute of the Academy of Sciences in Moscow, the short plump woman had been able to identify colors and to read from a newspaper merely by touching them. Dr. Mikhail Smirnov, one of the men participating in the carefully planned laboratory trials, enthused: "The fingers have a retina. The fingers 'see' light." *Izvestia*, noting that eyeless vision was now an established fact, wondered if others had supersensitive fingers or if the gift were Rosa's alone.

The Russians were not aware that history was being repeated. What is known today as dermo-optical perception was investigated in Liverpool as far back as 1816. Margaret M'Avoy, then sixteen, amazed her physician when with a heavy, opaque shawl tied over her eyes she touched pieces of fabric and stained glass and called out the colors. After Dr. Thomas Renwick opened a book and selected a page at random, Margaret, moving her fingers across the page, read the words aloud. She perceived short words with a tap of her finger. Longer words required more extensive contact. She would put her left forefinger on the first letter and her right forefinger on the last, then, sliding them along the surface, bring the two fingers together. When they met, she spoke the word. Timing his patient with a pocket watch, the physician learned she could read thirty words in as many seconds.

All this would have been remarkable enough if Margaret M'Avoy had had normal vision without a blindfold, but she was thought to be almost totally blind. As a child, she had suffered from scarlet fever, whooping cough, and nose and ear infections. When her eyesight began to deteriorate, applications of a diluted brandy solution and poultices of watered bread were of little aid. Then a family friend recommended a pharmaceutical product, "Johnson's Golden Ointment." Until this treatment, Margaret had stayed in darkened rooms; bright sunlight caused her almost unbearable optic pain.

Sight returned to her right eye, but when she forced the lids of her left eye apart, she found she could see only indistinctly through it. Following a severe cold, she had a relapse. She told the physician she could only make out vague shapes of objects near her—unless she wore a blindfold.

A long report on the curious case by Egerton Smith appeared on August 5, 1817, in the *Liverpool Mercury*. For almost a year the writer had been visiting the M'Avoy residence on St. Paul's Square. Margaret, an attractive girl with an amiable nature and an "artless disposition," permitted visitors to test her strange gift in whatever way they chose. She did not perform for money; her family had ample means. After years as an invalid, she enjoyed her new role as a celebrity.

Margaret told Smith she had first become aware of her strange power when she was fifteen. Her sensitivity, she admitted, varied. She was at her best when her hands were warm. If they were cold, it was futile even to attempt to "see" with them. Generally, she said, she was at the peak of her power on alternate days between the hours of ten and noon.

Sometimes skeptical visitors put a book or a heavy cloth between her face and the objects she touched. She failed then, Margaret explained, because it was vital that she feel her breath on her fingers. When a barrier had been interposed, her fingers lost their sense of sight.

Smith noted that Margaret had never been tested in absolute

darkness. Even to make such a proposal, however, would imply that this charming member of a respectable family had been cheating. Further, it was "perfectly ridiculous" to expect her to see in the dark. How could anyone identify colors under those circumstances? Everything looks black when there is no light. Margaret did not profess to see what the human eye could not see; she claimed that her sense of sight had been transferred to her fingertips.

Yet Smith was not entirely convinced; on his second visit to the M'Avoy home, he was bold enough to suggest that the candle, which was usually close at hand when Margaret was blindfolded, be extinguished. Only a faint glow from the fireplace illuminated the room, and Mrs. M'Avoy stood between the hearth and her daughter. Margaret sat in a chair with her back to the fireplace and, despite the blindfold and the feeble light, had no difficulty in reading from the small book Smith had brought with him.

So many friends and acquaintances of the M'Avoy family came to see the incredible demonstrations that Margaret began wearing a mask. It was too hot and uncomfortable, she said, for her to have a heavy shawl tied around her head on humid days. This mask was made from a pair of "gogglers"—glasses designed to keep dust from the eyes of travelers who rode in open carriages were then in vogue. Consisting of two transparent disks of green glass fitted snugly into a wide band of leather that was tied at the back of the head, Margaret's "gogglers" were made opaque by two cardboard circles glued onto the glass.

A Mr. Nichol, who had come to Liverpool to deliver a series of philosophical lectures, went with Egerton Smith and another man to the M'Avoy house that summer. Nichol examined the "gogglers" and confessed he could not see even a glimmer of light when they were tied in place. Before Margaret put them on, she told Smith she had made a discovery since his previous visit: she could now "see" with the back of her hand as well as her fingers. That day her most brilliant perception occurred when she named the colors of seven pieces of stained glass which Smith had provided for the test.

Only one gave her trouble. She held the piece of glass and hesitated. It was not black or dark blue or dark brown, she stated.

She paused again, then said it was crimson. The three men took the glass to the window. It was a cloudy day and practically impossible for them to be sure of the hue. At that moment the sun came out. In the sunlight the color could be perceived. It *was* crimson.

Other investigators were more demanding than Smith. Some, doubting the effectiveness of either the shawl blindfold or the opaque "gogglers," covered her closed eyes with goldbeater's skin or with halves of the white portion of hard-boiled eggs. Still her finger vision was not impaired. The experiments made by an unnamed visitor in July and August 1817 are described in Volume Six of *Kirby's Wonderful and Eccentric Museum: or Magazine,* published in London three years later. By then Margaret could "see" with another portion of her anatomy. Her tongue had not been sensitive to color, but when the petals of various flowers were held between her lips, she correctly identified their hues.

She also proved she could "see" at a distance. Placing her fingers on a window pane, she was able to describe a laborer, a young woman carrying a child in her arms, and three wagons in the street below. And she tried to go one step further. If her fingers could "see," perhaps they could also taste. Margaret dipped them into two glasses, one filled with pure water, the other with water to which salt had been added. The attempt failed. She could not tell the difference.

Smith, who had been dropping by at the M'Avoys' every few days, finally stopped going. He said Margaret was always cordial, but he could never really believe her puzzling feats were accomplished solely by touch. He was positive "that the eye was in some way concerned in these mysteries." It would not have been polite for him as a guest to insist on certain precautions that would have completely ruled out the use of eyesight.

Smith later heard that Margaret was making further fantastic claims. She would ask a visitor to set the hands of his gold hunting-case watch and close the metal lid before she touched it. Holding the watch in her hand, she would then call off the location of the hour and minute hands, explaining she had developed the power to see through metal. She would also describe objects placed behind her back after stretching out her fingers in their direction. These demonstrations, Smith thought, were too much for even a gullible man to swallow.

Margaret M'Avoy's repertoire is the first-known, complete eyeless-vision routine; it encompasses most of the marvels performed by those who profess to see while blindfolded today. Margaret, however, was not the only person in Liverpool at that time to exhibit the talent of eyeless sight. One of her contemporaries, a Dennis Hendrick, won a ten-guinea bet with an outdoor demonstration, according to *Curiosities for the Ingenious,* which was published in London in 1821. In telling of Hendrick's "extraordinary" accomplishment, the author stresses how difficult it is for anyone to walk even a short distance in a straight line without seeing where he is going. Yet "sometime ago" Hendrick, a stone mason, had walked blindfolded for three quarters of a mile from the Liverpool Exchange, rolling a coach wheel beside him. Hendrick's eyes had been sealed with "two plasters of Burgundy pitch" before the blindfold was knotted in place.

How did Margaret M'Avoy and Dennis Hendrick perform their feats? The methods are well known to magicians. Plasters do not adhere as firmly to the skin as most people suppose. A facial grimace can loosen them slightly. Only a small space between cheek and nose is required for a downward peek under a blindfold. An occasional unobtrusive lift of the head increases the distance one can see forward. There is little doubt that Hendrick and Margaret M'Avoy peered down the sides of their noses. Some children discover this ruse when they are blindfolded for party games. Those with long or turned-up noses have an advantage, but with practice others can also master the technique.

A blindfold did not hinder the rope dancers of antiquity, nor does it make the feats of modern circus high-wire walkers more dangerous. In addition to peeks made from under a blindfold, ingenious entertainers have for years used specially prepared blindfolds. For example, the cloth on the side that is to cover the eyes may be scraped in advance to make the material more transparent. This method is a favorite of jugglers.

The subjects of Charles Poyen, a French mesmerist, excited widespread interest with their apparent ability to see while blindfolded during his demonstrations in New England in 1836. Poyen believed he transmitted his thoughts to them. In his *Let-*

ter to Col. Wm. L. Stone, published in Boston the following year, Poyen cited an example. The blindfolded woman could not identify the object held over her head until he "mentally articulated the word *'grape,'* willing her to repeat it. Instantly she shook her head, signifying she understood me, and repeated aloud, 'It is a bunch of grapes.' "

Skeptical critics in some cities insisted Cynthia Gleason, who had joined him in Providence for a tour, peeked; others credited her with clairvoyance. In his book Poyen, annoyed by charges of deception, defended the subjects of other mesmerists as well as his partner on the stage:

> I have seen a number of that species of somnambulists who could see objects and read several lines through the top of their head, their forehead, or the pit of their stomach; there could be no collusion or deception in the case, as their eyes were either kept shut with the fingers of another person, or very carefully bandaged.

Perhaps the best American performer of eyeless vision during this period was Loraina Brackett, a twenty-year-old woman, who like her predecessor in Liverpool was said to be almost completely blind. William L. Stone, the editor of the New York *Commercial Advertiser,* described one of her routines in his *Letter to Doctor A. Brigham on Animal Magnetism,* published in New York in 1837. She wore opaque glasses in the Margaret M'Avoy fashion; after she had been mesmerized, investigators tried to block out peripheral vision with bits of absorbent cotton. Having glimpsed the test pictures placed on the wall of the room behind her back, she would stand facing away from them and describe them accurately.

Shireen, who was billed as "A Psychological Mystery" in American vaudeville shortly after the First World War, had her eyes covered with cotton, strips of adhesive tape, and a black blindfold. She won audience approval with her "blind" sharpshooting skill, then walked through the aisles describing how the spectators were dressed. Finally, back on stage, she named playing cards that were handed to her from a shuffled pack and called out the numbers written on a blackboard by an assistant after members of the audience had held up fingers indicating the numbers silently. Shireen was accepted for what she was—a clever entertainer.

When subjects, blindfolded much as Shireen had been, were tested by the French novelist Jules Romains (Louis Farigoule), he decided they saw with their skin. In *Vision Extra-Rétinienne,* published in Paris in 1919, Romains pointed out that the skin of some people's noses, in particular, was unusually perceptive.

In 1924, the year *Eyeless Vision,* the English translation of Romains's book, was published in the United States, "The Spaniard with X-Ray Eyes" came to the United States. In Europe, Joaquin Maria Argamasilla's ability to see through silver and gold had been attested to by many distinguished scientists; among them, Nobel prize winner, Charles Richet.

Dr. Walter Franklin Prince, research officer for the American Society for Psychical Research, was dubious, but he had no clue to the mystery. The Spaniard, a tall, hefty nineteen-year-old, put wads of cotton over his eyes and held them in place with a hand-kerchief blindfold tied at the back of his head. Houdini, the magician, knew the Spaniard could peek. How Argamasilla could tell in what position volunteers from the audience had set the hour and minute hands of their hunting-case gold watches with the lids snapped shut was something else again.

Houdini was present when Argamasilla performed for the press at the Newspaper Feature Syndicate in New York. As soon as the Spaniard had fastened on his blindfold, the magician tip-toed behind him and looked over Argamasilla's shoulder. There he saw something those in front were unable to see. With the back of his hand held toward the reporters, the performer pressed the catch on the watch case and permitted the lid to spring open slightly, while holding the watch at precisely the right angle for a downward peek. Once the hands had been glimpsed, Argamasilla raised the watch until it was near his fore-head, closing the lid in the process.

After that, Seeing Through Metal became a favorite Houdini close-up trick. He taught the routine to Horace Goldin, the illu-sionist, who in turn, many years later, showed it to me. Even though I knew exactly what Goldin was doing, he handled the watch so adroitly that when I watched from in front, there seemed no possibility for him to have secretly opened the case. Then Goldin let me look over his shoulder as he explained the technique to me.

Harlan Tarbell, the author of an outstanding course in magic, saw Shireen's vaudeville act in Chicago and read Houdini's explanation of Argamasilla's mysterious feat in a booklet the magician published in 1924. Tarbell worked out an impressive blindfold routine, which became the feature of his coast-to-coast lecture-hall tours. Tarbell admitted to magician friends that he could see better blindfolded than when he wore glasses. The tiny point of vision seemed to magnify the objects he described.

The revival of sightless vision in Russia was first reported in 1962 in *Uralsky Rabocy*, which told of Rosa Kuleshova's success before a group of psychologists in Nizhni Tagil, an industrial city located on the eastern side of the Ural Mountains. "The Tagil Phenomenon," as Rosa became known, said she had perfected her sense of touch while employed by a training school for the blind. She had learned to read Braille to understand the problems of the sightless. Following a siege of rheumatic encephalitis, she astonished her doctor by identifying colors with her eyes blindfolded—a remarkable parallel to Margaret M'Avoy's story. Rosa's physician arranged for her to appear before psychologists in her hometown several months later. By then she was describing photographs, reading periodicals with her fingers, and reaching into bags to remove playing cards or spools of various colored threads as they were requested.

Her greatest triumph came in Moscow. After she was tested at the Biophysics Institute in December 1962, scientists there proclaimed her as an authentic marvel. Unfortunately the Russian scientists did not bother to ask a professional magician, who would have been familiar with the ingenious tricks practiced by a M'Avoy, Hendrick, or Shireen, to join their investigating committee. The scientists—as professional scientists so often do in cases of this sort—concluded on their own that Rosa was not cheating, even though they had taken only the most perfunctory precautions to prevent her doing so, and instead proceeded to use their laboratory equipment to demonstrate how closely "finger sight" resembled normal eyesight.

A number of theories were proposed to account for Rosa's

feats. When the blindfolded Rosa indicated the light and dark areas of a picture as well as colors projected on a frosted-glass surface, someone suggested that dark areas might feel colder than light portions—that black, for example, might feel colder to the touch than red. More tests were made, and this conjecture was rejected. Finally an article appeared in *Izvestia* "explaining" how Rosa performed her wonders. As quoted in the February 1964 issue of *USSR*, an English monthly published by the Soviet government for circulation abroad, it reported that Rosa had "real light receptors, organs of vision, in the skin of her fingers." This, the physicists said, accounted for her ability to read while blindfolded. As to color perception, there were "receptors—for red, blue and green—whose graph of spectral sensitivity corresponds exactly to the cones of the human eye."

The conclusion of the Moscow scientists that Rosa's feats could be explained in physiological terms was not accepted by the entire Russian academic world. One dissenter was Leonid Vasilieuv, a distinguished physiologist and an avid researcher in the area of extrasensory perception. His opinion, quoted in the *USSR* article on Rosa: "Telepathy on the border of psychic and parapsychic phenomena."

Vasilieuv conducted his own investigation in his Leningrad laboratory. His subject was one of the many Russian women who claimed to possess a gift equivalent to Rosa's. Ninel Kulagina, recovering from an illness, had read about "The Tagil Phenomenon." Experimenting with her eyes covered, Ninel found she, too, could peek. Attractive in appearance, and far more personable and ingenious than Rosa, she went along with Vasilieuv's suggestion that a mysterious radiation from her body accounted for her powers. She held a compass; the needle under the glass began to spin inexplicably. Later, using the stage name Nelya Nikhailova, she exerted her "invisible force" so strongly that objects moved without her touching them.

Parapsychologists in other countries were startled by a film showing Ninel seated at a table, staring at matches, a salt cellar, and other small objects that were covered by a large, bottomless transparent cube until the objects became animated and slid in her direction. (The reaction to this movie was quite different when it was shown in March 1973 at an Occult Night of the Society of American Magicians in New York City. For years conjurers had stood at a distance as selected cards, covered by a glass dome on an unprepared table, rose from a pack, and close-up performers had exhibited cigarettes, matchboxes, and dollar bills which behaved in the same way as the Russian's objects. Laughter rocked the hall.)

Among the other claimants to eyeless vision publicized in the Soviet Union following Rosa's "breakthrough" were several children. One youngster succeeded in naming color cards that had been wrapped in plastic, after a pair of opaque cyclist's goggles had been fitted over her eyes. The goggles, applied by a team from the Biophysics Institute, resembled the "gogglers" Margaret M'Avoy had worn so many years before in Liverpool.

The ten-year-old schoolgirl's face turned and twisted as the scientists held the colored cards in various positions—first to one side of her, then to the other, and eventually over her head. They realized that if she could peek, it would be easy for her to identify the colors. But how could she peek? They had tried the goggles and couldn't see through them.

Fortunately a woman writer, G. Bashkirova, was covering the story. She reported in *Znanie-Sila* that, after the child had gone home, she herself had donned the goggles. And she could see! Unlike the "straight-nosed scientists," she—and the child—had turned-up noses.

G. Bashkirova was also aware that Rosa, the original "Tagil Phenomenon," had peeked. Following her acclaim as an authenticated marvel, Rosa had appeared on television and performed professionally as an entertainer. In her hometown she had helped stage theatrical productions for the blind, then, as a celebrity, recited verses and told jokes as preliminaries to her amazing blindfold demonstration. When Bashkirova attended the show, Rosa had many opportunities to cheat, and she did. Who could blame Rosa, the writer asked, when her feats provoked such thunderous applause?

Vladimir Lvov, a Leningrad crusader, identified as "a long-time hatchet man in regard to parapsychology" in Sheila Ostrander and Lynn Schroeder's fascinating but naïve *Psychic Discoveries Behind the Iron Curtain,* suggested Ninel had used concealed magnets to make the compass needles revolve, and his explanations of how a blindfolded trickster could see prodded Soviet scientists to examine this mystery more thoroughly.

" 'Finger Vision' Claim Exposed as Fraud" was the headline for the Associated Press dispatch from Moscow, printed on August 19, 1970, in the Baltimore *Evening Sun*. Five investigators, a story in *Literaturnaya Gazeta* said, had revealed that the newsmaking experiments of 1963 had not been carefully controlled. Like G. Bashkirova these investigators were convinced that Rosa had peered down the side of her nose. They also discovered that a color machine creaked as different hues were projected. They repeated the earlier tests with the sound of the machine obscured by a louder "whirring noise." Without the helpful, hitherto unnoticed audio cues, Rosa's fingers were colorblind. Nor could they read newsprint when precautions ruling out any use of eyesight were taken.

Rosa's worldwide publicity in 1963 had inspired American researchers to seek out gifted subjects. Richard P. Youtz, a Barnard College psychologist, traveled to Flint, Michigan, to test Patricia Stanley, who as a high school pupil in Kentucky had puzzled her classmates with her ability to see while blindfolded. "Woman Who Tells Color by Touch Mystifies Psychologist" was the accurate headline on Robert K. Plumb's story in *The New York Times* of January 8, 1964. By then Youtz was eager to make further experiments. The following year his work was facilitated by grants from the Public Health Service and the National Institutes of Health, according to the November issue of the Duke University *Parapsychology Bulletin,* which gratefully acknowledged that "he has at least lowered the barriers to financial aid for a venturesome exploration, even at a very inconclusive stage."

Youtz, in a letter to *Scientific American,* printed in June 1965, commented on an article, which had appeared three months earlier, reporting that Soviet psychologists were no longer intrigued by women who professed to see with their "fingertips, elbows and toes," after Ninel Kulagina had been caught cheating in Leningrad. Youtz shared the magazine's view that it was practically impossible to cover someone's eyes with a blindfold so that they could not see—a conclusion also reached, it should be noted, by Richard Hodgson in the first volume of the

British Society for Psychical Research *Journal* in 1884. The Barnard psychologist's star subject, Patricia Stanley, wore a "sleepmask." He emphasized also that under his supervision she "put her arms through holes into a plywood box. She also had doublethickness heavy black sleeves tight around each arm." The room was well lighted, he continued, so her actions could be observed.

Martin Gardner, the *Scientific American*'s recreationalgames expert and a longtime student of conjuring, who has devised many subtle strategies for the profession, was understandably perplexed by Youtz's approach. The eyes, not the arms, should have been the focal point for precautionary measures. Earlier, Gardner had suggested to Youtz that he enclose the heads of his subjects in a peek-proof box; this advice had been ignored.

Gardner's "Dermo-optical Perception: A Peek Down the Nose" in the February 1966 issue of *Science* described such a sight-stopping box in detail. Made entirely of light aluminum, the lower side fitted under the chin, close to the neck. Air holes in the top panel permitted the subject to breathe with ease, and padding under the box protected the shoulders.

Youtz, however, employed another protective device when he ran tests with Barnard students in New York. He called it a "bib-screen." This was a heavy cloth draped from the neck over a wooden screen, under which the volunteers put their hands. Even so, after the first round with Patricia Stanley, her score dropped, and no one whom Youtz tested was able to read newsprint through their fingers.

The Barnard psychologist had looked on as an observer at a New York hospital when experiments were made in 1964 with Linda Anderson, a fifteen-year-old girl from Billerica, Massachusetts. Arthur Anderson, the youngster's father, worked as an electronic technician at the Lowell, Massachusetts, plant of the Avco Corporation. An amateur hypnotist, he frequently used his blue-eyed, blonde daughter as his subject, hoping to improve her skill in algebra, her weakest subject at the local high school. One day while Linda was entranced, Arthur gave her seven pieces of glass; she identified the color of each correctly. Then he heard about the blindfolded Russian women who read news-

papers with their fingers and suggested that Linda try to duplicate this. At first she could only perceive short words, and these
with some difficulty. Then she began reading blindfolded as rapidly as she did when her eyes were uncovered.

Anderson observed that his daughter's fingers were not the
source of her vision; some part of her face—he wasn't sure
which—seemed sensitive to newsprint. Eager to pinpoint the
area, the Andersons participated in exploratory tests in a bio-
metrics research laboratory of the New York State Department
of Mental Hygiene.

In a letter to *Science*, written in December 1964, but not
published until the following February, researcher Joseph
Zubin said the teen-ager's performance (her name was not given)
had perplexed the staff. Adhesive tape applied to the edges of an
opaque blindfold did not restrict her vision.

According to Linda, as she concentrated, a reddish light
switched on in her mind; when it changed to white, her skin was
able to read. Visiting scientists who watched the blindfolding
process and her performance in the laboratory were as baffled as
the initial investigators had been. Then an unnamed professional
magician was added to the team.

Eventually someone noticed that when the girl wrinkled her
face in deep concentration the adhesive tape on the lower side of
the blindfold loosened a bit. A very small bit, but enough to permit normal vision. When these tiny gaps were stopped up, Linda
complained of the extra pressure on her skin.

Zubin noted that the girl continued to read a few sentences
after each hole was covered. She obviously had glimpsed several
lines and thus was able to quote the words from memory after the
tape was repaired.

Eventually the blindfold was discarded, and her eyelids
were sealed with two small strips of adhesive. With zinc ointment applied around the sides of the tiny tapes, Linda could not
use her eyes—nor could Linda "see" with her skin.

People in and around Massachusetts did not know about the
experiments in New York. Linda to them was the pretty high
school girl who volunteered to use her extrasensory perception
to help the police in their search for Kenneth Mason, a five-year-

Fig. M.

THE HOLDING TEST.

Anna Eva Fay permitted blindfolded spectators to "control" her in her cabinet, but they always said later they had no idea how she did her amazing feats.

Fig K

GENERAL MANIFESTATIONS, THROUGH THE COTTON BANDAGE TIE

Anna Eva Fay reached the horns, guitars, and other objects that had been placed in her lap by sliding her body back and bringing her tied hands forward.

Anna Eva Fay convinced many of the genuineness of her paranormal manifestations by producing them even while her hands were "tied" by an electrical circuit.

Sir William Crookes, who devised the electrical test for Anna Eva Fay, and who was taken in by her. Years later, she told Houdini how she had deceived this distinguished researcher.

Henry Slade, an ingenious American medium, enthralled clients by coaxing spirits to write messages for them on thoroughly examined, blank slates as he held the slates beneath a table.

Slade and Professor Zöllner, University of Leipzig physicist. Zöllner wrote of the medium's incredible feats in a book that is itself surpassingly strange, *Transcendental Psychics*.

THE EGYPTIAN HALL,

PICCADILLY, LONDON.

MANAGER ... ... Mr. W. MORTON

EVERY DAY AT 3.   EVERY EVENING AT 8.

MASKELYNE AND COOKE,

The Royal Illusionists

AND ANTI-SPIRITUALISTS.

An Original and

UNIQUE ENTERTAINMENT!

CONJURING EXTRAODINARY,

Spirit-Rapping, the Trance Medium, Floating in Mid Air,

THE NEW LIGHT AND DARK SEANCES

WHICH WILL INCLUDE

Spirit-Forms, Spirit-Hands, Spirit-Voices,

And many marvellous manifestations, under test conditions. Only to be witnessed at this Entertainment.

Pianist   - -   **Mr. CHAS. MELLON.**

The Room Furnished and Decorated by Messrs. LYON, Theatrical Upholsterers, Southampton Row.

FAUTEUILS, 5s. STALLS, 3s. AREA, 2s. BALCONY, 1s.

Box-Office at the Hall open daily from Ten till Five, where Fauteuils and Stalls, can be obtained six days in advance.

John Nevil Maskelyne, the British magician, duplicated Slade's slate trick in court and with his co-worker, Cooke, reproduced Anna Eva Fay's feats onstage.

Margaret M'Avoy devised the first known "eyeless vision" routine in Liverpool in 1817. She wore "gogglers" over her eyes as she read from books, told the colors of various objects, and performed other amazing feats.

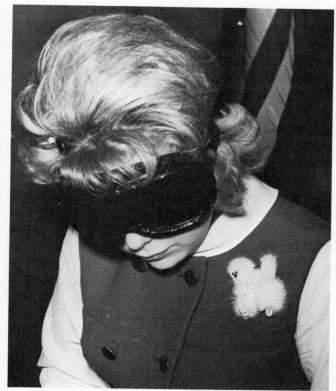

A recent claimant to this supernormal ability, Linda Anderson, had her eyes covered with a sleepmask; some observers believed she "saw" with her skin.

A séance, American-style, not long before the turn of the century. The artist has attempted to show what the sitters think is happening in the dark around them.

old Lowell boy, who had been missing since November 11, 1964. After her father hypnotized her, she said, "The boy is not in the river. The boy is in a house."

The lost child had not been found by February 12, 1965, the day Linda accepted a challenge from James A. Coleman, a skeptical American International College physics professor. Coleman had offered her a hundred dollars if she was able to convince a committee of the authenticity of her "facial vision."

Reporters and photographers from nearby cities traveled to the Yankee Drummer Inn in Auburn, Massachusetts, for the confrontation. Professor Coleman introduced the three committeemen who would judge the test: Wallace E. Dibble, a Springfield architect; Sidney H. Radner, proprietor of a Holyoke rug-cleaning concern, and Harry Eagen, a supervisor at the plant where Linda's father worked.

The opaque mask Linda planned to use provoked controversy. Jean Cole, a reporter from the Boston *Record American,* tried it and said she could see down through a triangle of space between her nose and her cheek. Coleman suggested that Linda merely shut her eyes, promise not to peek, and demonstrate her talent. Linda objected. It was vital, she declared, that all light be kept from her eyes; that was why she needed a mask.

Finally she permitted the professor to fasten pieces of adhesive tape over her eyes, which was easier said than done. Linda was wearing heavy makeup; the tape would not stick until she wiped some of the cosmetics away. Then she waited for Coleman to cover her face with her mask. This, he refused to do. She said it would take more time for her to get in the proper condition for skin-reading without the mask but that she would try.

The tape exerted too much pressure, Linda added. She reached up, loosened the bottom edges with her fingers, and pushed the tape up a bit. When she asked for something to read, an opening in the lower side of the tape was apparent to Coleman. He covered the spot with zinc oxide. After more openings in the tape were spotted and sealed, Linda read several words from a newspaper, "In 1961—among his—anthology." Upon checking, the latter word was found to be anthologies.

Coleman turned his attention to Linda's father, asking if he would like to say something about the scientific tests Linda had recently undergone. When Arthur Anderson replied that he would not, since those experiments were still incomplete, Coleman announced that a man at the back of the hall had participated in the New York tests. A short, slender bearded onlooker walked quickly to the front.

James Randi, the versatile Canadian magician and escapologist, then the host of a midnight to 5 A.M. talk show on WOR radio in New York City, was the unnamed conjurer in Joseph Zubin's letter to *Science*. Wearing white hospital attire, Randi had been in the lab. Linda's mask had been discarded at his suggestion. He then cut two minimal ellipses, just large enough to cover the girl's closed eyes, from a piece of tape and fastened them in place. These had terminated her "skin-reading" in the laboratory.

Committeeman Sidney Radner came forward. He said that Linda's performance should be reviewed like any other act in the theatrical pages of the newspaper. There was nothing remarkable about her demonstration; it had been presented by many past entertainers. The other two judges agreed that Linda had not earned the professor's hundred-dollar award.

A month later, Linda's extrasensory prowess suffered another blow. The body of the missing five-year-old boy, whom she had visualized as being "in a house," washed ashore on a bank of the Merrimack River.

Not all Americans who professed to have supernormal vision were girls. Pat Marquis, a thirteen-year-old Glendale, California, boy, amazed everyone but West Coast magicians by being able to read, play Ping Pong, swim, and walk around obstacles placed in his way, after his closed eyes had been heavily wrapped in bandage and sealed with strips of adhesive tape. The April 19, 1937, issue of *Life* followed the lead of Los Angeles newspapers and extolled his wonders in picture and prose. He was brash enough to go to Durham, North Carolina, and submit to tests in Dr. J. B. Rhine's parapsychology laboratory. Rhine quickly discovered that Pat peeked.

The most unusual blindfold specialist of recent years came from Oklahoma. At the age of twelve, Ronald Coyne lost an eye in an accident. By the time he was twenty-five, he had attracted crowds to revival meetings as far away as Miami with his God-given paranormal sight. After his good left eye had been covered by a blindfold, he demonstrated he could still "see"—with the empty socket of his right eye!

Dr. Richard Ireland, another evangelist, has presented his act in Greenwich Village and Las Vegas nightclubs and on television, as well as in more sacred surroundings. He reads written questions while blindfolded and gives answers of a sort. I have seen him at work; he is not among the most efficient practitioners in this field, yet he attracts audiences. A segment of the public yearns for advice from psychics; these credulous spectators are Ireland's patrons.

A story in the *Philadelphia Daily News* about Mary Donahue, an eleven-year-old "finger-reader," aroused national interest in 1970. Heralded by Merv Griffin on his syndicated television show as the psychic marvel of the age, Mary was led blindfolded through the audience. She described the objects she touched with the tips of her fingers as Merv expressed awe. Protests from magicians who saw the show, pointing out that Mary was scarcely the phenomenon Griffin claimed her to be, led to the cancellation of her second scheduled appearance with him.

Several weeks later I was invited to test Mary on the "Betty Hughes and Friends" program in Philadelphia. Alvin Hollander, WCAU-TV program director, was sold on the youngster's psychic ability. Still, in fairness to the viewers, he thought an effort should be made to authenticate her powers. Hollander asked if I could test her without enclosing her head in a box or causing her physical discomfort. I replied that I could. Betty Hughes, the wife of former New Jersey governor Richard Hughes, introduced Mary, a slender girl with long hair and a freckled face, to the studio audience. Mary's eyes were covered with pads, over which an opaque mask was fastened. She ran her fingers across the pages of a magazine opened at random by Mrs. Hughes, calmly described the pictures, and read from the text. The spectators applauded enthusiastically.

I sat beside Mary, who had removed her blindfold, and asked her various key questions: Was she an entertainer, or did she profess to have a mysterious power? Mary answered she had a God-given gift. Did she claim to have sight in her fingers? She said she did.

I tried two simple experiments. In the first her eyes were again covered as they had been originally. I took a piece of cardboard from my pocket, held it before her, and asked her to touch the *under* side and read the word lettered there. If the word had been on the upper side, she could have read it by peeking. She failed. Her eyes could not see through the card.

The station staff told me Mary had "finger-read" for them earlier when a man stood behind her and covered her eyelids with his fingers. Though fingers pressing on the eyelids can feel the eyeballs pulsing beneath the skin, it is still possible for the subject to see. A slight downward movement of the head can raise the lids just enough for a peek. During the TV-taping, with Mary's blindfold removed, I asked her to close her eyes. I extended two fingers and gently placed one *at the bottom* of each of her eyelids, then suggested she read an open magazine. She touched the pages; meanwhile I could feel her trying desperately to force her eyelids up a tiny bit. She failed—and she failed to describe the words or the photographs with her fingers.

There was consternation in the studio, conferences on the set, agitated talk in the control room. While the hubbub continued, I met Mary's parents and the family priest; they had been in the audience. I asked Mary's mother how her daughter had discovered she could "see" with her fingers. Mrs. Donahue said Mary and some other girls her age had played a game in which while blindfolded, they attempted to describe objects and pictures presented to them and that only Mary had been successful. Mrs. Donahue, who had read about extrasensory perception, tried various other experiments with her daughter. Mary's fingers seemingly could read. Devout Roman Catholics, the Donahues then asked the opinion of several nuns: Was this Satan's work? The nuns thought it was evidence of a gift from God. Joseph Geller, the family's physician, tested Mary. He could offer no explanation for her newly discovered talent. A newspaper account of the girl's phenomenal achievement had brought offers for television appearances and interviews with other publications.

"Are you convinced Mary uses a trick to see?" I was asked by someone at the studio. I said I was: I myself had performed while blindfolded for many years. Once, in Havana, I had bicycled with my eyes blindfolded and a bag placed over my head and tied at the neck. Mary was listening. "With a bag over your head," she said as her eyes widened. "How do you do that?" I decided it was safer not to tell her.

A few moments later Alvin Hollander took me aside. He said he had made a decision. The program we had taped would not be televised. Harry Harris, TV critic of the *Philadelphia Inquirer*, called the station that afternoon. Hollander denied the show had been scrapped because it showed Mary's talent in an unfavorable light. "She requires a highly positive atmosphere and was unable to perform in the crucible of the studio," the program director of WCAU-TV asserted.

Harris, in his *Inquirer* article the next day, noted that I was not the only investigator to turn in an adverse report on Mary's "gift." Dr. Carroll Nash, a St. Joseph's College parapsychologist, said Mary was unable to "see" with her fingers after he put a box over her head nor was she able to identify objects placed behind her back. Nash found, as other conscientious researchers have discovered throughout the years, that when the blindfolded subject can no longer cheat, the phenomena abruptly ceases.

A word of caution to future investigators: hundreds of diabolically clever blindfold methods have been devised. My friend Kuda Bux, a Kashmir conjurer who now lives in the United States, permits volunteers to cover his closed eyelids with dough. Thick pads of cotton are pressed over the dough; yards of surgical bandage are wound in every direction around his head; and several folded hand towels are tied over the bandage. Still, Kuda takes aim with a rifle, fires, and breaks targets placed on the opposite side of the stage; he duplicates signatures written on a large pad held by an easel; and he performs many other baffling stunts.

Conjurers drive automobiles, not only blindfolded, but with inverted metal buckets over their heads. Skillful blindfolded magicians can see straight ahead, and they can create the illusion that they have eyes at the back of their heads. They present these feats as entertainment, not to foster belief in the occult.

Unless an investigator is familiar with the extensive literature, circulated privately among conjurers, unless he has learned the details of the various systems designed to misdirect intelligent spectators, it will be extremely difficult for him to cope with claimants to dermo-optical perception who have devised new ways to cheat. Margaret M'Avoy's "spiritual" descendants are a highly ingenious lot.

ESP IN OUTER SPACE

The first experiments in extrasensory perception in outer space, though they occurred during the Apollo 14 mission in 1971, were not part of the National Aeronautics and Space Administration's carefully supervised program. Although twice on his way to the moon and twice on the return journey, Captain Edgar D. Mitchell tried to send his thoughts to friends in the United States, NASA officials were unaware of this history-making event; Mitchell said later he had carried out the tests during the hours allotted to him as rest periods.

The forty-year-old astronaut, who was born in Hereford, Texas, and grew up in Artesia, New Mexico, had become intrigued with parapsychology in 1967, a year after he arrived at NASA's Manned Spacecraft Center in Houston. Until then, the stocky, soft-spoken Texan, with receding brown hair and clear green eyes, had been too busy with technical and military problems to investigate the controversial subject that in later life would become his passion. After his graduation from Naval Officers' Candidate School, Mitchell flew with a patrol squadron in the Pacific, worked on research projects as a pilot, headed the Navy Project Management Division, whose main concern was to orbit an experimental laboratory, and earned a Ph.D. in aeronautics and astronautics from the Massachusetts Institute of Technology. An outstanding student who was distressed by orthodox theology and dissatisfied with accepted beliefs about man and his relation to the universe, Mitchell turned to mysticism.

For thousands of years there had been men whose talents seemed to reach beyond the pale of normal existence; some were seers; others, healers. Is there anything in psychic phenomena? the astronaut mused. Were all those who claimed to be clairvoyants and sensitives merely charlatans or were some in touch with a universal source of knowledge? Mitchell began to make his own investigation.

An acquaintance suggested that he arrange for a sitting with the Reverend Arthur Ford, a noted medium who claimed to relay messages from the dead. They met in December 1969 and became friends. Ford thought a man in a rocket would be in an advantageous position for an ESP test. A similar view had been expressed earlier by neurologist-parapsychologist Andrija Puharich in his book *Beyond Telepathy*. Puharich visualized an experiment with a sender in one elevator, a receiver in another. The sender would concentrate as his car ascended, and the receiver would be alert for the messages in the descending car. The higher the structure that housed the elevators, the better.

Ford was fascinated by Mitchell's plan for a rocket-to-earth test of extrasensory perception during the Apollo 14 mission but did not live to witness the event. He died on January 4, 1971, just twenty-seven days before the mission launch, which he had been invited to attend as the astronaut's guest.

NASA had vetoed a proposal from the American Society for Psychical Research for a telepathy experiment in 1970; Mitchell therefore decided not to risk another refusal by submitting his plan to the authorities. What he did during his rest periods aloft was a matter of concern only to himself.

Three unidentified friends made test runs with Mitchell before the flight. The fourth participant, Olof Jonsson, was a psychic whom the astronaut had never personally met but he had been highly recommended. Quarantined before the takeoff, Mitchell telephoned his friends and concentrated as they tried to guess whether he was thinking of a square, a circle, a star, a plus sign, or three wavy lines—the five symbols used on standard ESP-testing cards. The hits were slightly above the chance average of one in five, but not enough so to indicate that Mitchell was a strong sender or that any of his friends was an exceptional receiver. As Mitchell had not included Jonsson in this preflight test, his potential as a receiver remained an even more unknown factor.

Mitchell wrote down two hundred numbers in eight columns of twenty-five numbers each on a piece of paper. The figures, chosen at random, ranged from one to five. The numbers would represent the five ESP symbols in a sequence to be chosen each time he attempted to transmit his thoughts earthward. The receivers were given the days and hours they should be receptive to the images Mitchell hoped would reach them.

The spaceship-to-earth ESP experiments did not proceed exactly as planned, Mitchell admitted to Alan Vaughan in the October 1971 issue of *Psychic* magazine. Because of a forty-minute delay in the launching of Apollo 14 on January thirty-first, his first try at transmitting thoughts during his rest period began the following night, forty minutes after the receivers on earth were expecting his signals. His second transmitting session, on February third, was also held forty minutes later than scheduled.

Mitchell gathered rocks and carried out other official tasks on the surface of the moon on February fifth, and did not again try to send thoughts until the eighth, when Apollo 14 headed back toward Earth. He made his final try on the ninth. He sent four columns of data—one during each session—but he later learned that Jonsson, the receiver in Chicago, and one of the astronaut's friends had both made notations of the symbols they thought they were receiving on six occasions. The other two participants had found time to concentrate only twice. Result: Mitchell had transmitted four columns of figures, but there were sixteen columns of guesses—some made on days when he had not been sending.

Another complication was that Jonsson had leaked the news of the unofficial ESP experiment to the press, though all the receivers had promised to keep their part in the program secret. Understandably Mitchell was furious. There was, however, some consolation in the sympathetic messages he received from Joseph Banks Rhine and Karlis Osis. Rhine offered the facilities of his Foundation for Research on the Nature of Man, and Osis offered the cooperation of the research laboratory at the American Society for Psychical Research to aid in evaluating the receivers' scores.

The methods used to interpret Mitchell's tests were curious, to say the least. In the telepathy test Mitchell devised, he thought of the symbols only at the times he tried to beam his thoughts to Earth. This, he said, was why he had jotted down the rows of numbers—to avoid possible precognition. If he had written symbols at the start, he thought these might be visualized by the people on Earth. By assigning symbols to the numbers at the times of the experiments, he believed only telepathy could be involved—a view, by the way, not shared by many parapsychologists. When telepathy was ruled out because of the lapse in time between the sending and the receiving, parapsychologists nevertheless suggested that evaluations for precognition be made. Rhine compared the symbols thought of by the astronaut with the lists made by two of the receivers; the other two had neglected to cooperate during the first two attempted transmissions. Fifty-one symbols matched, rather than the forty, which parapsychologists agree would indicate pure chance. This was hailed as a "victory," although the same parapsychologists would agree, when pressed, that the sample (two hundred guesses) was too small to be statistically significant.

Another evaluation was made after all the guesses had been checked against Mitchell's list. The three hundred guesses made closest to the actual time of the astronaut's thoughts yielded thirty-five hits whereas sixty could have been expected by chance. This, we are told, was also a victory! It supposedly indicated a significant degree of *negative* extrasensory perception.

There was no mention of this negative factor in the article entitled "Ex-Astronaut on ESP" that Mitchell later wrote for the January 9, 1974, issue of *The New York Times*. Speaking of the Apollo 14 experiment, he said the four receivers guessed the symbols so successfully that the score "could be duplicated by chance [only] in one out of 3,000 experiments."

Following the worldwide publicity he received as the sixth man to walk on the surface of the moon, Mitchell served as a member of the back-up crew of other lunar probes until he retired from NASA and the navy in 1972. Divorced by his wife, Louise, in 1971, Mitchell married again in the fall of 1973. His second wife, Anita, shares his absorption in extrasensory mental phenomena. She says a psychic healer cured her of an ailment that physicians could not treat effectively.

Since his return to civilian life, Mitchell has established the Institute of Noetic Sciences in Palo Alto, California, to explore areas of consciousness not yet acknowledged by more traditional researchers. (Noetic means "of, pertaining to, or originating in intellectual or rational activity," according to Funk & Wagnalls *Standard College Dictionary.*) He appears frequently on lecture circuits and on TV panel shows.

Mitchell was one of the fund raisers when Andrija Puharich was eager to have Uri Geller, the Israeli "mystic," tested in a research laboratory; the former astronaut supervised the experiments at the Stanford Research Institute. By his own account Mitchell, like Puharich, believes Geller can materialize and dematerialize solid objects, such as metal tie clips and pocket watches. When they appeared together on a Merv Griffin TV show, Geller told Alfred Drake, the star of many Broadway musicals, that one day he would bring back to Earth the camera Mitchell had left behind on the moon. The former astronaut seems to think this is feasible.

Critical of the mind-control and -development courses so popular today in many parts of the United States, Mitchell said in the April 8, 1974, issue of *People* that while these classes do to some extent make students more sensitive, "The dangers from the training are higher than the advantages." He hopes to perfect a consciousness-expanding course of his own, which will avoid the mental hazards of its predecessors.

So far Mitchell has not developed powers of his own of the sort he attributes to Arthur Ford and Uri Geller. It must not be too fulfilling to play the role of an observer when one is convinced others are able to tap the universal source of wisdom.

While astronauts have journeyed to the moon by rocket, Ingo Swann, an American medium, claims to have visited Mars during his "out-of-body" excursions. His painting of outer space, as seen by a mystic, was reproduced in part in the March 4, 1974, issue of *Time.*

Swann's is only the latest of a long series of psychic interplanetary voyages. Hélène Smith, a statuesque beauty with long black hair and dark eyes, gave the first mediumistic re-portage on the red planet back in November 1894. Born Catherine Elise Muller in Geneva, Switzerland, in 1861, she was in her early thirties when she began conversing with spirits who answered her questions by rapping on and tilting tables.

Victor Hugo, the distinguished French writer, was one of Hélène's early invisible guides; later Cagliostro, who preferred to be known as Leopold in the séance room, replaced him. The psychic, while entranced, imagined herself to be Lorenza Feliciana, Cagliostro's medium in Alexandre Dumas's novel *The Diamond Necklace*. Learning that Lorenza was an entirely fictitious character, Hélène became the reincarnation of Marie-Antoinette instead.

The mystic played herself for her visits to Mars. Pantomiming her descent from a space vehicle, she clapped her hands, patted her nose, mouth, and chin, and went through a series of bodily gyrations. These actions, she explained, were the salutations with which one polite Martian greeted another.

The inhabitants, she said, were similar in physique to their earthly counterparts, but they dressed alike, both males and females, in baggy pants and ornamented jackets which fitted snugly at the waist. Some Martians lived in buildings with rooftop fountains, and there was a huge hall where crowds gathered. They traveled in horseless carriages without wheels which emitted sparks.

Camille Flammarion, founder of the French Astronomical Society, had conjectured about the possibility of life on Mars and other planets in his *La Planète Mars et ses conditions d'habitabilité*, published in 1892; one day, he said, new scientific techniques might "give us direct evidence of the existence of the inhabitants of other worlds, and . . . put us in communication with our brothers in space."

As there was then considerable speculation about what appeared to be canals on Mars, Hélène's patrons of 1896 were not too surprised when she reported having seen a lovely, pinkish-blue lake there and peculiar trees that tapered down rather than up. Earlier she had said all Martians wore the same garb; now, she added, the women had platelike hats. She also observed a new form of transportation—a car similar in shape to a carriage lantern which belched flame and propelled a single rider from place to place.

The psychic space traveler from Switzerland even learned the Martian language: *métiche,* "man"; *méche,* "great"; *dodé,* "this"; and *haudan,* "house" were a few of the words included in the Martian-French dictionary the medium worked on for more than thirty months.

To be sure her friends understood her descriptions of Martian people, houses, and scenes, Hélène painted pictures of them. The men had yellow skins; the buildings were Oriental in style; and the exotic flowers were of many vivid colors.

On a later visit to a remote part of the planet, the medium said, she saw grotesque creatures similar to those depicted in modern cartoons. Most of them were less than three feet tall; they had tiny heads, wide mouths, small eyes, and long, thin noses. Their feet and hands were unusually large, and sizeable black nails extended from their fingertips. Until one spoke, she thought it was an animal.

A fascinating account of Hélène Smith's mediumship appeared in Theodore Flournoy's *Des Indes à la Planète Mars,* published in 1900. The author, a professor of psychology at the University of Geneva, told the medium that the first Martians she had described seemed reminiscent of Orientals. Thereafter she created others in her imagination which she thought would be more acceptable. Flournoy analyzed her version of the Martian language and found it based largely on French.

In his *Encyclopaedia of Psychic Science,* Nandor Fodor, a disciple of Freud, said Flournoy's excellent examination of Hélène Smith's thought processes invalidated her claims to out-of-body experiences on Mars.

Former astronaut Mitchell has been intrigued by the efforts of modern mediums to project themselves and to describe the atmospheric conditions and vegetation of distant planets that will be targets of NASA projects. He also yearns to prove that at least some of the many psychic healers have indisputable supernormal powers.

One can only hope that his experiments in this area will be better designed, better executed, and more realistically evaluated than the one that brought him fame in the field of parapsychology—the first attempt to send ESP symbols telepathically from Apollo 14 to Earth.

TED SERIOS –
THOUGHT PHOTOGRAPHER

Balancing a Polaroid Land camera on his knee, as he sat facing its lens on June 10, 1962, Ted Serios squeezed the shutter release. The Wink light flashed; the shutter clicked. He passed the camera to one of the onlookers in the living room of the Wilmette, Illinois, house. Seconds later a print emerged from the camera—a hazy oblique view of a building fifteen miles away!

David Techter, president of the Illinois Society for Psychic Research, recognized the facade immediately. It was that of the Field Museum of Natural History in Chicago; he worked there as a paleontologist. Pauline Oehler, vice-president of the society, owned the camera, and she had purchased the film. Serios had not loaded the camera, nor had he touched the print.

When Curtis Fuller, publisher of *Fate* magazine, a monthly that features "true reports on the strange and unknown," saw this remarkable photograph and others Serios had snapped that were equally inexplicable, he wrote the Polaroid Corporation, asking for a possible explanation.

Vice-president Stanford Calderwood replied that an ingenious person by "a long and complicated procedure" could doctor the film, if he had access to it in advance, or that something might be inserted "in front of or behind the lens."

Mrs. Oehler's article in the December 1962 issue of *Fate*

stressed that before the test Serios had not handled either the film or the camera nor had he attached a supplementary lens.

Serios, a Roman Catholic, merely gripped a rosary in his right hand as he steadied the camera and pressed a short cardboard cylinder, which he held with his left thumb and forefinger, against the lens. He did this, he explained, so that his fingers would not accidentally cover the lens as the shutter clicked. The cylinder was examined both before and after the amazing photographs were taken. Without leaving the Midwest, Serios had photographed the Capitol and the Pentagon in Washington and a building halfway around the world—the Red Fort in Delhi, India.

Here, Mrs. Oehler pointed out, was a repeatable experiment that might validate one of the elusive phases of extrasensory perception. She hoped an organization with more money and better testing facilities than the Illinois Society for Psychic Research would probe this phenomena.

More than a year passed before Jule Eisenbud, associate clinical professor of psychiatry at the University of Colorado Medical School and a member of the American Society for Psychical Research, began an extensive investigation. He had to foot the bill for the research himself. Funds were available for efforts to prove there was a life after death and to study telepathy and clairvoyance, but the major research centers drew the line at giving grants to sponsor tests on a man who claimed he photographed his thoughts.

The story of psychic photography is an old one filled with credulity and eventual disillusionment. Framed on the walls of many Victorian homes were eerie portraits of mothers with the misty faces of their deceased children hovering over their heads and of bearded men with their dead and, to some extent, transparent wives. The most curious of these early spirit photographs portrayed Abraham Lincoln's grim-faced widow, Mary, being consoled by the assassinated President.

The inventor of spirit photography said he discovered the process by accident in 1862. William H. Mumler, chief engraver for Bigelow, Kennard & Company, a Boston jewelry firm, took what he thought was a self-portrait in a friend's studio. The figure of a young woman materialized beside him on the plate.

Mumler recognized her immediately; she was a dead cousin. Mumler showed the weird photograph to a spiritualist. This man wondered if a spirit would appear if he had Mumler take his picture. One did; and soon Mumler had more customers than he could take care of. When the demand for his five-dollar photographs mounted, he raised the price to ten.

If a client paid more, famous personages of the past would materialize. William Cornell Jewett, a fervent crusader for peace during the American Civil War years, was photographed with John Adams, Daniel Webster, and Andrew Jackson. These distinguished men supported his cause, Jewett proclaimed. Henry Clay and Stephen A. Douglas also appeared in shadowy form with him. Only George Washington, of all the spirits Jewett requested, refused to show himself even momentarily in front of Mumler's camera, though Jewett had offered fifty dollars for a single print.

P. T. Barnum told of the Jewett episode in his book, *Humbugs of the World*, published in London in 1866. Several photographs of Jewett and his spirit supporters were on display in Barnum's American Museum in New York City, including one with Henry Clay and another with Napoleon Buonaparte.

Mumler's popularity waned in Boston when someone discovered that a "spirit" in one of his remarkable pictures was still alive. A second disclosure of a living ghost practically ruined his business. In 1868 Mumler moved to New York City, where he made sure only the dead manifested themselves on his plates. Despite criticism from Barnum and other skeptics, he prospered there until a reporter accused him of fraud.

Arrested by order of the mayor, the by-then famous spirit photographer stood trial. No evidence was admitted from Boston, and the prosecutor was not allowed to bring Mumler's photographic equipment into court. Photographers, however, demonstrated how the glass plates used in a camera could be prepared. With an image of a "ghost" already on the plate, a second exposure was made of the customer.

Other photographers testified for the defense. They said they had examined Mumler's camera, plates, and chemicals, and could find no traces of trickery.

John Worth Edmonds, Mumler's most ardent supporter and

the city's most prominent spiritualist, made an impressive appearance on the stand. A former state supreme court judge, he recalled how the spirit of a man who had killed himself had once materialized in court before the judge, who alone could see and hear him. At the spirit's urging, the judge had asked questions of a witness, provoking answers so startling that the judge reached a decision contrary to the one he had been contemplating.

Barnum, testifying for the prosecution, told of the cheats he had unmasked in his recent book. Mumler's attorney, attempting to discredit the showman, said his testimony was just another of his famous humbugs. If the facts were as Barnum stated, then contrary to the "great precept," there was no "honor among thieves."

While the trial gave the public an insight into the methods used by charlatans who claimed psychic powers, the prosecution failed to present a real case against Mumler. The presiding judge in his summation declared, "I may be convinced there may have been trickery and deception practiced by the prisoner," but no real evidence had been offered in court to prove it. He ordered the prisoner released.

Personal Experiences of William H. Mumler in Spirit Photography, published in Boston in 1875, includes some of the quaint pictures accepted by the credulous of the time. The year it was published in the United States, Edouard Buguet, a French photographer, was arrested in Paris. He like his American predecessor seemingly coaxed the famous dead to return and pose with the living.

During a brief stay in London in 1874, Buguet had delighted British spiritualists with the pictures he took at 33 Baker Street. The specters included Charles Dickens, who during his lifetime had been critical of the famous spiritualist D. D. Home and other psychics. The Reverend William Stainton Moses became one of Buguet's patrons; Moses, a master at the University College School, gave private séances himself. When Buguet returned to Paris, Moses's spirit appeared on one of the Frenchman's photographic plates. This did not disturb Moses as much as one would think. The British medium said that at the time the picture was taken, he had been entranced across the channel.

The police raided Buguet's Paris studio in the spring of 1875 and confiscated his unusual paraphernalia. Included in the haul was a headless mannequin and the heads, wigs, whiskers, eyeglasses, gowns, and suits needed to convert it into an assortment of images.

Buguet confessed on the stand that he employed these props in the double exposures he passed off to his customers as spirit photographs. Earlier he had used live models, but as the risk of detection and exposure increased, he switched to the dummy. If he had a portrait to work from, his task was simpler. This did not really matter, however, since his patrons only saw what they wanted to see in his pictures.

This was evident in the transcript of the trial issued by Marina Leymarie, whose husband, the editor of *Revue Spirite*, a spiritualistic paper, was codefendant. An art dealer named Dessenon swore his dead wife appeared with him in a Buguet photograph; their children and his wife's cousin could testify to that. No, none of the ridiculous false heads bore any resemblance to her.

Questioned about this, Buguet said that he had never seen a portrait of Madame Dessenon; if the ghost looked like her, it was by "pure chance." Various sitters believed the same misty photograph represented totally different people. A police official made this point clear. Buguet had shown him the photograph of a woman which had been accepted as the sister of one patron, the mother of another, and the friend of a third.

Pierre Gaëton Leymarie, the codefendant, had read about Mumler's success in the United States. After suggesting that Buguet should cash in on the technique in Europe, Leymarie had sent many people to the studio and had written enthusiastically about the spirit photographs in his publication. Buguet and Leymarie were found guilty; they received identical sentences: a year in jail and a fine of five hundred francs.

Frederick A. Hudson introduced spirit photography to Britain in 1872. He varied his methods through the years. Though frequently caught practicing deception, he was never arrested. Hudson at one time used a trick camera, made by a craftsman who sold conjuring apparatus. Harry Price described how the camera worked in his book, *Confessions of a Ghost-Hunter*, published in London in 1936. When the plate slide was inserted, this action brought the paper positive of the "ghost" up against the sensitive plate. When the shutter bulb was pressed, this image and the picture of the sitter were captured on the plate. Thus a single exposure on this plate carried both images.

Price explained numerous other ways spirit photographs might be taken. He had seen a small box, which could be concealed in the curled fingers of one hand, containing a tiny bulb, a small battery, and a miniature positive transparency. When the hand palming the box touched a sensitive plate, a slight pressure caused the bulb to light, and the image on the film was transferred to the plate.

Even more ingenious was the system devised by C. P. MacCarthy, a Sheffield (England) investigator of psychic phenomena. To prove that even the most alert researcher could be deceived, he gave a demonstration in London. "Conditions were imposed which appeared to make faking impossible," the July 4, 1935, issue of *Light,* the British spiritualists' weekly periodical, reported.

A photographer supplied an unprepared camera and plate slide. A committee purchased the plates. MacCarthy was searched; handcuffs were locked on his wrists. Still, five specters appeared on as many plates. Three sitters identified three of the spirits as people they once had known.

These likenesses had been projected by ultraviolet rays from a gadget fastened under one of MacCarthy's fingers. As he pointed to each plate, he beamed the images a distance of approximately eighteen inches. This miniature projector had not been found when the committee searched his body, nor had they suspected such a device could be used.

Jule Eisenbud, the Denver psychiatrist-parapsychologist, who told about his study of modern thought pictures in *The World of Ted Serios: "Thoughtographic" Studies of an Extraordinary Mind,* had read some of the books about spirit photography. There had been fraud, he noted, but many distinguished witnesses vouched for the phenomena.

Eisenbud labeled Sir Arthur Conan Doyle's book *The Case for Spirit Photography,* "a real thriller." He cautioned readers not to consult the works of Gustave Geley, Charles Richet, and

Baron Schrenck-Notzing until they had cleared their minds of "cant." Even if this could be done, I doubt that many would accept the obviously spurious spirit figures that appear in the photographs illustrating the baron's *Phenomena of Materialization.*

Eisenbud saw Serios at work for the first time in a Chicago hotel room. After seven tries with the psychiatrist's Polaroid, the forty-three-year-old former bellhop came up with a tilting view of the Michigan Boulevard water tower. Eventually he snapped a shot of a building that Eisenbud later learned no longer existed.

Ted had taken a rosary, small change, and keys from a trouser pocket before the session began, explaining that metallic objects on his person hampered his ability to take psychic pictures. He chain-smoked, drank a double Scotch, and took a shower between photographic attempts.

Eisenbud was overwhelmed. He slept little that night. He wondered why "this clearly remarkable phenomena" had not been thoroughly investigated by "responsible" scientists. He recalled the papers he had contributed to professional journals endeavoring to show that everyone "had latent capacities to do unconsciously essentially what Ted was doing."

A week or so later, Serios flew to Denver, at Eisenbud's invitation and expense, to undergo a series of tests. He had been drinking heavily on the plane; he continued to down immense quantities of liquor and beer during his stay. Often he was late; sometimes he left the city; and at least once, the psychiatrist said, his "medical photographer," as he identified Serios, was jailed for disturbing the peace.

Eisenbud's professional and academic associates were as perplexed by Serios's thought pictures as he had been. Even when it was learned that some were fuzzy duplicates of portions of photographs that had been published in magazines, Eisenbud did not become disenchanted. The vital question, he insisted, was how did the images get on the Polaroid film?

I read the psychiatrist's book carefully in the summer of 1967. His descriptions of Ted handling the tube as he pressed it to the camera lens indicated to me, if not to the author, that something must have been loaded into it before each psychic photograph was snapped, then palmed away as the cylinder was tossed aside or passed for examination. The first clue I had to what this certain something might be came when I rummaged through an old cardboard box and found a souvenir of Washington, D.C., I had stored there many years before.

Attached to a key chain was an optical toy; when put to one eye and held to the light, it revealed a view of the Capitol. A few minutes later I pressed this toy to the lens of my Polaroid camera and took a picture. The first print was disappointing, but thirty minutes later, after experimentation, I produced an image like those of Serios.

I phoned Charles Reynolds, a knowledgeable photographer and a fellow member of the Society of American Magicians. He said he and a team from *Popular Photography* had been in Colorado investigating Serios. After observing Ted in action, Reynolds and his friends had devised a gadget similar to mine; the report on Serios would appear in the October issue of the magazine.

That was in August 1967. Later at lunch, Reynolds told me about his weekend in Denver. The visit had been carefully planned. Realizing that he and David B. Eisendrath, Jr., another noted photographer, might be distracted as they took pictures, Reynolds had arranged for Persi Diaconis, a skillful sleight-of-hand performer, to keep a constant watch on Ted's fingers.

In the studios of KOA-TV, Serios had attempted to produce images on the marked Polaroid film supplied by the investigators. He prepared for the encounter by drinking a great quantity of beer. Though he tried to concentrate on photographs which at Eisenbud's suggestion had been sealed in opaque envelopes by the team earlier, he did not succeed in imprinting any image of these, or of distant buildings, on the dozens of prints made in the studio.

The next day Eisenbud ran a film of a Denver TV show on which Ted had performed a remarkable feat. He held a cardboard cylinder in his hand, pressed it firmly against a TV camera lens, and bizarre shadowy images appeared.

Later that afternoon in the psychiatrist's living room, Serios tried again with the Polaroid. After many failures, he made a suspicious move which both Reynolds and Diaconis, the sleight-of-hand specialist, observed. Once more he pressed the cardboard tube to the camera lens. Once more Reynolds squeezed the shutter release. As Serios dropped his hand holding the cylinder to his side, Diaconis reached for it. Ted backed away, and Eisenbud blocked Diaconis. By then Serios had crammed the tube into his trouser pocket. When Eisenbud asked for it, Ted pulled it out and gave it to him. The cylinder was empty. Had Serios loaded something into the tube? Did he leave it in his pocket when he passed the cylinder to the psychiatrist? The photograph made just before the magician reached for the tube was what Eisenbud called a "blackie." A solid object held inside a paper tube (by pressure of the thumb and forefinger outside) would block the light and produce a black picture.

A two-page report on the "Man Who Thinks Pictures" in the September 22, 1967, issue of *Life* did not mention that Serios had put a tube over the camera lens when the "thoughtographic" illustrations were made. Nor could the cylinder be seen in the photograph of Ted, one eye shut and the other open wide, as he glared toward the Polaroid. Paul Welch, the writer, had known Serios for four years. He had heard him talk about the possibility of getting pictures of secret Soviet missile sites with his strange talent. This never occurred. "He drank a lot and cried a lot," Welch said, "and couldn't hold a job, missed appointments and disappeared for weeks." As to whether the "thoughtographs" were legitimate or produced by a trick, Welch said "I just plain don't know." But it made a good story for *Life*.

By contrast, the October issue of *Popular Photography* ran lengthy articles by Reynolds and Eisendrath telling in detail of their experiences with Serios. Their research established that the Polaroid film had not been doctored. They centered their attention on the tube Ted pressed against the lens. By following an accompanying diagram, readers could construct a device with a small lens and a miniature transparency that would fit into a tube. With this they themselves could take thought pictures.

That month I attended the lecture Dr. Eisenbud gave for the American Society for Psychical Research in New York. Dapper, slender, with wavy graying hair, he left no doubt about his belief in the Serios phenomena. Enlargements of several "thought-ographs" gave him the opportunity to point out their peculiar-ities—the odd angles of buildings, the objects that might be a lobster or an old airplane, depending upon the viewer's interpretation. Eisenbud stated emphatically that Ted was not a trickster; no trickster, he said, could repeat the same feat so many times without being detected.

When comments were invited from the audience, I said I knew magicians who had performed the same trick for years without other conjurers learning their precise methods. Eisenbud questioned my authority. Gerald L. Kaufman, a vice-president of the American Society for Psychical Research and a member of the Society of American Magicians, stood up and briefly told of my background.

After the lecture I met Dr. Eisenbud. He said a new series of tests was being run on Serios in Denver. As yet, Ted had not produced pictures under close observation, but as soon as this passive streak passed, the psychiatrist would phone me; then I could come to Colorado and watch the experiments myself. The following day Eisenbud called; we talked for more than an hour on the telephone. Again he promised to inform me as soon as Ted began to produce images.

I also saw Eisenbud and Serios on the NBC-TV "Today" show. Host Hugh Downs asked Serios to give a demonstration. He was not in the mood. Another guest on the panel, James Randi, the magician, startled Eisenbud, Serios, and Downs by taking a tube that Downs had examined, holding it to the lens of a studio camera, and producing shapes and patterns of the sort Serios had materialized on a local program in Denver. There was nothing psychic about this, Randi asserted; it was a trick. Serios looked uncomfortable. Eisenbud frowned.

I did not see the psychiatrist again until July 16, 1970, when I joined him for lunch at the Stanhope Hotel in New York City. He hadn't telephoned me earlier, he said, because during the interim Serios had been unable to imprint his thoughts on film. Some "whities" (all white prints) and "blackies" (all black) but no images. I asked Eisenbud if he still believed in the Serios's power. The psychiatrist coughed several times and had difficulty answering. He drank some water, then assured me he had not changed his mind. He was positive Serios had a highly developed ESP talent. He said William Edward Cox, Jr., who works with Dr. Rhine in Durham, North Carolina, had tested Ted. Cox had an opaque envelope containing a target picture. Serios sketched a house and trees and said the house was red. This was correct, but during the session Ted had projected no images on Polaroid film. Cox, a part-time magician, whose letterhead says that he presents "Entertaining Programs for all Occasions" and "Lectures in Psychical Research and allied topics," is quoted in Eisenbud's book on Serios. After he had seen Ted produce "blackies," Cox stated: "I say absolutely and unequivocally that no lens or microfilm could be hidden in a gismo barrel [Ted's tube] under these conditions. No conjuring techniques are remotely conceivable under the conditions."

It should be noted that Cox more recently has said that Uri Geller bent an object and started a watch running in his presence without trickery.

Eisenbud told me he had been investigating psychic photography of another type. He had traveled to Waterville, Maine, to meet the Veilleux family. They produced curious birdlike markings on prints. Though there were ghostlike figures on the photographs they had mailed to him, they never caused similar specters to materialize while he was present.

They also had taken photographs of tombstones, and mysterious leaflike patterns appeared on the prints. The family first communicated with the unknown by means of a Ouija board. Then they heard raps, which sometimes predicted the future by spelling out by the number of knocks the various letters of the alphabet. The raps said that Eisenbud would die just five months later, on December sixteenth, he informed me. He smiled and did not seem disturbed by the ominous prophecy which has since proved to be false.

Another earlier prophecy also went astray. On the dust jacket of Eisenbud's book about Serios, "John Beloff, Ph. D., Lecturer in Psychology, Edinburgh University, author of *The Existence of the Mind*," is quoted: "likely to prove the most remarkable paranormal phenomenon of our time."

The prediction was made, of course, before parapsychologists learned that they, too, could take pictures, Serios style, with the aid of an optical gadget concealed inside a cardboard tube. Shortly after this revelation appeared in print, Ted seemed to lose the psychic ability to project his thoughts. Like a Polaroid print that has not been coated with fixative, he soon faded from view.

ARTHUR FORD — MESSAGES FROM THE DEAD

During his lifetime Arthur Ford was the storm center of two bitter psychic controversies. He made headlines in 1929 by "breaking Houdini's secret code" and conveying a spirit message to the magician's grieving widow. In 1967 he again became front-page news when the Right Reverend James A. Pike, former Bishop of California, firmly avowed in an interview with a *New York Times* reporter that he had talked with his dead son, James junior, during a séance with Ford in a Toronto television studio.

Charges of fraud were hurled in each instance, but Ford weathered the gales. A clairaudient (clear hearer), not a producer of ghostly forms, his claim to fame rested on the accuracy of the revelations that came from his lips while entranced.

Ford often named names and related incidents that his sitters had forgotten. Those who believed in telepathy were therefore convinced that mind-to-mind communication was not involved. If the sitters themselves did not remember certain people and events in their past, Ford could not have gained his knowledge by intercepting their thoughts. Ergo, the data must have come from the dead. How else could he disclose forgotten facts?

Skeptics suggested that Ford researched his subjects. His adherents disagreed. They said not even the FBI or the CIA could ferret out the evidential material the medium brought to light. After the famous psychic's death in 1971, indisputable evidence of his sources was found—and by his friends, not his critics.

Born on January 8, 1897, in Titusville, Florida, a town near Fort Pierce on the eastern coast of the state, Ford studied for the ministry at Transylvania College and the adjacent College of the Bible in Lexington, Kentucky. World War I delayed his graduation; he served briefly as a second lieutenant at Camp Grant, Illinois. Ordained by the Disciples of Christ, the slender young man with dark, slicked-back hair, handsome features, and a well-modulated voice was called in 1922 to the pulpit of the Barboursville, Kentucky, Christian Church. A personable preacher, Arthur Ford doubled the membership before moving on to a new field—show business—where his charm and talent for convincingly expressing himself again won him quick acceptance.

As a lecturer and unit supervisor for the Swathmore Chautauqua Association, an agency that booked traveling shows, ranging from political orators to variety entertainers, Ford toured the New England States. Appearing between the acts of S. S. Henry's illusion production at Athol, Massachusetts, in August 1924, he gave "one of the finest talks on magic" the local correspondent for *The Sphinx,* a conjuring periodical, "had ever heard."

Ford complimented Henry on his presentation of "The Spirit Paintings"—producing paintings on blank canvas—a trick based on a deception practiced by the Bangs sisters, two notorious Chicago mediums. While Ford enjoyed this and other magic shows, he was far more fascinated by the occult. During his college days he had experimented with tilting tables and blindfold tests, and he had joined the American Society for Psychical Research. His chautauqua lecture, "The Witching Hour," enthralled audiences as he told of unexplained phenomena and miracles dating back to biblical times. Then, as a professional medium, he began demonstrating marvels himself.

Slips of paper and envelopes were distributed to members of the audience. They were told to write questions, sign their names or initials, then seal the slips in the envelopes. These were collected in a basket; the basket was placed on a table on the platform. Taking up one of the envelopes, Ford would press it to his forehead, stare into space, and seemingly receive communications from the dead. For example, he would say he had a message for someone in the audience whose initials were M. B. This lady suffered from a nagging ache in her back. Would M. B. raise her hand? As soon as a hand was raised, Ford said: "Thank you, *Margaret*." This revelation of the first name of a person he had never met frequently caused M. B. to gasp. Margaret was not the only member of her family to experience such pains, the medium continued. An older woman was present in the spirit; she informed Ford that she, too, had had trouble in this area. She said her name was B-r-o-c-k, *Brock*. He paused to ask if the name meant anything to the woman in the audience. She replied it was the name of her grandmother who had died ten years ago. Mrs. Brock, the psychic went on, said Margaret should not worry, her condition was not serious, but she should go to a doctor; he would ease the pain.

How, spectators wondered, could the medium have known so much about the woman, unless her dead grandmother had given him this information? They did not realize she had signed her name, rather than her initials, to her question and that the question had been: "Like my grandmother before me, I frequently have trouble with my back. What should I do?"

In the 1920's many other "billet readers" presented similar routines—some in churches, others on the stage. Sealed questions were secretly scanned in various ways. A small strong light concealed in a basket or palmed in the performer's hand and held against the envelope is one method. A thumb rubbed on the envelope will make the paper transparent if the thumb has already pressed against a concealed sponge saturated with pure odorless alcohol, and the alcohol will have evaporated by the time the medium has answered the question.

The most prevalent system, still practiced with subtle improvements that will baffle those who know only the basic secret, is the "one ahead." After the first "answer" has been made to a nonexistent spectator, the psychic rips off the end of an envelope and removes the slip to "confirm" the question. Actually the information gleaned will be revealed when the next closed envelope is held aloft. The data obtained when the second answer is being "confirmed" will be used for the third envelope, and so on.

Usually the torn envelopes and the slips of paper are crumpled and tossed into a waste basket. Sometimes adroit performers palm a slip as they discard an envelope, then switch it for the one taken from the next envelope, so that the envelope and the question they have answered can be passed to the writer in the audience for verification.

The mediums who employ concealed light and alcohol ruses can and do return sealed envelopes without opening them. Ford, however, claimed the gift of clairaudience, which as he later explained in the July 25, 1940, issue of *The Psychic Observer,* was

> a matter of assuming a certain mental attitude and then listening for the sound of a subjective voice. I sometimes hear the voice audibly . . . sometimes it is simply an inner awareness.
>
> My job is to repeat exactly what I hear, or interpret . . . I must be constantly on guard not to embellish or read into the message anything that might spring from a desire to comfort or convince the person addressed.

The first of a series of strange events leading to Ford's initial national publicity break occurred on February 8, 1928, when he was pastor of the First Spiritualist Church in New York City, which met in the Carnegie Hall building on West 57 Street. Entranced and talking in the voice of Fletcher, his spirit guide, he said a woman identifying herself as the mother of Harry Houdini, the magician, was anxious to speak. (Houdini had died two years earlier, and his widow, Beatrice, had offered ten thousand dollars for an authentic spirit message from him.)

Mrs. Weiss—Weiss was Houdini's real name—then said that her son Harry had hoped for years to receive one particular word from her: "His wife knew the word, and no one else in all the world knew it." That word was "forgive."

This information was relayed to Beatrice Houdini. The following morning, February ninth, she sent a reply. A facsimile, which Ford himself gave me, reads:

> My Dear Mr. Ford,
>
> Today I received a special delivery letter signed by members of the First Spiritualist Church, who testify to a purported message from Houdini's mother, received through you.

Strange that the word "forgive" is the word Houdini awaited in vain all of his life. It was indeed the message for which he always secretly hoped, and if it had been given to him while he was still alive, it would I know have changed the entire course of his life— but it came too late. Aside from this there are one or two trivial inaccuracies—Houdini's mother called him Ehrich—there was nothing in the message which could be contradicted. I might also say that this is the first message which I have received which has an appearance of truth.

Sincerely yours,

Beatrice Houdini

This letter is not reproduced in *The Houdini Messages: The Facts Concerning the Messages Received Through the Mediumship of Arthur Ford,* a 24-page booklet written and published in 1929 by Francis R. Fast, one of the medium's closest friends. Instead the author states that Mrs. Houdini affirmed "the entire correctness of the message," and misquotes her, attributing to her letter the statement that this message was, "The sole communication received among thousands up to that date that contained the one secret key-word known only to Houdini, his Mother and myself."

Furthermore the "one secret key-word" had already been published nearly a year before, on March 13, 1927, in the *Brooklyn Eagle*. Beatrice Houdini had told a reporter about her late husband's desire to hear from his dead mother. Any authentic communication, Mrs. Houdini stressed, would have included the word "forgive."

The magician had never really believed the dead could return. He had crusaded from coast to coast, exposing the tricks of fakers who preyed on the bereaved after World War I. A master of escape, he nevertheless did think that if anyone could free himself from the oblivion of death, he would be the man. He had assured his wife that he would try to send her a message in the code they had used in a second-sight routine.

Nine months went by after Ford received the alleged communication from Houdini's mother. In November 1928, according to Francis Fast, the first word from Houdini himself came through; the tenth and final code word was taken down on January 5, 1929. The next day Fast and John W. Stafford, another member of the Ford circle, took the complete message to Mrs. Houdini. Fast said, "She lay on a couch suffering from a fall sustained the week before, and a troublesome cold. To say that she was other than clear-minded, withal, is beside the mark."

How "clear-minded" Beatrice Houdini was may be judged from an article published on January sixth in the *New York Evening Graphic*. Reporter Rea Jaure's story headlined, "Widow Ill, Communes with Houdini," said Mrs. Houdini had been ill with influenza for several weeks, and on New Year's Day had fallen down a flight of stairs and injured her spine. While in a "semidelirium," the widow had cried: "Harry, dear, why don't you come back to me from the other side?" Reaching out her arms as though to grasp him, she then called out: "I knew you would come back to me, my dear." She blacked out from time to time, the reporter said, and "was under constant care of physicians." This account had been written before Ford's friends arrived.

Fast said in his booklet that when Mrs. Houdini read the message in code, "stirred with emotion," she "undertook to carry out the plan agreed upon with her husband." There is, however, aside from Fast's statement, no evidence that Houdini had told her to stage a séance after she received the code words and go through the ritual that was carried out two days later.

Shortly past noon on January eighth, Arthur Ford went into a trance in the living room of Mrs. Houdini's Payson Avenue home. With witnesses present and speaking in a voice he ascribed to the magician, the medium repeated the words: "Rosabelle, answer, tell, pray, answer, look, tell, answer, answer, tell."

The Houdini voice asked if the words were correct; his widow replied in a whisper that they were. "Thank you, sweetheart, now take off your wedding ring and tell them what 'Rosabelle' means." Beatrice, whose head was bandaged—another result of her fall down the stairs—was lying on a sofa, covered with blankets. She took off her ring and began to sing:

> Rosabelle, sweet Rosabelle,
> I love you more than I can tell.
> Over me you cast a spell.
> I love you, my sweet Rosabelle.

The Houdini voice said his wife had sung this song in their first performance together, then added "What do you say now?" She answered: "Je tire le rideau comme ça," (I close the curtain so.)—the same words she had used in France after she moved a cloth-sided cabinet forward on the stage to hide a locked-and-roped trunk from which the magician was to escape and in which she would appear.

The voice of Fletcher, Ford's spirit guide, took over to explain the message conveyed by the code words; it was "believe." Then the purported voice of Houdini, the ardent foe to fake spiritualists, recanted: "Spare no time or money to undo my attitude of doubt while on earth. Now that I have found my way back, I can come often, sweetheart. Give yourself to placing the truth before all those who have lost the faith and want to take hold again.

"Believe me, life is continuous. Tell the world there is no death. I will be close to you. I expect to use this instrument [Ford] many times in the future. Tell the world, sweetheart, that Harry Houdini lives and will prove it a thousand times."

According to Ford's own testimony, Houdini never returned through "this instrument." The first time I met Ford, he autographed a copy of the Fast booklet, then in its seventh printing, to me. "Did Houdini ever speak through you at another séance?" I asked. "No," the medium answered. At my request he added the words: "I have had no contact with Houdini since."

The story of the sensational séance broke the day it was held in the *New York Graphic* and the *Brooklyn Daily Times*. The following morning it appeared in newspapers across the nation. The "secret code," it was explained, consisted of ten units—nine separate words and one two-word phrase—with each unit standing for a digit, and each digit, in turn, representing the position in the alphabet of a letter in the coded message. Thus:

Pray = 1 = A	Please = 6 = F
Answer = 2 = B	Speak = 7 = G
Say = 3 = C	Quickly = 8 = H
Now = 4 = D	Look = 9 = I
Tell = 5 = E	Be quick = 10 or 0 = J

Double-digit letters were indicated by combinations of the code words. For example, the fifteenth letter in the alphabet, *O*, would be signaled by the phrase "pray (1); tell (5)," and "answer, be quick," would indicate the twentieth letter or T. In Ford's message, the nine words following "Rosabelle," spelled out "believe" in this manner: Answer = B; tell = E; pray, answer = L; look = I; tell = E; answer, answer = V; tell = E.

Follow-up reports quoted Mrs. Houdini as saying that only two people had known the code—her husband and herself. Joseph Dunninger, a magician-mentalist and one of the escapologist's friends, said this was untrue; the code had been printed on page 105 of Harold Kellock's *Houdini, His Life-Story*, published the previous year by Harcourt, Brace and Company, which as the remainder of the title indicates was taken from *The Recollections and Documents of Beatrice Houdini*.

Mrs. Houdini also told reporters her husband had planned, if possible, to send messages to Sir Arthur Conan Doyle and Remigius Weiss (Weiss, not a relative, had worked with the magician in exposing psychic fraud). Doyle, in London, denied Houdini had made an after-death pact with him, as did Weiss, in Philadelphia.

Mrs. Houdini said copies of the three messages, the only ones in existence, were locked in her safe-deposit box at the "Manufacturers Bank on Fifth Avenue." When her "sick brain" was better, she would go there and obtain the documents to show to the press.

At the insistence of Ford's friends, she issued another statement. Written on her personal stationery but not in her own hand, this declaration, attested to by three witnesses, read:

> Regardless of any statements made to the contrary, I wish to declare that the message in its entirety and in the agreed-upon sequence, given to me by Arthur Ford is the correct message pre-arranged between Mr. Houdini and myself.

Under this sentence, she signed her name.

The supposed messages in the bank vault were never displayed by Mrs. Houdini after she recovered from her illness. B. M. L. Ernst, Mrs. Houdini's lawyer, told me later these documents had existed only in her imagination. In a letter dated September 7, 1935, Ernst also wrote Will Goldston, London magic dealer, prolific writer of conjuring books, and himself a spiritualist: "As to the alleged Ford message . . . when Mrs. Houdini signed the paper to the effect that the message was genuine, she was confined to her bed after a fall, had been taking drugs and was not in a position to know what she was doing." (This letter is in my collection.)

Overlooked in most of the accounts that have been written about the Houdini séance is the statement his widow made to a *New York World* reporter on January ninth, the day after the sitting: "I had no idea what combination of words Harry would use, and when he said 'believe,' it was a surprise." She had hoped to get a ten-word message from him in code, but she did not know what the message would be.

Rosabelle, the first word of the message allegedly relayed by Ford was not a part of the code. Her husband had had four lines of this song engraved, along with a miniature likeness of his head, inside the wide gold wedding ring Beatrice wore. This was scarcely a secret; Mrs. Houdini had shown the unusual inscription to many people.

On January 10, 1929, two days after the séance, a five-column-wide headline in the *Graphic* branded the "HOUDINI MESSAGE A BIG HOAX!" The subhead proclaimed, "Ford Admits He Got Secret Code from Magician's Widow," and Edward Churchill's article called the séance "one of the most monumental 'psychic' hoaxes ever perpetrated on the American public." According to this account, Rea Jaure, who had written the original story on the séance, had invited the medium to her apartment the previous evening, January ninth. Ford arrived late after attending a lecture.

The newswoman recalled a party Ford had gone to with Mrs. Houdini the previous month "where all those temperamental people were," and asked if he remembered it. "Indeed I do," the medium answered, "My, it was funny, wasn't it?" He said they had had "a great time."

The reporter then mentioned she had seen the letter Ford's friends had taken to Mrs. Houdini two days before the séance, listing the ten words and that she had made a photographic copy of the letter with Mrs. Houdini's permission. The medium's mood changed; the *Graphic* article repeated the conversation:

"But you must play ball. Really, I'd be glad to make financial compensation," said Ford.

"Reporters don't accept money."

"Then I'll give you tips on big stories."

"I get all I want."

"Then I'll give you friendship—undying friendship."

"The first thing you know . . . you'll be proposing."

They laughed, then Rea Jaure said she had heard that Ford and Mrs. Houdini were to make a lecture tour together.

"Well, I'm going to—I'm always making lecture tours."

"Who is financing this?"

"I am. Mrs. Houdini supplied the code as her part of the bargain."

"If Mrs. Houdini supplied the code, you didn't get it spiritualistically, did you?"

"You know, Rea, I couldn't do that."

How could readers of the tabloid be sure this conversation had actually taken place? Writer Edward Churchill and managing editor William E. Plummer had been in another room of the apartment; they signed sworn statements that they had taken down the verbal exchange word for word.

In a subsequent story the *Graphic* claimed the medium had known the magician's widow long before the séance on Payson Avenue. The paper said it had letters Ford had written her, including one dated April 10, 1928, mailed from England.

The day the hoax story appeared, Ford, flanked by an attorney, called it a "blackmail attempt." He said he had not gone to the newswoman's apartment; instead he had a late dinner with a friend—Francis R. Fast. Medium Ford offered a motive for Rea Jaure's "lies." Mrs. Houdini had refused to let her make copies of the letters that Charles Chapin, former city editor of the *New York World*, then serving a life term in Sing Sing prison, had written explaining why he had murdered his wife. Furious, Rea threatened to expose the séance as a fraud unless he, Ford, got those letters for her. According to Ford, when the newswoman phoned him shortly after midnight, he told her, "Well, you can go to hell," and slammed down the receiver.

Dunninger, the mentalist, introduced still another element

into the controversy—a curvaceous redhead named Daisy White, who had moved for some years on the fringes of the magic business. It was suggested that she had had an affair with Houdini, that he told her the message he planned to transmit to his wife after death, and that she had passed this along to Ford. A fellow tenant of her building, Joseph Bantino, testified that Ford often visited Daisy's apartment; he also said he had heard her talk with the medium on the hallway telephone. Daisy admitted she knew the code and said most magicians did, but denied the romance with Houdini and said he had not revealed the message to her.

Meanwhile Beatrice Houdini, the magician's widow, wrote a moving letter to Walter Winchell, the columnist, which was published in the *Graphic:*

This letter is not for publicity, I do not need publicity. I want to let Houdini's old friends know that I did not betray his trust. I am writing this personally because I wish to tell you emphatically that I was no party to any fraud.

Now, regarding the séance: For two years I have been praying to receive the message from my husband; for two years every day I have received messages from all parts of the world. Had I wanted a publicity stunt I could no doubt have chosen any of these sensational messages. When I repudiated these messages no one said a word, excepting the writers who said I did not have the nerve to admit the truth.

When the real message, THE message that Houdini and I agreed upon, came to me and I accepted it as the truth, I was greeted with jeers. Why? Those who denounce the whole thing as a fraud claim that I had given Mr. Arthur Ford the message. If Mr. Ford said this I brand him a liar. Mr. Ford has stoutly denied saying this ugly thing, and knowing the reporter as well as I do I prefer to believe Mr. Ford. Others say the message has been common property and known to them for some time. Why do they tell me this now, when they know my heart was hungry for the true words from my husband? The many stories told about me I have no way to tell the world the truth of or the untruth, for I have no paper at my beck and call; everyone has a different opinion of how the message was obtained. With all these different tales I would not even argue. However, when anyone accuses me of GIVING the words that my husband and I labored so long to convince ourselves of the truth of communication, then I will fight and fight until the breath leaves my body.

If anyone claims I gave the code, I can only repeat they lie. Why should I want to cheat myself? I do not need publicity. I have no intention of going on the stage, or, as some paper said, on a lecture tour. My husband made it possible for me to live in the greatest comfort. I do not need to earn money. I have gotten the message I have been waiting for from my husband, how, if not by spiritual aid, I do not know.

And now, after I told the world that I have received the true message, everyone seems to have known of the code, yet never told me. They left it to Mr. Ford to tell me, and I am accused of giving the words. It is all so confusing. In conclusion, may I say that God and Houdini and I know that I did not betray my trust. For the rest of the world I really ought not to care a hang, but somehow I do, therefore this letter. Forgive its length.

Sincerely yours,

Beatrice Houdini

Despite this letter, members of Ford's own church charged him with fraud. On January twenty-fifth the *New York Sun* reported he had been expelled from the United Spiritualist League. On February tenth, the executive council of this league and the governing board of the First Spiritualist Church met at the Martinique Hotel to decide whether or not he should be ousted from his post at the church for "conduct unbecoming a spiritualist minister."

Three members of the *Graphic* staff—Plummer, Churchill, and Jaure—presented sworn statements affirming that the published account of Ford's meeting with Rea Jaure was true. James Lawlor, the doorman of her apartment house, identified Ford as the man he had seen enter and leave on the night in question.

Ford's attorney introduced three witnesses who said the medium had been elsewhere at the time. He also read the confession of an unnamed man, who four days before had sworn that he, not Ford, had been the person who had gone to the apartment that night. The man stated that he had been paid to impersonate the medium. This witness did not attend the hearing in person, nor were the names of those who had allegedly paid him ever released to the press. Following six hours of heated debate, the hearing adjourned at 2 A.M. After pondering the evidence for nearly a week, a decision was reached. "On the ground of insufficient proof," Ford was exonerated.

In the April issue of *Science and Invention,* Rea Jaure repeated her charge that " 'Rev' Ford Faked Houdini Message." The article, illustrated with the copy she had made of the January fifth letter from Ford's friends to Mrs. Houdini, which listed the ten words, and a diagram showing where Plummer and Churchill had been concealed in the Jaure apartment, quoted the conversation published earlier in the *Graphic.* It is noteworthy that Ford did not sue her, the *Graphic,* or *Science and Invention.* Instead he told reporters he considered the Houdini case closed.

Beatrice Houdini disavowed the Ford message countless times before she died in 1943. She never spoke to the medium again after, as she put it, her "sick brain" healed. An article on March 26, 1933, in the magazine section of the *New York Sunday Mirror* quoted from a speech she had made several months before:

> There was a time when I wanted intensely to hear from Harry. I was ill, both physically and mentally, and such was my eagerness that spiritualists were able to prey upon my mind and make me believe that they had really heard from him.

As a result of the nationwide publicity the Houdini séance received, Ford became a stellar attraction in psychic circles. Until then John Slater, a small, elderly, white-haired Californian, had been the outstanding American platform performer.

Though advertised as a "test medium," Slater ignored challenges from magicians. Houdini, Joseph Rinn, and Dunninger had offered him thousands of dollars if he would read their sealed questions. Attending the twenty-fifth annual convention of the General Assembly of Spiritualists at the Waldorf-Astoria Hotel in New York in June 1921 with Houdini in order to test Slater, Rinn, a wealthy wholesale-produce dealer and an amateur conjurer, stood up and waved an envelope. Inside it, he said, was a message and a certified check for a thousand dollars. If Slater read the message, he could have the check. "The easy-going, sarcastic Ganymede of Spirit Land," as one paper termed Slater, refused. The assembled mediums rushed toward the interloper—some women tried to stab him with hat pins, Rinn later said—and until the hotel security police arrived on the scene, he feared serious bodily injury. Eight years later at the Hotel Pennsylvania in New York, Dunninger offered the medium twenty-one thousand dollars if he was able to read correctly the contents of two envelopes. Again the challenge was rejected, and Dunninger and his party were forcibly ejected from the ballroom.

Dunninger, who made a study of Slater's methods, said in his book *Inside the Medium's Cabinet* that psychic intuition had nothing to do with Slater's success on the platform. The members of the audience placed their sealed questions in baskets in the lobby. The baskets were then taken backstage before they reached the platform. There someone slit open one end of each envelope. After removing the questions and reading them, this person made notes on the envelopes in pencil, close to the slits. Once the questions were replaced, no one in the audience could tell that the envelopes had been opened. Later, when the envelopes were heaped on a table on the platform, Slater would pick them up one by one, glancing at the notations as he touched each envelope to his forehead and "communed" with the spirits. After a reading, he would tear off one end of the envelope—the one with his cues—and pass the envelope to the audience, so that the writer could regain the question.

In the summer of 1929, Ford replaced Slater as the outstanding guest performer in the spiritualist camps of America. These seasonal gatherings, still held today, offered believers the opportunity to attend lectures and demonstrations by famous psychics, as well as by regional specialists in clairvoyance, psychic healing, and similar phenomena.

Ford's bookings that year extended from Camp Chesterfield in Indiana to Maine. He scored his greatest triumph in Lily Dale, New York. Located fifty miles from Buffalo, where the Davenport Brothers, the most famous stage mediums of the nineteenth century, had been born, Lily Dale then boasted an unparalleled "permanent" attraction, which has since been destroyed by fire—the transplanted Hydesville house in which the Fox sisters, the founders of modern spiritualism, heard the first "spirit raps" on the historic night of March 31, 1848, and where the same sounds still occurred when a rapping medium was present.

There were perhaps a hundred other psychics available at the camp for consultation when Ford arrived, but visitors thronged to see the "Houdini medium" in action, and many attended the classes he gave in "spiritual development."

Ford's instructions did not explain how he obtained the

names and facts that made his message-reading demonstrations so effective. He lectured instead on a technique he said he had learned at the British College of Psychic Science in London.

His listeners were told to shut their eyes and visualize a spirit near and dear to them: a mother, father, sister, or brother. The spirit would materialize in their minds most clearly just before they went to sleep at night or shortly after they awoke in the morning. The image would be fleeting, unless they took a deep breath and held it. Once air was expelled from the lungs, Ford said, the vision would disintegrate.

Not all good mediums were beyond reproach in their private lives, Ford admitted in one of his Lily Dale lectures. "Degenerates" as well as those who lived exemplary lives had been notable psychics: "The best medium in England is now in the penitentiary for burglary." George S. Lawton, a sociologist who was at the camp gathering data, reported these details and the fact that the medium's class grew so large that it had to be moved from a smaller hall to the main auditorium in his book *The Drama of Life After Death,* published in 1932.

Ford's fame also grew overseas, following the Houdini episode. Two thousand people attended his performance at Queen's Hall in London in June 1930. Ford's urbane manner, witty asides, and uncanny ability to call names and describe events in the lives of those who had written questions delighted the audience. Author Upton Sinclair was equally astounded when he attended a Ford séance that July in Los Angeles. Sinclair brought with him five letters, carefully wrapped in protective paper and enclosed in an opaque envelope. Ford named one of the five correspondents, the late Jack London, and said that London referred to his wife as a squaw because she wore "something tight about her head." Sinclair had not known this. He wrote to London's widow, and she replied that before her husband died, it had been her custom to wind her hair around her head and tie it in place with a strip of cloth.

In December when Ford visited his mother in South Carolina, no spirit voice warned him not to drive back to New York. A truck struck his car; his younger sister was killed; a woman who had accompanied them died a few hours later; and the medium himself was seriously injured—broken ribs, fractured jaw, internal complications, and cuts on his face. Morphine eased his pains, then turned him briefly into an addict. He overcame this affliction and turned to alcohol to relieve his aches and tensions. This craving for liquor he never fully conquered, though he became a member of Alcoholics Anonymous.

Ford's appearance at Queen's Hall in London on June 9, 1931, drew the largest crowd "since the much regretted decease of Sir Arthur Conan Doyle," the July issue of *Psychic Science* reported; almost all of the twenty-five hundred seats were filled. He endorsed Margery, the Boston medium Houdini had said was a charlatan, and stated she had "never been detected in fraud of any kind." The thumbprints Margery produced in wax of her dead brother, Walter, were, Ford asserted, "final proofs of surviving personality." As to Houdini, the medium said he had confessed his mistakes during the séance Ford had held for the magician's widow; he added that the spirit of Houdini was now one of his "own helpers" on the other side.

When the fortieth annual convention of the General Assembly of Spiritualists opened at the Statler Hotel in Buffalo, New York, in June 1936 Ford told a *Buffalo Times* reporter that too many unqualified mystics were appearing publicly. "The trouble," he said, "is that as a certain type of person is able to see a clairvoyant picture or receive an impression he stops his development and takes to the platform. In other words, he gets a shiver and hangs out a shingle."

A year later Ford, who had been elected president of the National Association of Spiritualists, embarked for a tour of Australia. Crowds filled the Assembly Hall in Sydney for four nights. The final evening he made spiritualistic history; his stage séance was broadcast. This marked the first time an entranced medium had attempted to communicate with the dead on Australian radio.

Ford enjoyed the company of ministers who thought extrasensory perception might account for his ability to produce verifiable information during his séances. He was among those who founded Spiritual Frontiers Fellowship in 1956. This new organization of clergy and laymen sought to reaffirm the miracles of the Bible by encouraging psychic healers and sensitives who could demonstrate mental and physical phenomena.

Two years earlier at the Maine State Spiritualistic Association convention Ford had denounced the "quacks who give religion a bad name" and said genuine mediums practiced "extrasensory perception, carried as far as humans have been able to carry it." He showed a reporter from the *Portland Press Herald* the statement Mrs. Houdini had signed, but did not mention she had later disavowed any communication with her late husband.

In his autobiography, *Nothing So Strange,* published in 1958, the ageing psychic noted that clergymen of many faiths were interested in his work and were fascinated by parapsychology "because they have had psychic experiences of their own."

Not until 1967 did the seventy-year-old medium score the second big publicity coup of his career. A front-page story in *The New York Times* and subsequent wire-service accounts reported a séance almost as weird and wonderful as the one he had staged for Houdini's widow thirty-eight years before. Again the prominence of the sitter made the event newsworthy. The Right Reverend James A. Pike had been facing a possible trial for heresy by the Episcopal House of Bishops.

The stocky, bespectacled prelate, who called himself "God's maverick," had been christened a Roman Catholic in Oklahoma in 1913. While studying for the priesthood in California, he became an agnostic. He received a doctorate in law at Yale in 1938 and married a young woman he had met in California. They were divorced two years later. He married again in 1942, while working as a attorney for the Securities and Exchange Commission and teaching an evening course in law at George Washington University. The Pikes became Episcopalians in 1942, following the birth of the first of their four children. Ordained a deacon in 1946 and a priest in 1948, in 1952, at the age of thirty-nine, he had risen to the post of dean at the Cathedral of St. John the Divine in New York City. Pike's provocative sermons, television programs during which he and his family discussed sex, civil rights, and psychoanalysis, and his frank answers to reporters' questions on such diverse topics as foreign aid and contraception made him one of the most controversial religious leaders of his time. Called to California as bishop coadjutor in 1952, he was elected bishop in 1958.

As outspoken there as he has been in the East, Pike outraged conventional clergymen by questioning such theological doctrines as the Holy Trinity, the Virgin Birth, the Incarnation, Resurrection, and Ascension. Aware that his critics regarded these views as heretical, Pike resigned his high office in November 1965 and announced he would go to Santa Barbara to work at the Center for the Study of Democratic Institutions.

Though no longer head of the Episcopal diocese of California, Pike was still a bishop and as eager to reform the church as his opponents were to oust him for heretical opinions. He admitted in January 1966 that he was skeptical about personal immortality and a life after death. Pike at the time was in England, studying at Cambridge University. News that his twenty-two-year-old son, James junior, had committed suicide in a Manhattan hotel room on February 4, 1966, shattered him. Pike knew his son had taken LSD and consulted a psychiatrist about his emotional problems, but he had never suspected the young man would kill himself.

A terrible sense of guilt preyed upon the bishop's mind. Had he been too preoccupied with ecclesiastical problems to understand his boy's inner turmoil? It soon became evident to him that his dead son was trying to reach him. He had been told that James junior had shot himself between three and three thirty A.M. When Pike saw that two picture postcards lying on the floor of his Cambridge flat formed an angle of 140 degrees, he took this to be a first sign. There is a five-hour time difference between England and the United States; perhaps the angle of the cards indicated the exact moment of the suicide— 8:19 British time. Accepting this premise, he was startled one day to notice that a clock had stopped at 8:19, and on another day to find that two books on the floor formed the same angle.

A friend, Canon John Pearce-Higgins, vice-provost of Southwark Cathedral, took him to see a medium, Mrs. Ena Twigg, who lived in East Acton. The messages she conveyed from his dead son consoled the Bishop as did those he received later through another psychic, George Daisley, in Santa Barbara, California.

The public had not learned of Bishop Pike's interest in communication with the dead, but Allen Spraggett, religion editor of the *Toronto Star* and a believer in the supernormal, knew of it and sold the concept of a taped séance to the Canadian Television Network.

Spraggett says in his book *The Bishop Pike Story,* published in 1970, that he phoned Arthur Ford, whom he had met in Lily Dale, New York, and who was then in Philadelphia, to ask if he would participate in a séance; the sitter was to be James Pike. With some reluctance, Ford agreed. Spraggett's letter of August 28, 1967, to the medium outlined the format. After Ford had given a trance reading for Bishop Pike, they would discuss "what psychic phenomena means to traditional Christianity."

Six days later, on September third, the program was taped in the studios of CFTO-TV, Toronto; two weeks afterward, it was televised. It was not, however, until reporter John Leo wrote a front-page story headlined "Pike Asserts He Got Messages from Dead Son at TV Seance" for the September 27 issue of *The New York Times* that the public learned how the former Episcopal bishop had reacted to Ford's revelations. Interviewed by telephone, Pike pronounced the spirit messages he had received authentic. His son had expressed "a loving affirmation" of his philosophy. "I don't see how research by the medium could very well have brought out the role of Donald McKinnon [a friend in Cambridge, England] in my life, or the fact of his having had two cats," the clergyman told the reporter. A message from Karl M. Block, his predecessor as bishop of California, had also been convincing. "Everything matched up," Pike said. "All the long-forgotten facts and details matched up."

Pike went on to explain why he accepted the words relayed through Ford as his son's:

> In the context of what we know about man's psyche transcending the space-time continuum, about mystical experience, and the accumulating evidence of extrasensory perception, plus all the data about apparent communication with the deceased—not excluding the Resurrection—one can say that it is the most plausible explanation to accept it as true.

I saw the tape of the Toronto séance at WNEW-TV studios in New York. Hans Holzer—a prolific writer of affirmative books on the occult—and I had been invited there to give our comments by Sonny Fox, the host of a daily show. Holzer agreed with Bishop Pike's view that it would have been impossible for Ford to have gained the information by research. I dissented. The word "forgive" had been in print long before Houdini's Hungarian mother, who knew only a few words of English, had fluently expressed herself through Ford in an unfamiliar tongue. The "secret code" had been published before the Houdini séance. Beatrice Houdini herself had been so disillusioned by psychic fraud that, before she died, she promised, "When I go, I'll be gone for good. I won't even try to come back."

Edward Fiske, religion editor of *The New York Times*, interviewed me after Pike told the press about the manifestations in his Cambridge flat which he attributed to his dead son: postcards, books, and safety pins found at an 8:19 angle; photographs that disappeared from a bedroom and were discovered by the bishop's chaplain under clothes heaped in a pile at the bottom of a closet. I thought a living person, not a spirit, had been responsible. Moreover, I doubted that it was chance that had led the distraught bishop to his first sitting with a medium.

Worldwide publicity about the Pike séance brought Ford requests for more private sittings and public appearances than he had had in years. I talked with him when he came to New York in 1968 to appear in a filmed report on the rising American interest in the occult for CBS-TV's "Sixty Minutes." Earlier I had attended meetings of various psychics and psychic study groups with the producer of "Sixty Minutes," Alice Bigart (she died before she finished editing the material and the planned segment was never shown). Ford was invited to go into a trance before the cameras. He said he had been ill and did not feel up to a séance. He had not known I would be in the studio, but he did not seem overly distressed when I sat with him and Hughes Rudd, the commentator for the program. How, I asked, could a medium in a matter of seconds reach one of the billions upon billions of spirits? He chuckled and replied he was a sort of psychic switchboard operator; he put in person-to-person calls through Fletcher, his spirit control. Service on the long-distance line in the hereafter must be better than it was on earth, I said. He chuckled again and said it was.

What did people do in the afterlife? He replied he wasn't

sure; he had only their word for it, but it seemed they carried out routines similar to those that had occupied their time on earth. I visualized astral baseball players batting out home runs, ethereal plumbers repairing leaky faucets, and cloudlike muggers ready to pounce on angelic strollers. Ford interrupted my reverie by saying that few of his sitters made inquiries on the subject; they were more eager simply to talk with departed friends and relatives.

Ford was in the news again the following year—as a sidelight to the tragic story of Pike's death. On September 1, 1969, Bishop Pike and his third wife, his former secretary, Diane Kennedy, drove from Jerusalem across the Judean desert toward the valley of Qumran. The Dead Sea Scrolls, the earliest-known version of the Old Testament, had been discovered in a cave there in 1947. About two hours after their noon departure in a rented Ford Cortina, they made a wrong turn—to the right instead of the left. When the terrain became so rugged that Diane could drive no farther, she attempted to swing the car around. A rear wheel slipped into a deep hole, and both of the Pikes together could not budge the car. Sharing a single bottle of Coca Cola, the fifty-six-year-old bishop and his younger wife set out in search of help. When he, fatigued from walking in the scorching sun, could not go on, she continued without him. Ten hours later she reached an Arab camp. Soon the world knew that Bishop Pike was lost in the desert and that Israeli troops and a helicopter were trying to find him.

Newspapers reported that Ford sent word to Diane; he said he had seen a vision of her husband alive but ill in a cave. Mrs. Ena Twigg, the first psychic Pike consulted in England, said the bishop "was on the border trying to make the transition." A Tel Aviv mystic held a pendulum over two maps and marked a location. The body was found on September seventh, not at the point indicated by the pendulum, nor in a cave, but sprawled on the ledge of a canyon. He had died, an Israeli pathologist's statement indicated, a few hours after his wife had last seen him.

Ford himself, ill with heart trouble and other ailments, had little more than a year to live. He continued to give private séances, sitting relaxed in a comfortable chair with a dark silk handkerchief tied over his eyes. Racked with violent chest pains, he underwent emergency shock treatment on January fourth at the Baptist Hospital in Miami. "God help me," he pleaded when the suffering intensified shortly before he died. He was seventy-five.

Since the noted psychic's death, several of his friends claim to have received messages from him. One, Jerome Ellison, had aided Ford in the preparation of his book *Unknown but Known,* published in 1968, and collaborated with him in the posthumous volume *The Life Beyond Death,* published in 1971. Ellison discussed his communications with the dead medium on Long John Nebel's WMCA late-night talk show in New York.

Another friend, Ruth Montgomery, once a syndicated political columnist but in more recent years a medium and the author of a number of books on the occult, said she sat at her typewriter the day Ford died and he, she maintains, began writing through her fingers. Her book, *A World Beyond,* published in 1971, contains Ford's "eyewitness account of the hereafter." There are trees, streams, clothes, and foods of various sorts in the afterlife— if new arrivals imagine they see them. Atheists who admit their error are given an opportunity to be redeemed. Soon after his "transition," Ford chatted with Fletcher, his spirit guide, and later met Sir Arthur Conan Doyle and Sir Oliver Lodge. Dwight D. Eisenhower, Ford reported, had been greeted warmly by the soldiers who had fought under his command. John F. Kennedy was working for world peace, and his brother, Robert, still tried to use his influence to promote civil rights. Franklin D. Roosevelt and Winston Churchill enjoyed conversations together. All of them ignored the ranting Adolf Hitler. Houdini and his wife had been reincarnated. Bishop Pike and his son were closer than they had been in life. Rudolph Valentino had returned to earth, "and is now happily married and living in Paris."

The most important Ford revelations came not from his spirit speaking through Ruth Montgomery, but from the private papers he left behind. "Cheating in Pike's Séance Is Alleged" was the headline for Eleanor Blau's story in *The New York Times* on March 11. 1973. She said Allen Spraggett, the host of the sensational Toronto television program during which Ford had conveyed messages from the dead to Bishop Pike, and the Reverend Canon William V. Rauscher, custodian of the medium's files, had made a startling discovery while preparing a book about his life.

Evidential material that had impressed Pike as he listened to the "voice" of Karl Block, his immediate predecessor as bishop of California, talk through Ford was found in the medium's extensive collection of printed obituaries. For instance, "ecclesiastical panhandler," the term Block applied to his successor, and Ford's statement that Block had died "during some rite of the church" were in the *Times* obituary, which said the death had occurred as he conducted an ordination service.

A page from a Ford notebook listed "biographical data on his sitters," and a man who had worked as the medium's secretary admitted that Ford traveled with a suitcase filled with information about those who were to attend his séances.

Arthur Ford: The Man Who Talked with the Dead, the Spraggett-Rauscher "authoritative biography of the world's greatest medium," which was published by New American Library in April 1973, gave more details on the psychic's sources. After one man's name, for example, were notations that he had been a dean at the Massachusetts Institute of Technology and had been killed, along with fifty others, when a plane crashed in Egypt, not far from Cairo. The Bishop Pike dossier, the authors found, extended over many years.

One of the several male secretaries, who had worked for Ford, is described in the Spraggett-Rauscher work as "a middle-aged, effeminate individual," who "parted on unfriendly terms" with the medium. This man said Ford researched his clients at a Philadelphia library during the years he lived there. *Who's Who* and the directories of educational institutions provided information. Once the medium knew the school or college his prospective sitter had attended, it was easy to get convincing information from yearbooks and similar publications.

The former secretary's most amusing recollection was that prior to his séances Ford would "read a little poetry." This "poetry" was the factual material the medium had accumulated on his subject. It was carried, Ford's former associate said, in a leather bag that the medium hid in the secretary's car. Ford never dared take it with him to a hotel room. He had suffered heart attacks and did not want incriminating data to be found near him if he died.

As the name of this informant is not given in the book, I do not know if he was the same Ford secretary who tried to sell a complete exposure of the medium's methods to *The National Observer*. One of the medium's associates removed considerable material from Ford's files before they were received by William Rauscher. Rauscher worked his way through college as a magician, but he firmly believes in communication with the dead and other psychic phenomena. He is a past president of Spiritual Frontiers Fellowship. During Ford's later years, he was one of the medium's closest friends.

Spraggett shares Rauscher's belief in, and admiration for, Arthur Ford. They say the medium may have cheated on occasion, as other psychics did, when, because of his physical condition, he could not communicate psychically.

Despite the weight of the incriminating evidence in Ford's private files, and the knowledge that Mrs. Houdini later denied she had received an authentic spirit message during the séance that made the medium famous, some people still insist Arthur Ford actually spoke with the dead. "Anyone can talk to the dead," Houdini once said as he lectured about fraudulent psychics, "but the dead do not answer."

MYSTICS FROM THE EAST

Disciples of Maharaj Ji, a fifteen-year-old mystic from India, leased the Houston Astrodome in November 1973 for "the most holy and significant event in human history." This widely heralded but scarcely specific proclamation provoked considerable speculation. A rumor spread through the Haight-Ashbury section of San Francisco that the newly discovered comet Kohoutek would later streak down and destroy every man, woman, and child on earth except those who hailed Maharaj Ji as the new messiah. In New York City a hippy convert to the fast-growing cult of "The Lord of the Universe" discounted the story from California. He solemnly assured a street-corner crowd in Manhattan's East Village that on the third and final day of "Millennium '73" the world's largest enclosed arena would blast off like a gigantic rocket and carry Maharaj Ji and his followers to a more peaceful planet millions of light-years away in outer space.

Marvels are always expected from Eastern mystics who visit the West. Swami Vivekananda disappointed many who heard his lecture at the 1893 World Parliament of Religions in Chicago. The eloquent disciple of Ramakrishna, a venerated Calcutta yogi, spoke of the inner joy achieved by meditation but did not demonstrate the awesome powers of mind over matter which many Americans had expected. Swamis, it was said, could thrust swords through their hearts without bleeding, remain buried alive for long periods without dying, and levitate themselves by concentrating.

Swami Yogananda, another holy man from the East, traveled to Boston for the International Congress of Religious Liberals in October 1920. He made it clear to those who questioned him that authentic yogis did not display their accomplishments for public amusement. The fakirs who slept on beds of nails or produced mango trees from under the cover of empty cloths were not true mystics, he said. He admitted in his *Autobiography of a Yogi*, first published in 1946, that the feats of at least one respected yogi were too "marvelous" to be believed.

As a boy Yogananda had visited Vishudhananda, better known as Gandha Baba ("perfume saint"). The portly guru, who had unusually large eyes, skin the color of a chestnut, and a long beard, told the lad to extend his right hand and name a fragrance. "Rose," Yogananda said. The holy man did not touch him; yet the unmistakable scent of this flower mysteriously arose from the palm of the boy's hand.

Testing the holy man's power further, Yogananda removed an odorless blossom from an urn and suggested that Gandha Baba give it a jasmine aroma. Immediately this sweet perfume wafted up from the white petals. Yogananda thought autosuggestion might account for these marvels, until he went home and his sister noticed the rose fragrance on his hand and the jasmine scent emanating from the flower he was carrying.

Paul Brunton, a British journalist who spent his later years studying the mysteries of the East, vividly described a similar encounter with Vishudhananda in his book, *A Search in Secret India*. The guru took Brunton's silk handkerchief while one of the old man's assistants went into the courtyard with a mirror and tilted it so that the sun was reflected in the room. As the perfume saint held the handkerchief in one hand, he trained the sun's rays briefly on it with a magnifying glass. Seconds later, he put the glass aside and returned the silk.

The aroma of white jasmine, the scent Brunton had chosen, came from one of the corners. When the Englishman selected two other perfumes, rose and violet, these were produced in the same way on two other corners. Finally a fourth fragrance, which the yogi himself chose and which Brunton could not identify, emanated from the remaining corner.

Brunton was puzzled. He said the robe worn by the man could scarcely have concealed the vast supply of perfumes needed to produce whatever aroma was called for. The magnifying glass had not been tricked, and no suspicious moves had been made.

Vishudhananda himself attributed this feat to his mastery of solar science. He said he had learned the technique from a yogi in Tibet who was 1,002 years old.

Like other "miracles" which over the centuries have amazed travelers to the East, the perfume mystery is a trick. I have seen it performed in New York and London, as well as in Delhi.

The most effective of the several ways to do it is perhaps the oldest. A drop of perfume essence is enclosed in a pellet of wax. When the fingers break the wax, under the cover of a handkerchief or flower, the fragrance is released. The wax adheres to a fingernail while the mystic displays the open fingers and palm of his hand. When the hand is turned palm downward, the fingers close and bring the pellet under the thumb. A quick squeeze, and the trick is done.

Yogananda, who did not know how the feat was accomplished, erred in saying the yogi did not touch his hand before the rose fragrance came from it. In this presentation the performer secretly breaks the proper pellet as soon as a scent is named; the perfume wets the ball of his thumb. Instructing the spectator to extend his hand, the performer reaches across to grasp it with his thumb on the palm and his fingers on the back. As he does this, the performer says, "I want you to turn your hand palm down. I will not touch it." The spectator remembers the words, not the action, of the performer. The performer moves several feet away. While standing at a distance, he tells the spectator to turn his hand palm upward. The scent is not perceptible until the spectator's hand turns and the fragrance rises upward to his nostrils.

Contrary to Paul Brunton's thinking, a "vast supply" of perfume is not essential. With a dozen tiny pellets, an adept showman can convince a skeptical investigator that "any" perfume can be materialized. The pellets are easily concealed. One Indian I saw at work hid them in his beard; the wax had been colored to match his facial foliage.

While Brunton was mystified by the perfume saint, he was dubious about the predictions of Meher Baba, another mystic. The Parsee seer—a man with long brown hair, a moustache, and an amiable manner—sat on a rug in a cave seven miles from Ahmednager, a city east of Bombay, and spelled out his thoughts by moving his index finger rapidly from one letter to another on an alphabet board. He had taken a vow of silence on July 10, 1925. Only when catastrophies and wars brought the world to the brink of destruction would he open his lips to deliver a message of momentous importance. Meanwhile his disciples often eased the strain for visitors by voicing the words his finger spelled out too rapidly for most people to follow.

The time when he would speak out was rapidly approaching, Meher Baba prophesied. Following terrible battles and calamities, there would be years of peace, international amity, and tranquility between all races and religions. In this era he promised he would perform miracles of all sorts: he would heal the afflicted, cure the incurable, and raise the dead.

Meher Baba had moved to new quarters near another city, Nasik, when Brunton came to see him again months later. In the interim the Englishman had discovered that the holy man's powers were not as great as he had been told. For instance, Meher Baba had been credited with curing a man who was suffering from appendicitis; the physician who had treated the man attested that the "appendicitis" was in reality indigestion.

Brunton had also read through the voluminous files in which two of the mystic's followers recorded their leaders' activities. In the past, Meher Baba had predicted the coming of the holocaust on various dates. Once he saw it erupting in the East when tensions there mounted; again he saw it breaking out in the West. Whenever an old prophecy failed to come true, he would make a new one. As time went by, he did not give exact dates in his predictions but merely implied he knew them.

Brunton concluded that Meher Baba was kind, gentle, and sensitive in a religious way but that he also displayed symptoms of paranoia. Still, he showed skill as an organizer, and his cult spread.

The public was not aware that the Indian seer visited the United States late in 1931 to arrange for an ashram, or retreat, to be established at Harmon-on-the-Hudson, New York. When he returned aboard the *Bremen* the following year, the press turned out in force to greet the thirty-eight-year-old prophet.

The May 30 issue of the New York *Herald Tribune* noted that the Parsee mystic had landed without saying a word. Besieged by reporters, newsreel cameramen, and radio broadcasters, he smiled and answered questions by spelling out words on his wooden alphabet board. His disciples announced that Meher Baba would break his seven-year-silence in less than a week; then the world would hear a message of international import. A representative of a newsreel company and an agent from a broadcasting firm were said to be negotiating for exclusive rights to this epic speech. Years passed; Meher Baba continued to delay his crucial announcement. The Indian messiah died in January 1969 at the age of seventy-five. The long-awaited words that would offer salvation to mankind were never uttered.

Two years after Meher Baba came to New York on the *Bremen*, Swami See Ram Lia, another mystic who had taken a vow of silence, arrived on board the Munson liner *Pan America*. In May 1934 he shoved a silver trident through a hole in his tongue for the press. Mohammed Lala, a fakir, made the trip on the same vessel. He posed for photographers, wearing a turban and a loincloth, seated on a bed of nails with his legs crossed. A steward on the ship told a reporter for the *New York American* that Mohammed Lala had objected to the soft berth in his cabin; he had slept on the floor throughout the voyage.

These wonder-workers came not to expound Indian philosophy but to appear in Robert L. Ripley's "Believe It or Not" show at the Century of Progress world's fair in Chicago. Countless performers of their sort had traveled in previous years to astound the curious in Asia, Europe, Australia, and the Americas. Audiences were enthralled when they performed in circuses, sideshows, and theatres.

Devout Indian religious leaders do not perform miracles; they teach systems of thought and body control designed to produce increased mental awareness and physical well-being. Pain resisters are sometimes ascetics, but more often those who exhibit their self-tortures to the public are showmen.

The most famous exponents of this phase of fakirism in the twentieth century were not, however, Indian either by birth or ancestry. Tahra Bey was an Armenian, Rahman Bey and Hamid Bey claimed to be Egyptians. Paul Diebel labored in a Silesian mine before he toured as "The Invulnerable Man." Mirin Dajo was born in Holland. The various Beys were bearded, wore flowing robes and headdresses. Their self-impalements were, for the most part, preludes to living burials.

In 1926 Diebel's torture act headlined at the Scala Theatre in Berlin and other Continental variety halls. He forced long needles, nails, and slender knives through the fleshy part of his body without drawing blood. After he jammed a dagger through his left forearm, he would walk through the audience to give the spectators a close-up look at the blade extending four or five inches from his skin. Then he would approach the footlights and under a powerful spotlight make drops of blood ooze from his chest to form a cross.

His finale brought cheers and rounds of applause. A spectator, standing several feet away from Diebel on the stage, would take aim with a powerful slingshot and send a large metal bolt flying toward his chest. Stepping back slightly as the missile struck, the European fakir would then pause, pry the bolt from his midsection, turn from right to left so that everyone could see the wound, then bow.

Diebel's stunts were not illusions. He really did force needles and thin blades through his flesh. If the portion of the skin to be penetrated is pinched between the fingers only a slight stinging sensation will be felt. This pressure anesthesia has been used by physicians. The cross formed as blood emerged through the tiny slits Diebel had cut in his skin earlier. His mental and muscular control were such that he could withstand the pain and take the impact of the catapulted bolt without flinching.

Diebel was daring but not rash enough to attempt the dangerous impalements which brought Mirin Dajo fame. It is one thing to force sharp skewers through the cheeks and arms, another to risk death as sword blades are pushed through the abdomen. Dajo believed a supernatural power protected him.

The son of a Dutch butcher, he had been born Arthur Hensckes in Rotterdam on August 6, 1912. His stage name came from an Esperanto term *mirindajo*, meaning "admirable deed."

A dedicated crusader for world peace, he said that if he was able to triumph over pain and death by sheer will power, international pacifist organizations should be able to stop wars by similar means.

After spending more than three years perfecting his sensational demonstrations in Holland, Mirin Dajo opened in Zurich in the spring of 1947. H. Otter, a Dutch hypnotist, presented the attraction. J. de Groot, another friend, had the task of inserting and removing the blades. Like the star of the show, De Groot had worked in a butcher shop.

Bare to the waist, the thin, balding, bearded Dajo stood erect as De Groot carefully positioned the point of an epée in his friend's back and applied pressure. The mystic's face reddened; he became tense, then seemed to enter a trance. De Groot carefully, steadily, forced the weapon through the body. The tip broke skin on the far side and extended more than twelve inches. There was no blood. Even skeptics were convinced when a thin hollow sword penetrated the body and when water sent through it spurted out from the protruding tip on the far side.

The torture instruments were rigorously examined by a committee from the audience; they were not sterilized before being put into use.

The removal of the blades by De Groot was effected with the same meticulous precision he had displayed during the insertion. Dajo pressed a finger forcibly on each wound in the front when the tip of a sword disappeared, and De Groot did likewise as a blade was withdrawn from the back.

Then Dajo made an impassioned plea for peace.

Night after night this incredible performance was repeated. One evening Dajo lost consciousness in the course of a transfixion. Until then the authorities had not realized he might be killed during his performance. The license for the show was canceled.

After Dajo was barred from theatres, he volunteered to perform privately for Swiss surgeons and physicians, and to permit them to make any scientific tests of his body they wished. He claimed his God-given power enabled him to stop the circulation of his blood and circumvent hemorrhages when vital organs were pierced. X rays revealed no interior damage, disclosed no infected areas, though blades had penetrated his torso more than five hundred times.

Professor Albert Bessemans, a distinguished physician who taught at the University of Gent in Belgium and investigated occult phenomena, read the extensive reports of Dajo's feats in *La Suisse, National Zeitung,* and other Swiss periodicals and in articles by R. Massini and E. Undritz in the *Schweizerische Medizinische Wochenschrift,* a medical journal. Fascinated by the mystery for which there seemed to be no rational solution, the Belgian researcher ordered smaller blades of precisely the same shape as those employed by Dajo. Then in his laboratory Bessemans inserted them as carefully as De Groot had done in mice, guinea pigs, rabbits, and eventually, a dog. The animals lived despite these impalements, even though they did not—presumably—have any special psychic powers. It seemed obvious, however, to Bessemans, as it had to the physicians in Switzerland, that if the Dutch mystic continued to submit to these tortures, almost inevitably he would suffer a tragic accident.

Professor Rex (Charles Emile Sauty), the publisher of *La Baguette Magique,* a Geneva magic magazine, printed Bessemans's findings in June 1948. Mirin Dajo's obituary ran on another page in the same issue. The preceding month he had announced he would dematerialize a thin pointed metal rod, thirty-five centimeters (almost fourteen inches) long, in his gullet. After he placed the rod in his throat, "The Invulnerable Hollander" became violently ill. An operation at a Zurich hospital on May thirteenth disclosed that the lower end of the rod had penetrated the inner wall of his stomach; he died seventeen days later.

Accidental death is a professional hazard for fakirs. Many more have died in the course of living burials than while performing feats of "invulnerability." A chapter on this subject is included in *ESP, Seers & Psychics,* published in 1970.

A mystic from Andhra, Madras, who believed he had mastered hatha yoga, a system of mind and body control, to the point where a lethal diet would not affect him adversely, demonstrated his immunity before an audience of government officials, physicists, and physicians at the Presidency College in Calcutta. Narasingha Swami, a dark-skinned ascetic with long brown hair and a beard, swallowed poisons and ate broken glass and handfuls of nails. Then he traveled to Burma to repeat the same feats in Rangoon. An Associated Press dispatch in the *New York World-Telegram* on March 26, 1932, said he had gulped down nearly a quart of corrosive liquids followed by the usual fragments of glass. "Two hours later he said he felt ill. In another hour he was dead."

Yogananda, Meher Baba, and other swamis who established cults in the United States shunned this facet of yoga. They appealed to people who yearned to share the mysterious secrets of the East and to be in tune with the rhythm of the universe.

Maharishi Mahesh Yogi was forty-eight when he came from India to London in 1959 to set up the first of his meditation centers in the Western world; he has since expanded his operations on a global scale. The Beatles, the biggest rock-music box-office attraction of the early 60's, fell under his spell and visited his ashram in Rishikesh to seek a greater understanding of themselves and the meaning of life. Actresses Mia Farrow and Shirley MacLaine were among the luminaries of the entertainment business who found the small man with an almost birdlike voice inspiring—at least for a time.

The Maharishi lives simply at home, but he travels in his own private jet and limousines during his frequent tours abroad. Normally he carries a flower in his hand as he speaks and seems serene amid the confusion of modern times. Yet he is far from an altruist. Those who attend the classes taught by his instructors pay for the privilege according to their means. Devotees of school age are charged a thirty-five dollar initiation fee, and women who do not work pay seventy-five dollars. Followers with steady jobs are asked to contribute a week's salary. Each initiate receives a personal *mantra*, a sound to use as a focal point of concentration. The mental repetition of this—twice daily in seclusion—drives away conscious thought, the Maharishi's disciples say, and opens up new frontiers of the mind.

Unlike Sai Baba, a younger competitor who was born in 1928 and lives in Puttaparthi, a town to the north of Bangalore, the Maharishi does not startle visitors by performing miracles. Sai Baba, a genial mystic who wears his dark hair Afro style, produces objects and sacred ashes from nowhere. To viewers unacquainted with sleight-of-hand techniques, this is very impressive. Arnold Schulman, for instance, tells of the marvels he saw in his book, *Baba,* published in 1971. Sai Baba has not as yet made a personal appearance tour in the Western world, though it is said he has projected himself here astrally on several occasions.

In the Felt Forum of New York's Madison Square Garden, where several years before Maharishi Mahesh Yogi had addressed his American followers, a "World Festival of Magic and Occult" was presented in December 1971. Fakir Rayo, one of the attractions, ate fire, plunged blades through his hand and arm, and after inserting in his tongue a hook attached to chains, which ran to the base of a heavy metal cylinder, pulled the cylinder across the stage by walking backward, tongue extended.

Earlier in his career this paunchy, bearded European mystic staged several weird feats that netted him worldwide publicity. Born Rudolf Schmied in Wels, Austria, Rayo left school at sixteen to work for a butcher. Finding this trade boring, he volunteered for the army. Back in civilian life, seven years later, he began his travels as secretary to the wealthy mother of an Italian banker. In North Africa he had the opportunity to observe several fakirs. Yoga had been his hobby; now it became his dominant interest. At the age of twenty-eight he sailed for India where he learned the methods that were to provide him with his future livelihood.

The self-torture routine Rayo presented after returning to Europe created little talk. While performing in Romania, he developed his first sensation. For eighty days in Bucharest, he was on exhibit, stretched out full length, with his extended tongue fastened by a nail to a heavy plank. He sustained himself through this long ordeal with a liquid diet. The next year he was back in Bucharest again in the same uncomfortable position. At the end of a month, he offered an extra attraction by hammering a second nail through his tongue into the board. This forty-four–day run turned out to be more profitable than his initial longer engagement.

Rayo's chief claim to fakirism's hall of fame is that he lived for a year in a "bottle." The press dubbed it a bottle, but the contraption resembled a giant lantern: a sturdy metal framework with glass sides, wider at the middle than at the top and bottom. Sealed inside it at Linz, on December 13, 1952, the fakir was trucked from town to town in Austria, then into Switzerland, Germany, and France. At each stop the "bottle" was taken to a showroom. For a fee the curious could stare at him through the transparent panels.

Rayo was not alone in the "bottle"; one of his pets, a three-foot-long snake, traveled with him. Food for man and reptile was lowered through a small opening at the top of the enclosure. He had planned to stay inside precisely a year, but Rayo extended the period of confinement for several days. On December 20, 1953, in Linz, where the venture started, he smashed a glass panel from the inside with a hammer as the thousands gathered on the Hessenplatz for the coming-out celebration cheered.

Rayo had planned to defy strangulation during his performances in New York in 1971. As he visualized the feat, a long chain would be tied around his neck. Each end would be locked to a motorcycle. Then he would revolve as cyclists drew the chain taut and raced at top speed in circles around him. The stage, unfortunately, was too shallow for this provocative demonstration.

By contrast the platform erected in the Houston Astrodome for Maharaj Ji's "Millennium '73" was gigantic. One section held fifty-six musicians and band leader Bhole, Jr., the guru's taller, five-year-older brother. Another area was used for folk dances and special presentations. Twenty-four of the "perfect master's" mahatmas—the upper echelon of his disciples—sat in a tier at the center of the stage. Above them, the mother and two other brothers of the mystic of the moment relaxed on orange thrones. On the highest level the short, pudgy fifteen-year-old "Lord of the Universe" reigned on a larger blue one.

The growth of Maharaj Ji's Divine Light Mission in the United States had been phenomenal. There were six converts in California in 1971; two years later an estimated fifty thousand Americans had accepted him as the true messiah.

The young guru traveled by private plane, Rolls Royce, or Mercedes 600. He owned ashrams in Los Angeles, Denver, and New York. He offered his followers inner serenity and spiritual knowledge; onetime campus activists, crusaders for world peace and other lost causes showered him with gifts, frequently gave him their personal wealth, and vowed to abide by his principles.

Previous mystics had condemned the materialism of the West. Maharaj Ji's converts, while living frugally, thought it fitting that their leader should have the trappings of a potentate. "What do you expect him to do, travel from L. A. to Houston on a donkey?" a disciple was quoted as saying in Ted Morgan's "Oz in the Astrodome" in the December 9, 1973, issue of *The New York Times Magazine.*

The rites in Texas were filmed for "The Lord of the Universe," a devastating documentary that was shown by the Public Broadcasting Service in February 1974. One segment pictured reporters questioning him during a press conference at the Astroworld Hotel. Someone wanted to know why he wasn't in the Middle East stopping the war then in progress. The young mystic replied: "When a war begins, a general doesn't have to be on the spot." Another asked if Maharaj Ji was the son of God. He snapped back: "Everybody's the son of God. You ain't the uncle or aunt of God, are you?"

Billy Graham had drawn a capacity crowd, sixty-six thousand people, to the Astrodome for one of his sermons; fewer than twenty thousand turned out for "the most holy and significant event in human history."

A disciple of the messiah, whose favorite reading matter is said to be *Superman* comic books, announced on the third and final day that plans had been drawn up for a Divine City in the United States. Solar energy would supply power. Computerized transportation would replace the gasoline-fueled cars and buses that blight modern metropolises. Food and other supplies would be dispatched directly to living quarters through a network of pressurized tubes. There would be every imaginable convenience; toothbrushes would eject toothpaste through their handles directly onto the bristles.

When Maharaj Ji delivered his closing-night oration, he compared his teachings to a filter in an automobile fuel line; the knowledge his devotees acquired would eliminate the dirt and waste material that clogged up so many lives. There was no great revelation; no miracle came to pass. The Astrodome did not soar up into the clouds. The earth did not tremble.

Maharaj Ji lost heavily on the "Millennium '73" venture. Months afterward, Texas bills were still unpaid. His *And It's*

Divine magazine suspended publication. The Divine Light Mission, a tax-exempt religious conglomerate that supervises various corporations, among them home-repair and office-equipment businesses, suffered in the wake of the Houston fiasco. The Divine City project was indefinitely postponed.

Yet the messiah did not seem especially perturbed. A Colorado judge ruled in May 1974 that the sixteen-year-old guru was sufficiently mature to marry Morilyn Lois Johnson, a tall, twenty-four-year-old former airline stewardess, who had been working as his personal secretary. After the wedding she continued to stand up when the "perfect master" entered one of the rooms in their $80,000 house in Denver and, like his other disciples, bow and touch his feet.

Messiahs and fakirs almost invariably promise more than they can deliver. Their words stimulate the imagination, intrigue the mind, but their systems of meditation and body control are all too often falsely claimed to be conducive to the development of extrasensory perception and supernormal powers. Hard-working disciples of successful mystics seldom miss an opportunity to promote their cause. One of Maharaj Ji's ardent campaigners was told that visitors from another planet might land in Houston. His immediate response was, "If you see any, just give them some of our literature."

THE INDESCRIBABLE
PHENOMENON

Scientists who test psychics are often so preoccupied with their technical procedures that they do not realize that what seems at the moment to be a perfectly controlled experiment is actually one that allows considerable leeway for a charlatan to cheat.

Moscow researchers were so busy verifying colors and words as a blindfolded woman identified them with her fingers that their attention was diverted from the insecure bandages that covered her eyes.

Frequently investigators are misdirected by the words or actions of the ingenious people they have planned to observe carefully. Arigó, the Brazilian psychic surgeon, told American Andrija Puharich not to look before an incision was made in his arm. Obediently Puharich turned his head.

When a scientist is predisposed to accept the miraculous, this attitude blurs his normally keen perception. Psychics who shy away from experiments made by doubting researchers have little fear of exposure from those who seek to document the impossible. A classical case in the latter category occurred in England in 1875.

Mrs. Fay—she was married, but most people knew her as Miss Fay and believed her to be her husband's much younger sister—sat in the library, facing the wall, near the open doorway to William Crookes's laboratory in London. After dipping her hands in a solution of salt and water, she gripped two brass handles wrapped in linen which had been saturated with the same salt-and-water mixture. Wires attached to the handles ran through the wall to a galvanometer, resistance coils, and a battery in the adjacent laboratory, where the investigators were seated. The lights in the library were extinguished; the curtain between the two rooms was closed.

Though Annie Fay was alone behind the drape, Crookes was able to tell by watching the luminous index of the galvanometer if she released even momentarily her grasp on the handles. In his enthusiastic report, published in the March 12, 1875, issue of *The Spiritualist,* the baffled scientist stated that sixty seconds after the séance started a handbell began ringing in the library. A moment later a hand appeared from behind the curtain—at a point three feet away from the handles—then disappeared. The hand returned to offer a copy of *The Spiritualist* to the man who edited it, to extend three books—last seen on the shelves of the library—to their respective authors, to toss a package of cigarettes to a smoker, and to give out a small clock that had also last been seen in the library, on the mantelpiece. Crookes had been too occupied with his monitoring device to vouch for the most remarkable manifestation himself; but two of his author friends assured him they had glimpsed the full-form materialization of a woman when the hand with their books came from behind the curtain. Finally, nine minutes after the handbell sounded, the illuminated index of the galvanometer showed a sudden break in the electric circuit.

Crookes and his guests threw open the curtain and rushed into the library. They found the medium slumped in her chair, her hands hanging limply at her sides. She had fainted, Crookes reported, and thirty minutes passed before they could revive her.

Hailed by the famous investigator, who would be knighted for his contributions to chemistry and physics and serve as president of the British Society for Psychical Research, Annie Eva Fay advertised in other countries that she had been endorsed not only by a fellow of the Royal Society but by the Royal Society itself.

The medium, whose performances on both sides of the Atlantic were as puzzling to theatre and concert-hall audiences as they were to Crookes, had been born as Anna Eva Heathman in a Southington, Ohio, cabin in the 1850's; the exact year of her birth she preferred to keep to herself. Driven from home by her father's spiteful second wife, Annie had given her first professional exhibition in an old schoolhouse in New Portage, Ohio. After investing in candles to light the room and handbills to advertise the show, she had, as she would later say in her souvenir books that sold by the thousands in theatre lobbies, "ten cents capital to begin life."

Where, when, or how she met her first husband, Henry Cummings Melville Fay, is not known. Emma Hardinge, a medium, denounced Fay in her book, *Modern American Spiritualism,* published in New York in 1870; she said his deceptions had been "openly exposed by the Spiritualists themselves." John W. Truesdell, a well-informed skeptic, agreed that Fay was a rascal; in his book, *The Bottom Facts Concerning the Science of Spiritualism,* published thirteen years later, Truesdell noted that Annie's cotton-bandage tie, her featured stage mystery, had been introduced by Laura Ellis when she was a young medium before Annie was even born.

Melville Fay may not have been a convincing psychic, but the slender, diminutive blonde he instructed, managed, and married became a strong attraction in the United States. Preceded in England by the Davenport Brothers, who were able to produce "startling wonders" after they had been securely tied inside a large wardrobe-like cabinet, Annie opened with some trepidation in London in 1874. John Nevil Maskelyne and George Alfred Cooke, two conjurers from Cheltenham who had exposed the Davenports, now had their own theatre at Egyptian Hall on Piccadilly. The American medium, billed as "The Indescribable Phenomenon" and booked into a Portland Square concert room, competed for audiences with these "Royal Illusionists and Anti-Spiritualists."

Annie's husband supervised the volunteers who mounted the platform to where she sat on a stool in her open-front cabinet. One tied her left wrist at the center of a long strip of cloth with many knots, one on top of another; a second volunteer followed suit with her right wrist. She held her hands behind her back as

Houdini made this photograph of himself with the "spirit" of Abraham Lincoln to show how easy it is for a clever deceptionist to picture the dead with the living.

The misty figure looming behind William Stead, the journalist who endorsed Elizabeth Tomson during her first season in London, is—some people say—a true spirit.

67 Payson Ave.
New York City

My Dear Mr. Ford
Today I recieved a spec-
ial delivery letter signed
by members of the First
Spiritualist church, who testify to a
purported message from Houdini's
mother, recieved through you.
Strange that the word "forgive" is
the word Houdini awaited in vain
all his life. It was indeed the message for which he always secretly
hoped, and if it had been given
him while he was still alive, it
would I know, have changed the
entire course of his life — but it
came too late. Aside from this
there are one or two trivial inaccuracies — Houdini's mother called him
Ehrich — there was nothing in the
message which could be contradicted
I might also say that this is the
first message which I have recieved
among thousands which has an
appearance of truth. Sincerely yours
Beatrice Houdini

Feb. 9-28

Mrs. Houdini's letter of Feb. 9, 1928, to Rev. Arthur Ford was misquoted in a pamphlet written by Francis Fast prior to the famous Houdini séance of 1929.

NEW YORK CITY.
JAN. 9TH, 1929.

REGARDLESS OF ANY STATE-
MENTS MADE TO THE CONTRARY,
I WISH TO DECLARE THAT THE
MESSAGE, IN ITS ENTIRETY, AND IN
THE AGREED UPON SEQUENCE,
GIVEN TO ME BY ARTHUR FORD,
IS THE CORRECT MESSAGE PRE-
ARRANGED BETWEEN MR. HOUDINI
AND MYSELF.

Beatrice Houdini

WITNESSED;

Harry R. Zander.
Minnie Chester
John W. Stafford —

Another hand lettered
the words that the
magician's widow
signed after the 1929
séance.

An old New York *Graphic* photo shows that Mrs. Houdini was ill and her head in bandages when Ford gave what he said was a spirit message from Houdini to her.

Joaquin Maria Argamasilla, a young Spanish psychic, stated he could see through metal. After Argamasilla had been blindfolded, Houdini stood on tiptoe, peered over the psychic's shoulder—and saw how the seemingly impossible feat was done.

One of the many ways to switch slates during a private séance is shown by the late John Mulholland, an adept magician, well-versed in ruses of fraudulent psychics.

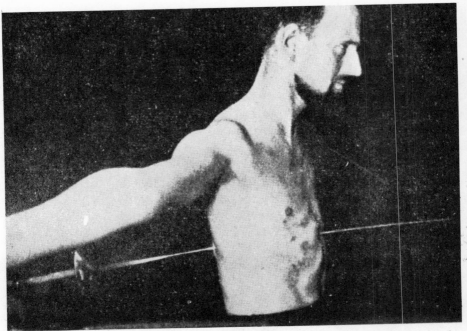

Mirin Dajo, a Dutch mystic, proved that thin blades could be thrust through a man's body without killing him, but an accident brought his career to an untimely end.

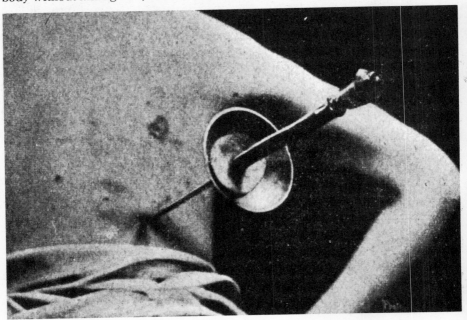

The Dutch psychic firmly believed he was invulnerable, and crusaded for world peace, drawing large audiences with this seemingly impossible feat.

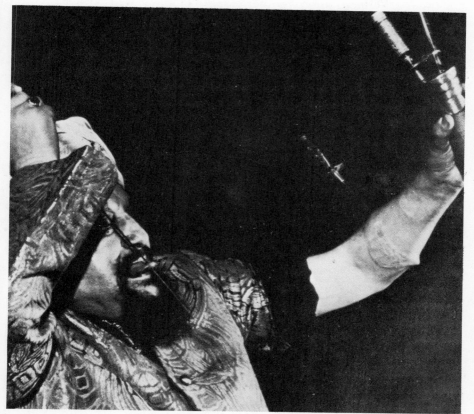

Yogi Rayo, an Austrian fakir, forces skewers and knives through his tongue and the flesh of his arm, but he has wisely chosen to avoid more dangerous impalements.

they bound the two strips together and knotted the cloth to a harness ring that was securely embedded in an upright post at the rear of the cabinet. Another piece of tape was tied at the back of the medium's neck, and the ends were fastened to a staple higher on the same post. One end of a long rope was lashed around her ankles; the other was held by a spectator throughout the performance that followed.

"Colonel" Fay placed a hoop in the medium's lap and closed the green curtain at the front of the cabinet. Almost immediately he threw open the drape; the hoop now encircled Annie's neck! Removing the hoop, he balanced a guitar on his wife's lap. The moment he closed the curtain, strumming sounds were heard. A bit of a melody echoed through the hall until he opened the curtain again. While he was doing so, the guitar fell to the floor. When the curtain was closed, there was more "spirit music" from a harmonica and other instruments, followed by an invisible carpenter who hammered several nails into a block of wood behind the curtain. When scissors and paper were put into the cabinet, an obliging phantom snipped out a string of paper dolls.

An empty pail, which had stood at the side of the medium's stool, apparently flew up and was next seen dangling from her neck by its handle. Finally a knife was placed in Annie's lap. Though the curtain was closed for only a few seconds, the spirits seemingly had time to sever her bonds. She stood up and came forward to take numerous bows.

Annie merited the applause she received. Split-second timing and skill created an astounding effect. Despite the careful tying (and usually the knots were sewn to hold them firmly), she was still able to use her hands. Because one knot had been tied on top of another when each of her wrists were bound, six inches of slack were obtained between them when the ends were tied together. More slack came when these ends were fastened to the harness ring.

The moment the curtain hid her from the spectators' view, Annie slid back from the stool, so that her body was to one side of the post, and she pulled her hands forward until she could reach the object on her lap. A flip upward put the hoop around her neck; her fingers strummed the guitar, cut the paper dolls, raised the pail so that she could lower her head inside the handle. As soon as an action had been completed, she quickly moved her body forward and brought her hands back behind her back. Slashes with the knife released her later from her restraints.

Critics were charmed and perplexed. Even those who doubted that spirits assisted her admitted Annie gave a sensational performance. Maskelyne and Cooke were not baffled by "The Indescribable Phenomenon." In October they added "An Indescribable Séance" to their program, with Cooke, tied in the same way as the American, duplicating her feats.

It was to counteract this that Annie went to William Crookes, "threw herself on his mercy and gave a series of tests," according to Houdini, who told of his conversations with the then elderly medium in A Magician Among the Spirits, published in 1924.

Though not a spiritualist, Crookes believed that phenomena could be produced by a "psychic force." He had written of the marvels he had seen in his own home in the Quarterly Journal of Science and The Spiritualist. Daniel Dunglas Home, for instance, had levitated himself and caused an accordion to play while holding it with one hand under a table, and Florence Cook had caused a beautiful feminine form to materialize, which walked, talked, and upon being touched, even felt like a real woman.

Home, the most famous psychic of the period, never performed for the general public, but he was willing, Crookes said, to submit to any test his friend the scientist could devise. Miss Cook, a young professional mystic, had been cooperative. She stayed in the investigator's home, sometimes for as long as a week, so she would be available at a moment's notice for his experiments.

What Mrs. Crookes thought of her husband's intense interest in the attractive sensitive we shall probably never know, but gossip at the time and Trevor Hall's book, The Spiritualists, published in London in 1962, indicates it was not strictly scientific. Indeed strong evidence is presented in the Hall book that Crookes's infatuation with his subject clouded his judgment.

Cromwell F. Varley, another fellow of the Royal Society, had provided an electrical control circuit for Florence Cook's séances; it was a modified version of this equipment that was employed during the Fay experiments.

While Crookes's article "A Scientific Examination of Mrs.

Fay's Mediumship" is largely concerned with the séance of February 19, 1875, two previous sittings are also mentioned. On February fifth, thirteen minutes after Annie gripped the handles and the curtain was drawn between the library and laboratory, rapping noises were heard. The sounds increased in volume two minutes later, then, after another two minutes, Crookes said the medium was "heard to sigh and sob." Musical instruments were heard playing behind the curtain, and several objects were thrown forward. A hand came into view with a violin which the scientist took; then the noise of a music box being wound was noted. After twenty-four minutes the circuit broke. The medium's hands were not on the handles when Crookes entered the library. She said, "So tired of holding these things," then collapsed.

The following evening at the end of a shorter séance, she was again found with her hands away from the control handles. Clearly she had discovered a way to free her hands without breaking the circuit—but had not learned how to replace them, though apparently Crookes was unaware of this. He admitted in his report:

> At first I always give new mediums who come to me their own conditions, for while I do not know what the phenomena may be, I am not in a position to suggest tests, nor, possibly, should I be able to get them before the mediums have confidence in me and that I will not play them any tricks, after which they have always shown a desire to help me as much as they can. All manifestations depend upon delicate conditions intimately connected with the nervous state of the sensitives, and most manifestations are checked when anything takes place to annoy them.

At the séance on February nineteenth, two of the guests— unidentified members of the Royal Society—were less gullible than their host. Before the session began, when they inspected the electrical-control system, they discovered, after experimentation, that a damp handkerchief stretched between the handles would keep the circuit open. At the suggestion of one of these men, Crookes nailed the handles so far apart that a handkerchief could not span them. Apparently no one considered the possibility that a longer strip of cloth or another type of resistor might be used. The medium was not searched, nor was any effort made to insure that she did not leave her chair when the curtain was closed.

It is unlikely that Annie had planned to produce a full-form manifestation of herself during this séance. This surely was an accidental marvel. Edward W. Cox, a well-known barrister, who was one of the two guests to see this figure, reported in the March 26, 1875, issue of *The Spiritualist* that when his book was being handed to him, the drape had opened enough for him to "see distinctly . . . the perfect form of Mrs. Fay—the hair, the face, the blue silk dress, the arms bare below the elbow, and the pearl armlets!"

Cox said "the form was either Mrs. Fay herself or her double." He was "strongly inclined to conclude" that it was Mrs. Fay. He suggested that "spirit-arms" may have held the handles while her body moved away. This seemed more feasible to him than the idea of her dress and armlets being duplicated by spirit matter. He made no mention of the possibility of fraud, though surely this must have occurred to him. A year earlier, when Mary Showers, another of the young mediums Crookes had tested, produced a full-form figure, the "spirit," at Crookes's instigation, dipped her fingers in a dye. After the "spirit" had evaporated, the dye was found on the medium's fingers!

Fortunately for science, Crookes terminated his psychic probe shortly after the Annie Eva Fay séances ended. She with his endorsement went on to become an even greater theatrical attraction.

Maskelyne, the magician, received a letter from the impresario who had booked the medium in Britain offering to reveal for a substantial sum how the Crookes experiments had been faked. When Maskelyne declined the offer, the man wrote again, saying he thought the medium would return to America but that he had another pretty mystic who could do the Fay tricks. After Annie left England, this woman went on tour with the same routine, using Annie's name.

A devastating exposure of the Fay stage séance appeared on April 12, 1876, in the *New York Daily Graphic*. The data was supplied by Washington Irving Bishop. Until a personality clash led to his dismissal, he had been a member of her American troupe. A month later Bishop became a professional "Anti-Spiritualist" and eventually achieved international fame as a thought-reader.

Mrs. Fay and Bishop, under the names of Evalina Gray and W. Sterling Bischoff, were characters in Allan Pinkerton's popular novel *Spiritualists and Detectives,* which was first published in 1877 and was still in print seventeen years later. In the book, Annie's mate is referred to as an "accommodation husband," and the medium says as she tells another Ohio mystic of her adventures in Europe:

> at Venice . . . I bilked a swarthy nobleman from the mountains out of five thousand dollars. At Rome I did a swell American out of everything he had. . . . At Berlin a German student killed himself for me; and at St. Petersburg I fooled the Czar himself.

In the preface, Pinkerton—the same Pinkerton who opened the first American private detective agency in Chicago in 1850—said the incidents were true, but that he had given fictional names to the characters. However, Pinkerton though thoroughly familiar with investigative procedures was not as well informed on mediumistic methods. He told his readers that the slender psychic extricated herself, after being bound with ropes, by releasing the air from an inflated jacket she wore concealed under her dress.

Anna—she used the more formal name, rather than the diminutive "Annie," after her return to the United States—gave birth to her first and only child, John Truesdell Fay, at Akron, Ohio, in 1877. Thereafter her son traveled with the show. Two illustrations published in the *Chicago World,* after one of her many engagements in that city, showed the five-year-old youngster clinging to his mother's leg under the cover of her bustlelike skirt, then hiding himself under the folds as she sat on a stool with her hands tied behind her back. A skeptical reporter claimed that the boy, not the medium, was responsible for the manifestations in the cabinet: "Of course, the committee of gentlemen would not dare to molest the lady's dress or to even feel for a boy under it." Arrangements were made to expose this ruse at her last performance. Perhaps Anna learned of this plan. That evening she appeared on stage in a tight-fitting gown, and it was obvious even to the suspicious that she and she alone produced the marvelous effects.

By then her first husband had been replaced by David H. Pingree, whom she married in 1881 when he was twenty-six. Pingree, as astute a businessman as his predecessor, sometimes overdid it as a promoter. For example, he lured some six thousand people to the Battery D Armory in Chicago on Sunday evening, March 6, 1887, with an advertisement, whose first sentence contained a cleverly worded qualification: "The following are some of the tests that usually take place. . . ." Many people, overlooking the caveat, were eager to see the table that soared several feet above the stage, the spirit faces, and the "large piano" that floated in midair and was "played upon without a living soul touching it." Two other female mediums were on the program, but "The Celebrated Anna Eva Fay" was the principal attraction. She appeared, the *Tribune* said, "in gorgeous evening dress, with a train a yard long" sweeping behind her. "She is a dainty little blue-eyed, diamond-bedecked piece of humanity—at least she seemed to have lots of diamonds last night. A necklet of diamonds, each as big as a bean, glistened on her white throat, and several others sparkled on her fingers." She gave her usual program with no soaring table, spirit faces, or floating piano. Shouts for her to show the advertised miracles were ignored. When she bowed off, an unruly mob surged up on the stage, pulled down the scenery, and smashed her props. "Without question," the *Tribune* reported, "it was the most impudent exhibition ever given in the city."

The *Inter-Ocean* was more sympathetic. "The exhibition is one that the intelligent public would enjoy under favorable conditions, and when Miss Fay appears in Chicago again, it is hoped she will not be overwhelmed by a concourse of idiots."

Despite such near riots, as well as frequent unmaskings, the much-publicized medium continued to draw capacity audiences. She added comedy to the show. A blindfolded volunteer seated with her behind the curtain of the cabinet had a bucket land upside down on his head. She introduced a second cabinet, smaller than the first, so that her head could be seen extending above it during some of her feats, and she perfected a clairvoyant act.

Pads were distributed, and members of the audience were invited by her husband to write questions, sign their names, tear off the sheets, and hold the pieces of paper folded in their hands.

Later Anna, blindfolded, sat on a chair near the front of the stage, covered from head to toe with an opaque sheet. "The name of S-h-e-r-w-o-o-d—Sherwood—comes to me," she said at the Majestic Theatre in Chicago one night in 1907. "This is Mrs. F. H. Sherwood, and she is on my left." This woman, acknowledging her name at Mr. Fay's request, raised her hand.

"Mrs. Sherwood wants to know what she should do with her mining stock. I say hold it—there is a rise coming. It will be good." The woman acknowledged this had been her question.

"I get the name of Winters, or maybe it is Withers— something like that," said the voice from under the sheet. "He is in the balcony." An acknowledgment came from the upper reaches of the house. "You are worried about a two-dollar bill. Oh, I have it now—you have bet two dollars with your friend that I cannot tell you the number on the two-dollar bill you have. I get the letter B and the number 7638724. Is that correct?" It was.

After giving a dozen more answers to questions, she called the name of a woman in the balcony. "You are worrying about John Smith. You want to know whether he is alive or dead. I seem to be floating away somewhere—oh, yes, it's in the Philippines. He is in the Philippines, and he's alive. Write to Dr. Jones, Hospital No. 7, Manila, and you will get news of your friend."

There seemed to be no key to this mystery. The folded pieces of paper containing the questions remained in the hands of the audience; no one approached the medium who sat alone on the stage.

The ingenious system that Anna used to perform this act had been devised by Samri S. Baldwin, "The White Mahatma." Baldwin had duplicated the cabinet feats of the Davenport Brothers and Anna Eva Fay in the United States before he began the first of his around-the-world tours. Born in Cincinnati, Ohio, he had served as a drummer boy during the Civil War. With his wife, the former Julia Clara Mansfield of Carthage, Missouri, Baldwin presented a full-evening show. While he revealed the tricks of mediums, he claimed his wife had "somnomistic" visions. To insure

that her visions would be accurate, his assistants distributed prepared pads to the audience. Each second sheet was coated on the
underside with paraffin. The pressure of the pencil, as questions
were written, transferred a wax impression of the words to the
third sheet. The pads, each previously marked on the back, were
then collected and taken backstage, where assistants rubbed
lampblack on the third sheets. The black powder adhered to the
wax as the sheets were tilted. The questions and the locations of
the writers, indicated by the marks on the pad, were then secretly conveyed to the "somnomist."

Baldwin called this portion of his entertainment "Som-
nomany"; Anna Eva Fay advertised hers as "Somnolency." Her
son John, who married Anna Norman, a girl from St. Louis, in
1898, taught his wife the system, and they worked on their own
as "The Fays." After his death in 1908, John's widow, billed as
Mrs. Eva Fay, "The High Priestess of Mysticism," became a
vaudeville headliner. Anna Eva Fay had adored her son, and she
built a handsome mausoleum to house his remains, but she had
never liked her daughter-in-law; she resented her using a stage
name so similar to her own.

Trouble came from another quarter in January 1911. Albini,
the magician, opened at the American Music Hall in New York
with an exposure of the Fay "Somnolency" act, showing how the
pads were collected and how the information was given to her
through a speaking tube, pushed up from beneath the stage and
hidden by the folds of the covering sheet. Anna started a suit
against him, then changed her mind when her husband reminded her that the evidence presented in court would be more
damaging than a revelation from the stage. She had been periodically exposed over the years; still the public filled theatres where
she was featured.

It was Pingree who arranged to have confederates in the audience to acknowledge her most astonishing "psychic" statements during the show, and once, according to a Brooklyn reporter, he paid two men to steal an automobile and park it at the
place where Anna said it would be found.

In addition to the money the medium made as a performer,
she also obtained a sizable income from answering questions by
mail. Anyone who bought one of her souvenir books was entitled

to send the enclosed coupon with a question to her home at Melrose Highlands, a Boston suburb, where five secretaries helped her answer about five hundred letters daily of the thousand she received.

During her 1913 tour of Britain, Anna Eva Fay received an unexpected tribute. She was elected the first Honorary Lady Associate of The Magic Circle in London. She wrote a letter of thanks, but never found time to attend one of the meetings.

For another eleven years the veteran mystic continued to attract capacity crowds wherever she performed. She played her final engagement in Milwaukee in 1924. An accidental injury brought her professional career to an end. Houdini visited her in the spacious Melrose Heights house filled with mementoes of her travels abroad. She, in turn, came to his lecture at Symphony Hall in Boston on January 2, 1925, when he denounced the famous medium Margery (Mina Crandon).

The now gray-haired woman, whose souvenir books had carried her signed statement, "I would rather be a Hottentot and dwell in the wilds of Africa than to betray a human Christ and be a Judas," explained to Houdini how she had tricked Sir William Crookes during the séance in his laboratory. While she held a handle with one hand, she gripped the other with "the bare flesh under her knee." With her free hand, she rapped against a table and the wall, then strummed the stringed instruments. She had no qualms about discussing her methods with another famous mystifier now that she had retired.

A year later she announced she planned to leave the ten houses on her Melrose Heights property to destitute actors and actresses, but she died on May 20, 1927, before working out the final details of this project.

Will F. Clarke recalled the career of the renowned medium, who had mystified audiences since the days of horse cars, hansom cabs, and fifty-cent dinners, in the June 5, 1927, issue of the *New York World*. He said she had understood the art of getting publicity better than any other woman on the stage. She predicted Republicans would win elections in Republican states and that Democrats would triumph in the areas where they were popular. "She courted attacks from the pulpit, and several times when the police in various cities threatened to refuse to permit her to appear she saw to it that the 'news' was broadcast."

No doubt, Anna Eva Fay would have been delighted had she known that her death caused considerable trouble for Eva Fay, her son's widow, to whom she had not spoken for years. Because of the similarity of their stage names, some of Eva's bank accounts were closed, and she lost several bookings because agents thought the obituaries referred to her, not to the older medium whose name and act she had taken.

THE "SCIENTIFIC AMERICAN" INVESTIGATIONS

In December 1922, *Scientific American,* the foremost periodical in its field, candidly admitted that "on the basis of existing
data," it could not "reach a definite conclusion as to the validity
of psychic claims." In an effort to resolve these controversial issues, the magazine announced two $2,500 awards: one for the
first person to take an authentic spirit photograph under test conditions; the other for the first medium to produce an authentic
"visible psychic manifestation."

Five eminent men were chosen as judges: Dr. William Mc-
Dougall, professor of psychology at Harvard; Dr. Daniel Fisk
Comstock, an inventor who had been a member of the Massachusetts Institute of Technology physics department; Dr.
Walter Franklin Prince, research officer of the American Society
for Psychical Research; Hereward Carrington, investigator of,
and writer on, paranormal phenomena; and Houdini, the foremost magician of his day. James Malcolm Bird, an associate editor of the periodical, acted as committee secretary but was to take
no part in their deliberations.

Elizabeth Allen Tomson, the first medium to volunteer,
lived in Chicago, where as a professional psychic she had a
flourishing business. She said she would come to New York immediately—if *Scientific American* would pay the traveling expenses for herself and her family. Learning of this early in 1923,

the *Chicago Tribune* offered to finance the journey. A *Tribune* reporter asked the medium when she would leave. Mrs. Tomson, a middle-aged woman with thinning hair and a plump figure, hesitated. As soon as her sick daughter recovered from an illness, she eventually replied. Months before the Tomsons arrived in Manhattan, several Midwestern papers erroneously reported that the Chicago medium had won the prize.

"Dr." Clarence H. Tomson telephoned Bird on November second, inviting the committee to attend a private séance his wife was to give two days later at the Great Neck, Long Island, home of Raymond Hitchcock, the Broadway star. The medium, Tomson said, wished to meet the investigators informally.

On such short notice, only one judge, Walter Franklin Prince, could be reached. Bird went with him to the séance, and wrote about the encounter in the January 1924 issue of the magazine:

> The "social contact" plea was a huge joke. The medium was held in seclusion in another part of the house. Our first glimpse of her was when she entered the cabinet, running through the circle at top speed to reach it; at the end she left with equal speed and greater suddenness. Two frantic flights through the semidarkened room were literally all we saw of her.

Bird and Prince were in a downstairs room watching the cabinet being erected, while Mrs. Tomson disrobed on the floor above. They later heard that Charles M. Niesley, a Manhasset, Long Island, physician, had examined the medium's vagina, but not the other anatomical passages. Following this limited examination, six women guests looked on as the medium donned one of Mrs. Hitchcock's colorful kimonos and came down the stairs. Dashing across the séance room, Elizabeth Tomson took a seat in the cabinet; then the curtains at the front were closed.

After the lights were lowered, the curtains opened, and the first of several figures swathed in a white, filmy material was seen. Sitters were asked to come forward when their dead relatives called to them. A woman who had never been to a séance before almost had hysterics when her "mother" cried, "My darling daughter," embraced, and kissed her. The other guests accepted the weird manifestations more calmly.

Hitchcock, the host, identified a bearded specter as his uncle or, possibly, his grandfather. Bird, on request, entered the cabinet twice. The first figure was so heavily veiled that he could not see the face. Then the veil dropped, and he recognized Mrs. Tomson. The second materialization "had a curious unfinished appearance, as though the features were but half formed."

Afterward, he talked with some of the thirty or so people who had been present at the séance. The general reaction, he reported, was not one of awe. Most wanted to know: "Where did she carry all that stuff?" He thought he knew, but he saved his speculations for print.

The medium, Bird pointed out in his article, "brushed against her daughter" as she ran from the hall to her cabinet. After the final materialization, when Mrs. Tomson "burst through the curtains like a firecracker," her daughter jumped up, put her arms around the medium, and hustled her away.

Compressible white gauze, packed tightly in a small bundle, could have been passed from daughter to mother in the first instance and from mother to daughter in the second, Bird surmised. The séance at the Hitchcock residence had not been part of the formal *Scientific American* investigation; that was to be scheduled later.

Though Bird made no mention of it, Elizabeth Tomson had been tested fourteen years earlier. In 1909, while she and her husband were performing at the London Hippodrome, where she produced small animals as well as ghosts and flowers, she accepted a challenge from William T. Stead, founder of the *Review of Reviews* and one of most respected journalists of his time.

The Tomsons came to his house, as the challenge stipulated, without baggage. Each was stripped to the skin and searched by three persons of the same sex. Then, wearing black garments provided by Stead, they were taken to a room where Sir Oliver Lodge, the distinguished physicist, had supervised the construction of a cabinet, made from some folding screens and a curtain.

Despite these precautions, ghostly forms materialized, and fresh flowers, appearing from nowhere, were passed to the sitters. Stead publicly proclaimed that he had witnessed authentic phenomena; he said he and his friends had seen and talked with the dead.

P. T. Selbit, editor of *The Wizard*, a monthly periodical for magicians, and himself an ingenious illusionist, tried to arrange an interview with the Tomsons. They would not meet with him, so he visited Stead instead.

The bearded writer greeted him cordially. Their conversation, as reported by Selbit, began: "Sir Oliver Lodge tells me you are 'resolutely credulous.' Do you not lay yourself open to being deceived?"

"No," Stead replied emphatically. "If you came here and said by waving your umbrella over the Thames you could turn water into treacle, I should say, 'Come on, and let me see you do it.' If you did, I should be very interested."

"But don't you think you may, occasionally, have cleverly been gulled?"

"I have often been deceived by conjuring, and enjoy it completely," Stead admitted. "But when investigating phenomenon produced under my own test conditions, there has been no loophole for deception."

Selbit said Mrs. Tomson produced small animals during her stage séances. Wouldn't it be more spectacular if she conjured up a horse?

Stead answered: "You may as well ask me why Moses didn't turn his rod into an elephant instead of a snake."

In the March 1909 issue of *The Wizard*, Selbit published photographs of three bits of material that had been snipped from one of the medium's veiled apparitions during a Stead séance. The smaller ones, he said, were "woven out of some West Indian vegetable product; the larger piece could not be matched at Liberty's [a famous silk store in London]."

"If the performance of the Tomsons is conjuring, and we see no reason for believing otherwise," Selbit stated, "the only mystery is the exact way she hides her 'load,' so that it cannot be found."

Returning to the United States that spring to capitalize on their London triumph, the Tomsons were reviewed in the April 17 issue of *Variety*. Their act, the critic said, was just another cabinet routine; the only novelty was that the medium stripped to tights. The cabinet had been assembled piece by piece in front of the audience. "A dirty portiere, which might have been grabbed from a tenement window," covered the front. The medium entered it with a piece of black netting draped over her tights. She threw out flowers and a bird, then came forward to pose in white and red veils. "Colored spotlights have a peculiar shading influence upon some material," the *Variety* critic noted. He said Stead, a noted British editor with an inclination toward the supernatural, had given the turn tremendous free publicity in London, but the Tomsons would have difficulty getting bookings in the larger American cities: "The woman's almost worse than nudity and her manner of becoming so" would stir only passing comment.

The Tomsons played in London again the following year. The manager of the Alhambra Theatre invited Sir Hiram Maxim, inventor of a machine gun and other less deadly but equally profitable contrivances, to investigate the manifestations, hoping he would give them his approval as Stead had earlier.

A private showing was arranged for the American-born scientist on the Alhambra stage. Sir Hiram, a portly man with a shock of white hair and a small but bristling beard, said later that three women had searched Mrs. Tomson but he suspected their examination had not been thorough. Elizabeth, clad in black form-hugging tights, entered a cabinet. Nothing was concealed in this structure; Maxim had scrutinized it himself.

Mrs. Tomson produced a dove. Sir Maxim noted it was white, small, and ruffled; the tail feathers had been snapped and turned forward. Then flowers materialized in a vase from behind the curtains. The bouquet was quite large: the stalks of some of the flowers were twelve inches long and thorny. Finally the medium "showed herself in a cloud of white chiffon in a dim blue light."

An article in the July 26, 1910, issue of *Pall Mall Gazette* said Sir Hiram had challenged the Tomsons, but there was no mention that he had exposed them. He set the editor straight the next day in a letter calling the séance, "Nothing more or less than a conjuring trick, and not a very good one at that." Now that Tomson had "thrown down the glove," he would write an article for an illustrated magazine giving the facts.

After seeing the act, Maxim revealed in the September 1910

issue of *Pearson's Magazine,* he returned to the theatre with equipment for a scientific examination. The Tomsons refused to accede to his requests. Finally the theatre manager issued an ultimatum: Either the performers would comply with Sir Hiram's plans, or their contract would be canceled.

Elizabeth, her husband, and their son drove to Maxim's factory in Norwood. To insure that her family could not assist her, Sir Hiram put them behind "wire netting" in his laboratory. In an adjacent room Mrs. Tomson took off her street clothes and donned the black tights provided for her. Then the inventor's secretary and her sister stitched the material, making it fit snugly at the neck, wrists, and back. Over the tights, they put a red cotton coverall, sewing it as they had the tights. Next, large, heavy stockings encased her feet and were sewn below the knees of the coverall. A brass chain in the neckband of the outer garment was fastened at the back with a Yale lock.

Red tapes were tied and sewn around the medium's waist and around her arms above the elbows. Finally a small sack made of transparent black chiffon was drawn over her head and tied and sewn to the upper part of the coverall.

This done, the medium was weighed. She tipped the Fairbank scales at 147¾ pounds. From the scales Mrs. Tomson was led to a cabinet Sir Hiram had made. In it was a chair. A ledge, firmly nailed to a side wall, served as a table. Sir Hiram closed the curtains.

Elizabeth had produced a dove in two minutes on the Alhambra stage. Thirty uneventful minutes dragged by in the factory. An occasional rustling noise could be heard behind the curtains, but no bird appeared nor did a figure in white emerge from behind the curtains. Fifty-five minutes passed before a voice from the cabinet called for the curtains to open.

Bits and pieces of flowers were strewn around inside the structure. The investigator walked forward to take a closer look. He jumped back: a live snake was coiled on the ledge. His assistants removed the three-and-a-half-foot-long reptile, and gathered up the debris.

The medium was perspiring profusely; there were streaks on her face from the black dye that had been used to color the chiffon sack. She drank some water, then walked to the scales. Mrs. Tomson now weighed 145 pounds; 2¾ pounds less than she had an hour before.

The snake and the crushed flowers were weighed. They accounted for two pounds; the rest had been lost by sheer exertion.

Sir Maxim asked the medium to raise her head. He found a tear, large enough for him to put his "hand through," in the chiffon below her chin. He left the dressing room while his women assistants helped Elizabeth extricate herself from the coverall and the damp tights. Fragments of the flowers, which had been concealed under her breasts, still clung to her moist skin. She sobbed and confessed that the snake had been hidden under one arm beneath the tights. The reptile had pressed so tightly against an artery that it stopped the flow of blood. This arm was numb when she reached through the chiffon to yank out the snake.

The Tomsons "assured me over and over again that they were not mediums, that they were not even Spiritualists," Sir Hiram said. They had been brought to his attention as mediums, and they so represented themselves to others; that was why he had revealed their deception.

During the years that followed, the Tomsons appeared in theatres and churches in the United States, and they also gave private séances. Houdini saw them perform in November 1920 at a special show at the Morosco Theatre in New York City; he attended another of their public séances at the Palace Theatre in Chicago. After the latter exhibition, he and several friends visited the home of Cyrus McCormick, Jr., chairman of the board of the International Harvester Company to discuss the performance. H. H. Windsor, publisher of *Popular Mechanics,* and the other guests agreed the séance had been a hoax.

Houdini was on tour in Texas when the Tomsons came to New York to compete for the *Scientific American* prize. Though a member of the committee, the magician was unaware that the test had been set for November seventh. That afternoon "Dr." Tomson asked to see the room where the investigation was to take place. J. Malcolm Bird, the committee secretary, showed him the law library of Munn, Anderson & Munn (Orson Munn was the publisher of *Scientific American*). This book-lined chamber did not meet with Tomson's approval. Where could his wife undress privately? he asked. Bird led him across the hall to a smaller room with all the required facilities. Unable to make up his mind, Tomson took another look at the law library. The atmosphere was unsuitable, he complained. Bird replied that Mrs. Tomson had often performed on the stage, as well as in churches and private homes. Tomson said the apartment of one of his friends would be more appropriate. Not for a *Scientific American* experiment, Bird countered. Tomson canceled the sitting.

The next day he came to Bird's office, proposing again that the séance be transferred to another place. Bird suggested the apartment of Orson Munn. Tomson vetoed this. Before he left, he charged that the Roman Catholic Church had financed the investigation to harass mediums. This statement was untrue, but the first medium to volunteer for the *Scientific American* award never contended for the prize.

Veteran investigator Joseph F. Rinn recalled in his *Sixty Years of Psychical Research,* published in 1930, that two days after the medium's husband stormed out of Bird's office, the Tomsons were arrested. On the evening of November ninth, Dick Gallagher a plain-clothes policeman, was called into the cabinet during a séance in Brooklyn. When the ghost embraced him, he bit it—and discovered it was Mrs. Tomson.

Bird ran a note on the first medium to apply for the *Scientific American* award in the April 1924 issue of the magazine. After returning to Chicago, Elizabeth Tomson advertised her séances in the newspapers as usual, but there was a new statement at the bottom of the ads: "Pay no attention to false stories of jealous people or publications. Mrs. Tomson's séances in New York were great triumphs. Proofs on file in our free reading room."

Fulton Oursler told of his encounters with the Tomsons in *Spirit Mediums Exposed,* purportedly written by Samri Frikell and published in 1930. (The name Samri Frikell, one of Oursler's several pseudonyms, was devised by taking the first name of a famous mentalist, S. S. Baldwin, and the last name of a once widely known magician, Wiljalba Frikell.)

Oursler offered two explanations for the ghosts that appeared in Mrs. Tomson's cabinets. The first was similar to the one Bird had published earlier in *Scientific American.* The highly compressible silk gauze, Oursler said, was carried in a container so obvious that no one noticed it—a woman's handbag. The medium took this from her daughter as she rushed through the séance room on her way to the cabinet and concealed it under her robe when she darted away at the end of her performance. Oursler's wife had been one of the women who watched as the medium changed back from the robe into her street clothes at the end of a New York séance in 1923. Mrs. Oursler noticed a purse she hadn't seen earlier in the dressing room and asked Mrs. Tomson to open it. The medium flew into a rage and demanded that the skeptic leave.

Oursler hinted he peeked as the medium was being examined on another occasion. Though he didn't actually claim to have seen the load, he was positive he knew where it was hidden. Twenty or thirty yards of the sheer fabric rolled tightly had been fastened with adhesive tape diagonally "down the groin" of Mrs. Tomson's left leg. She stripped to the waist, then modestly covered the upper part of her body with a borrowed garment as she let her white skirt fall. Then she raised the fabric, which now covered her naked body, until it reached the edge of the hidden bundle so that the women investigators could see the lower portion of her anatomy.

Under cover of the curtains of the cabinet, Oursler continued, she removed the adhesive tape, unfolded the silk gauze, and draped it over her head and shoulders.

Later, Oursler theorized, as her husband stood in front of the cabinet, Mrs. Tomson reached out and under the back of his coat to steal a second load. Such a technique had been employed by other mediums. Possibly it was one of Mrs. Tomson's methods; it is unlikely anyone will ever know for sure.

The manifestations produced by George Valiantine, the first medium actually tested by *Scientific American*, were less impressive than Elizabeth Tomson's. Valiantine staged his séances in the dark. Spirit voices spoke from a trumpet as it floated about the room, and sitters reported they had been touched by invisible hands.

The medium from Wilkes-Barre, Pennsylvania, did not know that the chair in which he sat during his third séance for the *Scientific American* committee had been wired. Men in an adjoining room checked a stopwatch, and noting a signal that flashed each time the medium left his seat in the dark, discovered "phenomena" occurred at precisely the moments Valiantine was on the prowl.

The Reverend Josie K. Stewart, who came from Cleveland to compete, did not require a darkened room. She produced handwritten messages from the dead on previously examined pieces of blank cardboard. Flower petals were inserted here and there in the stack of cards before the words appeared.

She summoned up the invisible writers through Effie, her spirit guide, and claimed she needed a sensitive sitter to generate electricity, which would give her the magnetism she required.

The first test in the *Scientific American* offices on October 9, 1923, was a failure. She tried again two days later and, apparently noticing that each of the committee's cards had been marked by a pinprick at one corner (to prevent substitution), failed again. A different method of marking the cards was used at the third sitting; their edges were trimmed. Once more, the medium failed.

At the fourth sitting, however, messages came through. The medium held the pack over Dr. Prince's head during the course of an outdoor séance in a Bayside, Long Island, garden on October sixteenth. After "a series of mild convulsions, she fell back toward her chair," moaning; then she cried: "Look at the cards! Look at the cards!"

Three of the cards carried an inscription apparently written by a ghostly hand. Two more mysterious communications appeared later, and that night, Bird reported in the December 1923 issue of *Scientific American*, Effie, the spirit guide, informed Josie that she would win the prize. Effie was wrong. The cards on which the messages appeared were not those the magazine had supplied for the experiments. They were longer, thinner, and of a slightly different color. Dr. Prince had also spotted the move she used to add them to the pack.

Test séances with a young Italian medium in December were more exciting. Nineteen months earlier, Nino Pecoraro had astounded Sir Arthur Conan Doyle and his wife during a private sitting in New York. Pecoraro claimed his spirit guide was Eusapia Palladino, the world-famous Neapolitan medium who died in 1918.

Sitting with his back to a curtained cabinet as Eusapia had done, Nino placed his fingers on the top of a table. The Doyles and eight other sitters followed suit as they sang "Nearer My God to Thee" and "Onward Christian Soldiers."

"Come, spirit," the creator of Sherlock Holmes pleaded, "we want you to know that we love you. We are friends." The table tilted. Two legs left the floor, then jolted back. The far legs rose and fell. Nino went into a trance. Hereward Carrington, a prolific writer on psychic phenomena, who had arranged the séance, tied first the medium's legs and then his wrists to his chair with picture wire.

The chair was pushed back into the cabinet, and the curtains were closed. A moan sounded from behind the curtains, then came loud snorting noises. The curtains blew forward; the table vibrated and shook. A cool breeze—one of the trademarks of a Palladino séance—was felt by the Doyles. A tambourine jangled and came spinning out from behind the drape. A handbell rang and a child's piano inside the cabinet tinkled. A small table emerged from the dark of the cabinet, toppled over, and crashed to the floor.

"Palladino, Palladino!" the medium called. Then he said, "Palladino is here. She will try to show you her hands, her face." Another voice spoke, a deeper voice with a heavier accent, "I who used to call the spirits back, now come back to be a spirit myself."

Carrington asked, "Is that you, Madame Palladino?" He had been Palladino's manager during her single visit to the United States. "Yes" was the almost whispered reply according to the account of this sensational séance in the New York *World* on April 19, 1922.

When Houdini, who was performing in Little Rock, Arkansas, received a telegram from Munn, the *Scientific American* publisher, urging him to come to New York and attend at least one of Pecoraro's test sittings in December 1923, the magician returned; he didn't trust Carrington, who was a fellow committeeman, and he was furious because Bird, the committee's secretary, had not informed him that the Pecoraro investigation was under way.

Houdini made a dramatic entrance at the fourth séance. Upon hearing that the contestant was to be bound with a sixty-foot length of rope, the magician literally exploded. He knew that even a rank amateur could gain slack enough to release his hands and feet when tied this way. The master escapologist took charge. He slashed the rope into many short pieces, then set about tying the psychic's wrists, arms, legs, ankles, and torso. There were no spirit manifestations that evening, and the ingenious Italian was no longer a contender for the award.

Eight years later, Pecoraro confessed to his trickery at a press conference called by Joseph Dunninger, the mentalist-magician who carried on Houdini's crusade against fraudulent spiritualists. A photographic copy of his signed and witnessed statement may be seen in Dunninger's *Inside the Medium's Cabinet,* published in 1935 by David Kemp and Company.

Four mediums had applied unsuccessfully for the *Scientific American* award: Elizabeth Tomson withdrew without being tested; Valiantine, Stewart, and Pecoraro tried strenuously to win before their tricks were detected.

The fifth applicant, unlike her predecessors, was not a professional. J. Malcolm Bird said, in the July 1924 issue of the magazine, that she was "a lady of refinement and culture," who shunned publicity. There is little doubt Bird thought the medium he called Margery merited the award. The committee, he reported, had had several sittings with her, and their attitude "has been distinctly favorable." Certainly the range of phenomena produced by this woman was so remarkable that she deserves a chapter to herself.

MARGERY –
THE BOSTON MEDIUM

It is unlikely that Mina Crandon, the blonde vivacious Canadian-born wife of an American surgeon, would ever have tried to produce fingerprints of the dead in the dark or won her prominent place in the annals of psychic research, if her husband had not read a book about an Irish medium.

One night in the spring of 1923 Dr. Le Roi Goddard Crandon, a wealthy, fifty-two-year-old physician, planned to read himself to sleep. A scoffer at tales of the supernatural, he opened William Jackson Crawford's *The Psychic Structures at the Goligher Circle*, believing he would doze off after a few pages. Instead the account written by a mechanical engineer and lecturer at Queens College, Belfast, kept him awake until dawn.

According to Crawford, a strange substance flowed from the body of Kathleen Goligher as she sat entranced in a chair. This substance extended down to the floor, then rose up beneath a table. Exerting force, it lifted the table into the air. When the table settled back into place, the mysterious substance disappeared.

Crandon, a tall saturnine man with graying hair and a neatly trimmed moustache, could not conceive how a bodily material—one he had never encountered in all of his years of medical practice—could become rigid enough to support a piece of furniture.

The former instructor in surgery at the Harvard Medical

School had a table built to the exact specifications given in the Crawford book, and invited four friends to join his wife and himself for an evening of experimentation.

The Crandons lived in a four-story brick house at 10 Lime Street in the Beacon Hill section of Boston. On the evening of May twenty-seventh, following dinner, they escorted their guests up the stairs and to their places around the unvarnished "Goligher" table in the front room of the fourth floor. The curtains were drawn, and all the lights turned out, except for a single shaded red bulb in a far corner.

Six pairs of hands were placed flat on the table; the sitters concentrated and called for the spirits. Nothing happened. Mina Crandon, exuberant, attractive, and about fifteen years younger than her husband, made sly disparaging remarks. There was laughter, rather than the prayers and hymn singing that would have preceded a séance conducted by people who accepted after-death communication as a part of their religion.

Then the table began to move, tilting high on two legs before it banged down to the floor. Someone suggested that a code be used to receive spirit messages. If the answer to a spoken question was yes, the table would bang once; no, twice; perhaps, three times. The table responded as they hoped it would.

It was discovered, when the participants took turns removing their hands from the surface, that only one person in the room had the power, whatever its nature, to control the table: Crandon's wife, Mina. That evening the woman who was to become the most versatile psychic ever known realized that she was a medium.

Mina Stinson, the daughter of an Ontarian farmer, had migrated to Boston in her middle teens. Pretty, personable, and talented, she played the piano and cornet with local dance bands and appeared as a cellist with the orchestra of the Union Congregational Church, where she worked as a secretary. She also acted in dramatic productions, and kept herself trim by swimming and playing tennis.

In September 1910 Mina married Earl P. Rand, the owner of a small grocery store. Three years later she gave birth to a son, John. Little is known about her life during this period, but in 1917 she entered a Dorchester, Massachusetts, hospital for an unspecified operation. The surgeon was Dr. Crandon; earlier that year he had been divorced from his second wife. In January 1918 Mina decided to sue Rand for divorce on the grounds that he treated her cruelly, a charge he did not contest.

Meanwhile Crandon, who served as a lieutenant commander during World War I, headed the surgical staff of a New England naval hospital. Mina, a civilian volunteer, drove an ambulance which took casualties there. A few months after she received her divorce, she became the third Mrs. Crandon, and moved into the house on Lime Street with her young son.

Five years after the wedding and five months after *Scientific American* had begun its search for authentic psychical phenomena, Mina became a medium. At her husband's suggestion, she became entranced during her third séance in June 1923. Thereafter the dead spoke through her vocal cords. Other guides sometimes took over, but the dominant spirit voice was that of her elder brother, Walter Stinson, who had died after a train wreck in 1911. Walter's voice was deeper than Mina's. He could also be sarcastic, and his profanity sometimes shocked sitters. It was also proof to believers that a boisterous spirit, not the doctor's wife, was speaking.

Mina enjoyed her new role. Eight séances were held in June; a dozen, in July. Eager to provide his wife with the paraphernalia usually associated with mediums, Crandon set up an open-front cabinet, made from a folding screen, in the room, and frequently played records on a Victrola to create a mystical atmosphere. Other music, apparently ghostly in origin, drifted up from the floors below. Sometimes "Taps" tinkled on invisible chimes, sounds of livelier tunes were heard from a distant harmonica and piano, and, on occasion, the "Call to Arms" blasted out from a phantom bugle.

No two séances were exactly the same. Soon after the doctor read about a psychic marvel, a variation of it occurred during one of Mina's séances. Flashes of light streaked across the dark room, unseen chains rattled, and a live pigeon materialized on a lower floor. Presumably it had flown through the solid walls of the house.

Delighted by his wife's progress as a psychic, the doctor wrote Sir Arthur Conan Doyle, who was then making a coast-to-coast American tour, lecturing on the comforts to be had from communicating with the dead, and expounding his philosophy that those who are loved are always with us. The famous British author passed on the news to J. Malcolm Bird, secretary to *Scientific American*'s investigating committee.

After an exchange of letters with Crandon, Bird accepted the doctor's invitation to come to Boston at his expense and stay on Lime Street while he evaluated Mina's mediumship.

Mrs. Crandon met Bird at the railway station in mid-November 1923. That night at dinner he was told that another investigation had been under way for some time.

The first of many extensive investigations of the Boston medium was being conducted by Professor William McDougall. The Harvard psychologist, a member of the *Scientific American* committee, was acting on his own in this case, having been invited to several séances. He had tried to solve some of the mysteries, but this was not an easy task. Dr. Crandon, not his guests, supervised the tests. He wrote the official accounts of the sittings to use as he saw fit, and stipulated that anyone who suspected trickery must voice this opinion. Those who did were rarely invited to attend another séance.

Crandon did allow the professor some leeway, however. McDougall, and two colleagues from the Harvard psychology department, A. A. Roback and Harry Helson, were permitted to search the house before a séance began on the evening of November 3, 1923.

After dinner, the doctor gave his servants the night off. When the last one departed, the Harvard men locked the various entrances to the house and sealed two doors that led to the cellar with hot wax. Before it hardened, McDougall pressed his thumb against it, as though his thumb were a sealing ring, and left two thumbprints in the wax.

Despite these precautions, the sitters still heard mysterious music. A phantom whistler on a lower floor trilled two bars of "Souvenir," Mina's favorite melody; "Taps" was played somewhere in the house on chimes. Then less than a minute after the clock on a nearby church steeple struck ten, ten musical notes echoed in the hallway by the séance room.

Walter offered to stop a clock at any hour McDougall suggested; he chose ten thirty. Mina came out of her trance to escort Roback down the stairs so that he could verify that the clocks on various floors were running. When they returned, the séance continued until eleven fifteen.

Then the investigators found the grandfather clock on a stair landing had stopped at precisely ten thirty, as had a smaller clock in the reception room. The doors to the house were still locked; the wax seals with the professor's thumbprints on the cellarway entrances had not been broken. If the men thought someone with a duplicate key had entered and left the house, they didn't mention this possibility to their host.

Dr. Crandon invited McDougall, Roback, and Helson to another session a week later. This evening the most exciting manifestation occurred on the ground floor. Crandon turned out the lights, except for a red bulb, put a record on a Victrola in the dining room, and told the men to sit, as Walter's voice had suggested earlier, on a large table in the doorway to the hall with their feet off the floor.

Suddenly a piano stool, which had been in the reception room, glided down the hall; it stopped abruptly about seven feet away from the men. They leaped up and examined the stool. They were able to see well enough to tell that no mechanical device was attached to its base. They found no clue to the sudden motivation.

Later in the séance room, McDougall asked Walter for a reprise of this astonishing feat. Walter consented, warning the investigators not to touch the stool if they wanted a third view of this phenomenon.

Once again the men went to the dining room, and, as before, the piano stool moved eerily down the corridor. They returned to the séance room, believing this manifestation would be repeated one more time, and that they would have the opportunity to search the ground floor thoroughly. This was not the case.

The first time Helson had seen the stool move he thought he knew how the trick was done. It had glided toward a register in the floor of the corridor. This grillwork was a remnant of an old hot-air heating system that had been replaced by steam radiators throughout the house. He reasoned that if a string were attached to the base of the stool, with the free end extending down the hall and through one of the small openings in the register, some-one in the cellar by pulling on the string could tug the stool toward the register.

The second time the stool slid down the corridor and stopped, Helson saw a short piece of string on the floor. He picked it up, and gave it to McDougall that evening after they left the house.

McDougall wrote a long and carefully worded letter to Dr. Crandon, suggesting that he had evidence of fraud. The doctor sent his wife to see McDougall. On the November 1923 evening Bird first had dinner with the Crandons, she told him about her confrontation with the psychologist earlier that day. Bird described the incident in his 518-page book, *"Margery" the Medium*, which was published in 1925. Convinced that the Crandons were not interested in personal publicity, he had given Mina the name "Margery" in the first articles he wrote about her for *Scientific American;* it was as Margery that the public came to know her.

According to her account, McDougall tried in every conceivable way to force a confession from her. When he displayed the evidence of her trickery, a short, scraggly piece of string, she was torn between "indignation and uncontrollable laughter."

That evening at the dinner table Margery passed Bird a string about seven inches long and asked him what he thought it was. Bird peered at it through his glasses; he said it appeared to be a strand from a carpet. He followed her into the reception room, where she pointed out the fringe of the rug from which she had taken it. Bird said that when the piano stool had been propelled across this rug and down the corridor it might well have carried a bit of fringe with it.

Before Bird returned to New York after his weekend with the Crandons, Helson came to Lime Street with *his* piece of string. Bird compared it with the one Margery had pulled from the rug; the pieces matched. Helson admitted his theory had been exploded. He said he regretted the charge he had made and hoped the Crandons would forgive him, but he was never again invited to another of Margery's séances.

There is another possible explanation for the mysterious moving stool. If someone had passed one end of a long strong thread up through the register, along the hall, around one leg of the stool, back down the corridor, and through the register, this secret operator could have drawn the stool down the hall by hiding in the cellar and pulling on both ends of the thread. Whenever he wished the stool to stop, he could have released one end and rapidly hauled in the other. By the time an observer reached the stool, the motivating force would be in the cellar.

Anxious to see how European experts would respond to his wife's phenomena, Dr. Crandon took Margery abroad in December 1923. Long before they sailed, he had written to the principal psychical-research centers in France and England. In Paris, Nobel-prize winner Charles Richet; Gustave Geley, director of the Institute Métapsychic International; and other eminent Frenchmen enthused as they watched Margery exert her psychic influence on a table. They shouted their approval and called for more when the open-front cabinet in which she sat collapsed. Not as demonstrative but enthusiastic in a more restrained manner were the researchers who attended the séances Margery gave for the British College of Psychic Science and the Society for Psychical Research in London.

During a private séance with Sir Arthur Conan Doyle, a table tilted and rose, and Walter talked and whistled. Margery herself sat in a cabinet, improvised from an open three-fold screen with a carpet top. Though the cabinet didn't topple over, it vibrated until the rug was dislodged from its position as a temporary roof. A dried flower on the mantelpiece apparently flew through the air and landed by Lady Doyle's feet in the darkened apartment. Sir Arthur had recommended Margery to Bird as a worthy medium before he met her. Now that he had seen her in action, he felt his endorsement more than justified.

Curious to learn if the presence of the invisible forces that gave his wife her uncanny power could be captured on film, Crandon took her to two of Britain's foremost spirit photographers, Ada Deane and William Hope. Two misty faces appeared in a cloudlike formation above the American medium's head in one of Mrs. Deane's prints. One face Margery recognized immediately; it was that of her dead brother Walter. The dark hair was combed in the same style. More important, with the aid of a magnifying glass, she could see a scar on the left eyebrow.

This mark, she later told Bird, dated back to the time "he had been kicked by a horse." Another face, this one on a Hope photograph, was eventually identified by Mrs. Stinson, Margery's mother; she had no doubt it was that of her late husband, the medium's father.

Returning to Boston in late December after their triumphant tour abroad, the Crandons spent more time than ever in the séance room, holding twelve sittings in January 1924, fifteen in February, and nineteen in March.

In April Dr. Crandon entered Margery in the *Scientific American* contest. The prize money didn't interest the wealthy surgeon; the prestige that would come from winning the endorsement of an outstanding journal did. In his letter the doctor explained that he himself was unable to come to New York because of his medical practice. He would be glad, however, to pay the travel expenses of the committee members and put them up at his house. Though it was his wife, not himself, who would be competing, he had no intention of letting her face a critical group in another city without his support.

Enamored as much by the medium as by her psychical manifestations, Bird attended fifty-one séances between his first visit to Lime Street in November 1923 and late December 1924. Dr. Crandon paid his New York-to-Boston expenses and entertained him at their home during his stays.

Bird made the initial preparations for the *Scientific American*'s probe of the mediumship without consulting the committee as a whole. In the past a few test sittings had been enough to establish the fraudulence of a contestant. Margery was another matter. Bird told his editor and publisher he believed her claim. He asked McDougall and Daniel F. Comstock, who lived in Boston, to act as a subcommittee for the preliminary experiments. Though Bird was not a voting member of the committee, he wrote enthusiastically for the magazine about the wonders he had seen in Boston.

The Crandons regarded Professor McDougall as an antagonist after the string episode, but were amused by and tolerant of physicist Comstock's friendly challenges.

Comstock arrived at 10 Lime Street on the evening of April 18, 1924, with a large glass bottle. He had sealed the cork earlier.

Firmly fixed to the lower side of the cork was a brass rod bent at the bottom to form a hook. A strip of flexible, springlike metal protected the point of the hook. One end of this spring was fastened to the rod; the other could be pushed back so that a ring could be put on the hook; then the spring snapped back so the ring would not drop off if shaken. There were three rings inside the bottle: one made of wood, one of brass, and the third of green string. Also in the bottle were a short pencil and a small slip of paper.

Before the séance started, the physicist put the bottle on Margery's table and suggested that she ask Walter to put one or more of the rings on the hook and write something on the paper without removing the cork or smashing the glass.

The lights were turned out, and sounds from the jar indicated that the bottle was being rolled and shaken. When the lights were turned on, the three rings were still at the bottom of the bottle, but the slip of paper was on the hook.

Comstock left the bottle at the Crandons. Two nights later, the loop of cord was found on the hook. He was not present when, at the end of another séance, dots were found on the surface of the slip of paper, the point of the pencil had broken, and a crack was discovered close to the neck of the bottle.

Comstock salvaged the mechanism. He bent the hook slightly and replaced the spring with another flexible strip of brass; then he fastened the rod to the bottom of a cork with a larger diameter. This time, along with the modified hook, three rings of string—Walter had expressed a preference for them—another blank piece of paper, and a pencil were sealed in a bottle with a wider neck, and the cork was held in place with wire as well as with wax.

To keep the bottle from being turned upside down and manipulated without his knowledge, Comstock also added a thin cylinder containing mercury to the upper part of the shaft that terminated in the hook. The second bottle remained at the Crandons' several days; Walter never succeeded in getting a ring on the hook or writing on the scrap of paper.

Comstock also brought with him a pair of scales, and periodically Walter attempted to tip them. They were broken one night when the table on which they rested was overturned in the dark, and this testing device was discarded.

A "bell box" devised by the physicist met the approval of Margery's spirit guide, and it was used during many séances. Inside the wooden container were a bell and batteries. When the lid of the box was pressed down, the wiring system closed and the bell rang.

Dr. Crandon had read that Eusapia Palladino, the famed Italian medium, had caused blasts of cold wind to manifest. Cold air was felt by many sitters who sat in the dark with Margery. (If a medium's lips are pursed and she blows in the direction of a sitter, her breath when it reached him would be cold. With the sweep of a free hand a psychic can also generate an "icy" current of air.)

Margery was "controlled" in the dark by the sitters on either side of her. They took her hands and held their legs against hers. This control was questionable as her husband usually sat at her right. Dr. Crandon, of course, insisted that he never released either her hand or her foot.

Walter Franklin Prince attended three séances in May. He stayed at a hotel. It did not seem reasonable to him that an investigator could live with the Crandons, accept their hospitality, and still maintain an impartial view of the case. Hereward Carrington, on the other hand, remained at the house on Lime Street throughout the weeks he was in Boston as a *Scientific American* observer.

Like Bird, Carrington found the medium to be a fascinating woman. In later years he reminisced with old friends about his amorous adventures with her. During the time he lived with the Crandons at least two committee members knew of his emotional involvement with the person he was investigating.

Born on Jersey, one of the British Channel islands, Carrington had been brought to the United States as a boy. In 1900 at the age of nineteen, while living in Minneapolis, he joined the American Society for Psychical Research. Widely read in both occultism and conjuring, he has been called an expert magician. This is not quite true. Though he studied the standard texts and subscribed to conjuring periodicals, he rarely performed and then usually for friends. He earned his keep by writing, lecturing, and introducing alleged psychics to vaudeville audiences.

During Carrington's prolonged stay with the Crandons, he arranged for Fred Keating, a young New York sleight-of-hand specialist, to stay for ten days at the Lime Street house and aid him in detecting possible fraud.

Later Keating became a star in nightclubs, theatres, and films with his sophisticated brand of wizardry. I met him at the peak of his career and in the years that followed often talked with him about Margery, Carrington, and Bird.

Margery, Keating said, was the most ingenious medium he had ever seen. Quick-thinking, amazingly adroit with her hands and feet, she had little difficulty in deceiving those who believed she was a psychic.

Carrington, according to Keating, pretended some of Margery's manifestations baffled him: he hoped to get Crandon's financial backing for a psychical research foundation.

Keating had known Bird before he met Carrington. Keating said Bird was intent on building up Margery as America's most gifted medium. He made voluminous notes during his visits and planned to write books about his close association with her and to lecture on her manifestations.

Until Houdini, another member of the *Scientific American* committee, received a letter from Bird in June—three months after the preliminary investigation started—the magician had not been informed that one was under way. Bird's letter said the case had reached a point where Orson Munn, the publisher, wanted the magician's opinion.

In *Houdini Exposes the tricks used by the Boston Medium "Margery,"* a forty-page booklet published in 1924, the magician said that when he called on Orson Munn, the publisher summoned Bird, and the following exchange took place:

> "Do you believe that this medium is genuine?"
> "Well, yes, she is genuine. She does resort to trickery at times, but I believe she is fifty or sixty per cent genuine."
> "Then you mean that this medium will be entitled to get the *Scientific American* prize?"
> "Most decidedly."

Stunned to learn that the committee was even considering making an award to a contestant he had never seen, Houdini said it was imperative that he be given an opportunity to test Margery. "If you give this award to a medium without the strictest examination," and she is later "detected in fraud *we would be the laughing stock of the world.*"

Houdini and Munn checked in at the Copley Plaza Hotel on Wednesday, July twenty-third. Bird had gone to Boston earlier—as usual, he stayed with the Crandons—and arranged for a séance that evening.

In New York Bird had told Houdini about the happenings at Margery's séances; Bird thought the ringing of the bell in the wooden box Comstock had constructed (while the medium's hands and feet were held in the dark) was strong evidence of her psychic powers. Learning that Margery's husband or another close friend always sat on her right, the magician hoped he might be permitted to take the chair on her left. He prepared for this possibility in a way he did not reveal until later.

It was hot that July night. The men took off their coats. Margery sat between Houdini and her husband. Munn and R. W. Conant, who worked in Comstock's laboratory, completed the circle. Bird, sitting outside it, put one hand around the linked hands of the medium and the surgeon. Her right leg pressed against her husband's left; her left leg touched Houdini's right one.

The lights were turned off. In the darkness Walter talked and whistled. He said the bell box should be placed on the floor between the magician's feet. The bell rang while it was there. Walter said a megaphone, one of the medium's props, was floating in the air; no one could see it. In reply to a question from Walter as to the direction in which the megaphone should be hurled, Houdini answered, "Toward me." It landed with a crash. There was more noise and confusion when the open-front cabinet behind Margery toppled over.

Houdini and Munn discussed the events of the evening as Bird drove them back to their hotel. The magician said the medium was a fraud. The ringing of the bell in the box, which puzzled Bird, was no mystery to Houdini. That morning he had slipped a tight elastic surgical bandage on his right leg below the knee; he knew from experience this would make his skin sensitive. He removed the bandage shortly before he left for the séance at the Crandons'.

In the dark room Houdini had pulled up his trouser leg. When Margery's leg touched the sensitive skin, he could detect her slightest movement. He felt her leg slide as she slowly inched her foot behind his until she could press it down on the top of the bell box.

The only trick he did not understand after a single sitting was the megaphone tossing. Bird recalled that one member of the committee had suggested it might have been balanced on her shoulder. Houdini thought a minute, then declared the megaphone had been on her head—like a dunce cap. With a snap of her head, she could hurl it wherever she wished.

Several times the séance had been interrupted, and the lights turned on. After one of these intermissions, Houdini explained, Margery could have quickly picked the megaphone up from the floor and put it on her head with her right hand, then tilted the cabinet back just enough for her right foot to slide under the nearest panel. There was always a brief delay while hands were being grasped to re-form the circle. She would then be ready to send the "floating" megaphone toward a sitter and to upset the cabinet with a swift kick.

This step-ahead procedure is akin to that used by a magician. The preparations for most tricks are over before the audience knows they have even begun; that is, the vital secret actions are completed before the trick, as the spectators see it, takes place. This technique, masked by misdirection—diverting the audience's attention—is as effective in a séance room as on a stage.

Suppose a professed medium wants to use a magnet during one of his or her feats. If the magnet has been hidden in the room earlier, the performer can be searched to the skin just prior to the demonstration.

Margery was searched by Comstock's female secretary before her appearance for the committee in the physicist's apartment at the Charlesgate Hotel on July twenty-fourth. Nothing in the routine she presented that night depended upon a concealed object.

The cabinet was still standing when the séance was over, but the three hinged sections had been pushed close together. A card table tilted and later overturned, spilling the bell box, which had been on it, to the floor.

The bell rang frequently though it was again on the floor; five rings sounded in succession when Munn chose that number. Once more Houdini pulled up his right trouser leg in the dark. Again he knew by the sense of touch each time Margery moved to press the lid of the box with her foot. Indeed her silk stocking caught in the buckle of his garter, and he had to free it.

He realized how the medium caused the table to rise without using her hands or feet—a ruse he might not have detected had he not released his grip on Munn's right hand and explored beneath the table top. Margery's head was there! She had leaned forward in the dark to get into this position. When she raised her head, she lifted the table. One fast thrust was sufficient to overturn it.

During the committee discussion afterward, Houdini said they should call the newspapers immediately and expose Margery's deception. Munn and Bird disagreed. Reports of the séances, they said, should appear first in the pages of *Scientific American*.

Houdini and Munn took the late train back to New York City; Bird stayed on in Boston at the Crandons'. On the train the publisher told Houdini that he was worried. The September issue of *Scientific American*, carrying an article by Bird lauding Margery's mediumship, was now on the press. The magician convinced Munn he must have these comments deleted, despite the additional expense, to avoid being embarrassed when the truth about Margery became known.

Several days later Walter Franklin Prince and Houdini met with Munn in New York to object to statements Bird had issued to the press concerning the investigation in Boston. Any information released should reflect the committee's views, not those of the secretary, they said. Munn told Bird to stay away from future committee séances.

The publisher had a countersuggestion. If Margery was a trickster, as Houdini thought, the committee should be able to offer proof of this to the public. Perhaps the best way to do so would be to control her actions, so that she could not produce manifestations by cheating. A device making it impossible for her to carry out her clever deceptions would be ready for the scheduled test sessions in August, the magician promised.

The Crandons and several of their friends were disturbed when they saw Houdini's contraption in Dr. Comstock's apartment on the night of August twenty-fifth. Similar to a crate for an old-fashioned, slant-top desk, it was large enough to hold the medium seated comfortably on a chair inside. Semicircular sections had been cut out of the hinged front and top sections, so that when they were closed around the medium's neck, only her head protruded. At the sides there were holes through which she could extend her hands. Extra strips of wood could be nailed over these openings should the committee decide to have her hands kept within the box.

Crandon said the "cage" made no allowance for "the theory and experience of the psychic structure or mechanism." Margery's followers now believed that a mysterious spirit rod extruded from between her legs to produce phenomena.

A familiarization séance with the medium in the new box was given behind closed doors for the Crandons' friends before Margery appeared for the committee and Orson Munn. When Margery's supporters left the room, the members of the committee filed in. The test session ended abruptly after the hinged front of the box clattered down in the dark. Crandon said Walter must have forced it open; Houdini claimed the medium had used her shoulders to loosen the narrow brass strips that held the panels closed. He had not challenged Margery to escape from the box; its sole purpose was to prevent trickery. The shouting match between Crandon and Houdini became so heated that Walter's voice called for a truce.

Once more the committee left the room, and the Crandons' group returned for another private session. Only they know what was said while the magazine's investigators were closed off in another room. This much is certain: when the members of the committee again entered the room and the séance resumed, Walter went on the attack. He asked Houdini how much he was being paid to stop the manifestations. There were no phenomena produced. Eventually Walter told Comstock to examine carefully the bell box under a light. Comstock did, and found a small round eraser, the sort usually seen on the end of a lead pencil, wedged under the lid. With this in place, the physicist estimated, four times the usual pressure would have been required to make the bell ring. Houdini made a statement for the record that he had not put the eraser there.

He reinforced the box for the test session the following night, adding heavy hasps, staples, and four padlocks. A surprise visitor was J. Malcolm Bird. He wanted to know why the publisher had given him express instructions not to attend this series of séances. Before Munn could answer, Houdini and Prince unburdened themselves. They knew Bird had told the Crandons of the committee's discoveries in July and, despite Munn's orders, he had continued to release misleading statements to the press. Bird denied these charges and offered to resign as committee secretary. This resignation was accepted; Prince was elected to fill the post before the writer left.

On the evening of August twenty-sixth Houdini held Margery's left hand as it came from his side of the box; Prince held her right one. This was an important procedural change. Until then, Crandon had been the "control" on that side. Before the séance began, Houdini warned Prince not to release the medium's hand even for a moment. Margery asked him why he made such an issue of this. The magician replied that as long as her hands were grasped, she could not reach any object that she might have smuggled inside.

Soon Walter spoke up and implied Houdini had put a ruler under the cushion on which the medium's feet rested. While the magician had not been in the room prior to the sitting, Walter said Houdini's assistant had been. Walter became loud, abusive, and profane: "Houdini, you Goddamned son of a bitch, get the hell out of here and never come back. If you don't, I will."

When the box was unlocked, a new carpenter's ruler, a two-foot length folded in four six-inch sections, was discovered under the pillow. Comstock suggested that it might have been left behind when the box was being strengthened. When Orson Munn sent for Jim Collins, Houdini's assistant, and questioned him, Collins said his ruler was still in his pocket. He took it out and showed it.

Houdini dictated a statement to the stenographer: "I wish it recorded that I demanded Collins to take a sacred oath on the life of his mother that he did not put the ruler into the box and knew positively nothing about it. I also pledge my sacred word of honor as a man that the first I knew of the ruler in the box was when I was so informed by Walter."

Years later when my friend William Lindsay Gresham wrote his biography of Houdini, he quoted Collins as admitting he had hidden the ruler in the box on Houdini's instructions. The source of this story, though not mentioned, was Fred Keating. I had shown Keating an unpublished Houdini manuscript in which Houdini referred critically to Keating, not as a magician, but as an observer when assisting Carrington in his investigations of Margery's mediumship.

Keating, who had admired Houdini since boyhood and who had an autographed photograph of the master showman in his apartment, had been annoyed. A short time later he told the Collins story to Gresham. When Keating read a set of galleys of the book (also in my collection), he added the comment, "Good!" by the side of the anecdote. I knew Collins, too. He idolized Houdini, and would have been the last person on earth to implicate him even if there had been some sort of a plot to set up Margery. Thus, the story falls of its own weight.

The committee's final verdict was released for publication in February 1925. Four of the members had already been quoted in the November 1924 issue of *Scientific American*, but the fifth did not report until three months later.

Prince said there had been no proof of supernormal powers. Carrington said the medium had produced some genuine phenomena. Houdini called her a fraud. Comstock said he had never witnessed a manifestation under strict scientific control. McDougall, the first committee member to attend a séance at the Crandons', was the last to send in his opinion. He had seen nothing that would lead him to believe that means other than normal had been employed. He suggested the Crandons had devised the séances to test the gullibility of scientists. By a 4 to 1 verdict, Margery did not receive the award.

There were repercussions. Influential members of the American Society for Psychical Research who sided with the Crandons forced Prince to resign as chief research officer of the organization. Bird replaced him. When Houdini heard this, he struck out the clause in his will which said that his library on the occult would go to the American Society for Psychical Research, and specified that these volumes, along with his conjuring collection, were to be sent to the Library of Congress.

Walter had predicted during a Margery séance the previous December that the magician would die in less than a year. He failed to oblige and continued to denounce the medium and duplicate her tricks during his performances. He even produced manifestations while locked in the box he had built to restrain her.

Performing on a brightly lit stage, Houdini explained that Margery cheated under the cover of darkness. Rather than turn out all the lights in the theatre, he would employ a cloth to hide his actions. Then the audience could see that he was not being aided by his assistants.

After he had been padlocked in the restraint, with his head extending from the top, his assistants moved a table with a bell box and a tambourine close to the front of the enclosure. The table was positioned just as it had been during Margery's unproductive sessions with the *Scientific American* committee. The magician's assistants covered the restraint and the table with a large black sheet. Houdini's head was in view as it protruded from a hole in the center of the cloth.

He described the tests made in Boston and advised the audience to pay close attention. Almost immediately the bell rang and the tambourine jingled.

While Bird and the American Society for Psychical Research continued to laud Margery, Houdini and Prince, who had been named research officer of the newly formed Boston Society for Psychic Research, stressed that nothing supernormal occurred when the medium was under proper control.

Even Bird, in his book *"Margery" the Medium*, admitted she could deceive investigators, if she wished. No other medium, Bird said, was more alert or could "get more fun" from doing this. Even so, he insisted that she produced genuine phenomena. A review in the ASPR *Journal* found little fault with the way the author covered his subject; but after all, that was scarcely surprising—the reviewer was Bird himself.

The villain of his account, the magician who had dared to denounce Margery as a cheat and who had duplicated her feats on the stage and lecture platform, studied the volume carefully. An unpublished forty-three–page Houdini manuscript, now in my collection, offers the escapologist's rebuttal.

Until he read the Bird book, Houdini considered a book by one of the famous Fox sisters, Ann Leah Fox Fish Underhill's *The Missing Link in Modern Spiritualism*, published in 1885, "the worst conglomerate mass of lies in print." (A similar view had been expressed earlier by Kate Fox Jencken, Mrs. Underhill's youngest sister. She is quoted in the October 10, 1888, issue of the *New York Herald:* "Now, there's nothing but falsehood in that book from beginning to end, excepting the fact that Horace Greeley educated me. The rest is nothing but a string of lies.")

Bird, Houdini asserted, eclipsed Mrs. Underhill as a "super liar. . . . He impeaches and questions the integrity of Professor William McDougall, Professor Daniel Comstock and Dr. Walter Franklin Prince. My personal opinion is that their integrity stands at 100%, and I would rather take them at their word, than J. Malcolm Bird at his oath.

"As to the competence of Bird as an investigator," the magician went on, "he is so gullible that he can not see through the simplest parlor tricks of magic." Bird's friend, Hereward Carrington, Houdini dismissed as the sort of investigator "who seriously attempts to photograph the soul of a rat as it leaves its rodent remains."

Bird's statement that *"Houdini absolutely refused to sit other than in total darkness,"* the magician said, "is an absolute falsehood." Before the séance when the ruler was found in the box under the cushion, Bird said the Crandons were willing to permit a physician of the committee's choice to give the medium "a full anatomical" probe. "To the contrary," Houdini countered. "Dr. Crandon emphatically refused to allow any such examination to be made and he further stipulated that this was not even to be put in the records and, if anyone demanded an anatomical examination of Mrs. Crandon, he would stop the séances."

A page in the Bird book had been labeled "The Deadly Parallel." At the top a line drawing from Houdini's booklet on Margery showed the medium reaching her left foot behind Houdini's right leg to ring the bell box. At the bottom of the page there was a photograph. Bird stressed that the size of the box, where it was placed on the floor, and the position of the legs and feet, as shown in the photograph, did not jibe with the Houdini illustration. The bell box is larger in the photograph, but Bird did not mention, as Houdini did in his notes, that the photograph was taken after the test, with the participants posing for the photographer.

Any photographs taken during or after a sitting were under Dr. Crandon's direct supervision; only those he approved were released for publication. With the arrival of Eric John Dingwall, research officer of the British Society for Psychical Research in Boston in December 1924, the mediumship entered a new phase, and some of the strangest pictures ever made at a séance resulted.

Dingwall, who had seen the medium at work during the Crandons' visit to London in 1923, urged Margery to produce the ectoplasm, or whatever it was, that her husband said extruded from her body in the dark. Since the psychic rod had first been suggested, the medium stripped to the skin before sittings and wore only a light robe or kimona during the séances. One memorable night in mid-January 1925 what appeared to be a dark misshapen hand came through a gap in the robe that covered her nude body and rested on the end of a table closest to her as a flash exposure illuminated the room. The "hand" was as limp as a dead fish and did not move when the light fell upon it. It disappeared as it had appeared in darkness.

In Dingwall's "Report on a Series of Sittings with the medium Margery," published more than a year later in June 1926 as part of the British society's *Proceedings,* Volume XXXVI, he said this object felt soft, cold, and wet like "raw beef" or "rubber."

Crandon, from time to time during these sittings, had flashed the red beam of a lamp on, but never at the right moment nor long enough as far as the investigator was concerned. Dingwall was given to understand that this substance had been modeled into its curious shape by an invisible force after it left Margery's body; he hoped to see this being done, but Crandon refused to turn on the red lamp during the process.

Professor McDougall had been invited by Dingwall to join

in the investigation; he agreed with his colleague that they should have more freedom to conduct the tests as they wished. This was not to be. If a suggestion made by them met with Crandon's approval, it was carried out; otherwise, it was ignored.

Dr. Crandon still refused to let a physician search his wife's body, so there was always the nagging suspicion that she extracted the "teleplasmic mass" from her vagina.

Perhaps remembering Sir Hiram Maxim's account of his encounter with a materializing medium, Elizabeth Tomson, Dingwall sought permission to enclose Margery's body in tights. After Mrs. Tomson had ripped open the neck of the outfit, which had been sewn tightly at her neck, wrists, waist, and ankles, Maxim discovered she concealed the flowers she "materialized" under her breasts.

Neither Margery nor her husband had any qualms about her being tested while she wore only silk stockings, shoes, and a loose-fitting wrapper, but they vetoed the proposal of tights. Instead she tried to divert the investigators' attention by seeming to extrude mysterious substances from her navel, mouth, or ear.

There is a similarity between the technique Margery used and that employed by East Indian fakirs during the presentation of their mango-tree feat. An Indian magician plants a seed in the ground, erects a tripod over the spot, then makes a cloak by wrapping cloths around the tripod, so that no one can see what is happening inside. Each time he removes the wrappings, the tree is larger, growing from a sprout into a fruit-bearing tree.

Darkness was Margery's cloak. The eerie emanations from her body would have expanded or changed form whenever Crandon decided to give the sitters a glimpse of the phenomena with his red lamp.

Dingwall, a member of the Inner Magic Circle in London, was well informed on the tricks of magicians and the deceits of charlatans. Three years earlier, with Harry Price, another noted investigator of psychic phenomena, he had added notes, a glossary, and a twenty-nine–page bibliography to the facsimile edition of *Revelations of a Spirit Medium,* published in London by Kegan Paul, Trench, Trubner & Co. This classic exposure of séances by an anonymous author who professed to be a reformed psychic was originally published in St. Paul, Minnesota, in 1891.

Even Houdini grudgingly admitted Dingwall was not a "shut-eye," as he referred to those who preferred not to see what was actually happening at a séance. In Houdini's copy of the above-mentioned book, which is now in my collection, there is this handwritten note: "Dingwall does know a lot for a man of his 'experience' but—I disagree with him as he believes anything he can't explain or has done so up until a few months ago."

Dingwall had been amazed by Margery's new phenomena; he admitted as much in a letter written from Boston to his friend Baron Schrenck-Notzing in Germany. By the time he prepared his report, however, he was less certain. He carefully described what had taken place, then offered possible explanations. He said a gynecologist had assured him the strange substance that Margery produced could be stored in the vagina. Dingwall also admitted that a crude mass of material could be exchanged for another better formed one between the flashes of Crandon's light. But, he emphasized, he himself had seen no evidence of trickery.

Was the mediumship of the Boston woman described in his meticulous account authentic? Dingwall reached no conclusion; he wasn't sure.

I visited Dingwall at his country home in England. An old framed photograph of Margery hung in the room that housed his occult library. He was a gracious host. One day I asked him if he planned to write a book about his adventures with mediums, especially the Margery episode. He assured me he did not; he had said what he wished to say about her in his report.

In Volume 1 of "The Margery Mediumship," published in 1928 as Volumes XX–XXI of the *Proceedings* of the American Society for Psychical Research, Bird says Professor McDougall was the culprit who swayed Dingwall from his initial favorable assessment of the medium, and led him to follow "the identical bungling course."

Far from being a bungler, McDougall had taken the photographs of "teleplasmic" substance, which Crandon said were conclusive proof of Margery's marvelous mediumship, to Harvard experts in physiology and zoology. Enlargements confirmed McDougall's initial opinion that the flabby material was animal lung tissue. Had someone skillful with a knife shaped it?

More trouble for the Crandons was in the offing from Cambridge. Hudson Hoagland, a graduate student at Harvard; Foster Damon, an English instructor; and a group of their associates, including Grant H. Code, whose hobbies were conjuring and acrobatic contortions; Robert Hillyer, a poet; and several other professors invited Margery to sit for them in Emerson Hall.

Seeking acclaim in academic circles, the Crandons accepted. Precautions were taken against deception. The medium, her husband, and two members of the committee wore luminous bands on their ankles, wrists, and heads so their movements could be observed in the dark. At these séances, when the sitters in the circle joined hands, they formed part of an electrical circuit. If two hands parted, theoretically this break would be indicated on a monitoring instrument. Years before, however, Anna Eva Fay had worked out a way to outwit her investigators when William Crookes used a similar device to control her hands. As long as some part of her bare flesh touched one of the two brass handles, she could free a hand without being detected.

The Margery séances held in May 1925 in Emerson Hall were great successes, but on June twenty-ninth, during a sitting at Hoagland's home as a "psychic rod" held one of Margery's new props, a luminous circle that Walter called a "doughnut," near another of her gadgets, a luminous board, Hoagland saw the dark bulk of the medium's right foot move; her toes were acting as fingers. He kept quiet. Committeeman Code also observed something peculiar. The luminous band that had been only partially visible on the medium's right ankle was on the floor.

Following Crandon's rule—report any trickery you see— Code spoke out. Almost at once a partial ring of light replaced what had been a full one. It was noted at the end of the sitting that the band which had been around the medium's right ankle before the lights were turned out was now in a different position.

Earlier that evening the committee had asked Walter to press the "teleplasmic" extrusion into modeling clay. This imprint was now visible. Once the séance was over, Margery was eager to leave, but she stayed long enough to put one of her bare feet on the clay, so that her footprint could be compared with the impression made in the dark.

In her rush to get away, Margery dropped one of the slippers she had worn during the séance. Hoagland did not realize she had lost it until his dog retrieved it the following day. The slipper was then microscopically examined along with the two impressions in the clay. The indentation made by the alleged psychic substance turned out to be an impression of the lower part of a human foot and very similar to the print made by the medium. Both contained tiny bits of lint and sand—and so did Margery's slipper!

The medium was as confident and cool as usual when she appeared that night for the next sitting in Emerson Hall. Code took her right hand. Alert for another view of the medium's foot, Hoagland was shocked to see, by the reflection of the luminous board, lengthy *fingers.* Walter permitted committee members to hold the "hand." Like the one Dingwall had described earlier, it was damp and limp. It left an entirely different impression in the clay from the footprint of the previous night.

The committee was stumped. A day passed; then Code confessed to the others that by prearrangement, he had worked with Margery to move the luminous circle up her arm, so she could reach with her right hand into her lap without the move being obvious in the dark. She used this hand to get the object they had touched in the dark from its hiding place.

Code explained that after having seen that the lint and sand in the clay impressions matched those in her slipper, he had visited the medium and confronted her with the evidence of her deceit. He told the committee he was now convinced that Crandon had used hypnosis or the power of suggestion so frequently on his wife that by now she was a split personality, who didn't know what she was doing when Walter possessed her. In Code's eyes, neither she nor her husband was really responsible for their abnormal behavior. Code feared that if the committee exposed Margery, the shock might mentally unbalance her husband. It was for this reason, he said, that he had offered to help the medium by pulling the luminous arm band higher at the séance so that she could perform as she had in the past. He asserted there was nothing supernormal about her feats; indeed he had exhibited some of them himself for the enlightenment of the committee. Code further reported that Margery at first feigned disinterest in his offer. He then asked to talk to Walter. In the séance room, sitting behind the table her husband had built, Margery entered a trance. Walter was disturbed by news of the committee's evidence; he agreed Code should be her confederate that night.

This was the story Code told his fellow investigators. Hoagland's official version, "Science and the Medium: The Climax of a Famous Investigation" appeared in the November 1925 issue of the *Atlantic Monthly*.

Crandon and his friends issued *Margery Harvard Veritas: A Study in Psychics*, a 109-page effort to combat the criticism, not only of the most recent Harvard group, but of the earlier investigators as well. A formal declaration by the participants in the test sittings at Emerson Hall and in Hoagland's home had stated that the phenomena had been produced by trickery: "the only possible difference of opinion . . . is to what extent the trickery was unconscious." Among those who signed this statement were Harlow Shapley, director of Harvard Astronomical Observatory; Edwin G. Boring, director of Harvard Psychological Laboratory; and Simeon B. Wolbach, Harvard Medical School's professor of pathology.

Alluding to this and other exposures in the first volume of "The Margery Mediumship," Bird wrote: "I am in the unique position of not having any urge toward the rapid promulgation of final conclusions of some sort." He added, "Published unfavorable conclusions are of no permanent scientific merit save as they turn out to be in line with the ultimate facts. They are, however, here and now a serious embarrassment to me."

These words prefaced his account of the preliminary work of a new American Society for Psychical Research team, headed by Princeton psychologist Henry Clay McComas. McComas and two professors from Johns Hopkins University, physicist Robert W. Wood and psychologist Knight Dunlap, traveled to Boston in January 1926. McComas, a polite, amiable man, had been to Lime Street before. The Crandons liked him, but they objected to his less tactful, outspoken companions for a variety of reasons. The medium's husband sent a letter to the American Society for Psychical Research officials in New York. He complained that Dunlap and Wood were deaf, one entirely so since childhood, while the other could hear only "soft whispers." This meant they were not capable of appreciating the voice phenomenon—the Walter personality. Moreover, Crandon continued, Dunlap revealed his bias in his writings.

Indeed, Dunlap had practically given his verdict before he came to Boston. In his book *Old and New Viewpoints in Psychology*, published in 1925, the psychologist wrote that a devotee of the occult with "failing facilities and decreasing energies," realizing that the end of his life is near, "grasps frantically at even the poor pitiful straw of psychic research, and shuts his eyes to its futility and insufficiency." He also flatly asserted, "If a medium claims that something is written on a slate without normal human agency or articles moved about, or bells rung without human or mechanical agency, or that voices or other sounds heard by sitters are produced by other than living beings, she is a fraud and nothing she produces is to be taken as other than deliberate fraud."

Wood, the physicist, was even less welcome in the fourth-floor séance room. This blunt cantankerous researcher, called "as American as a hickory tree" by his biographer, William Seabrook, had tried to trap Eusapia Palladino in 1909 with a cleverly rigged lighting system during her test sittings at Columbia University. Hidden from her view, lying flat on the top of an apparatus case in the laboratory, as a grille similar to a venetian blind was opened below to provide dim illumination on the floor, he spotted a black object moving across the patch of light, but didn't know what it was. Before the next sitting, Wood installed an X-ray machine that would permit him to see the bones in the medium's limbs on a concealed screen if she used one of them to reach back into the cabinet behind her table. The plump Neapolitan mystic was wary. She glanced at the unfamiliar equipment in the room, became conveniently ill, and canceled the session.

Wood arrived at the Crandons' with a satchelful of paraphernalia. He showed Dr. Crandon a lamp that he correctly described as a "black light," though he did not explain it produced ultraviolet rays. Crandon, not as well posted on scientific equipment as he was on postoperative techniques, had asked Walter earlier if Wood could switch on this seemingly ineffective source of illumination during the séance; Walter gave his permission.

It was Wood's intention secretly to photograph the manifestations: concealed under his coat was a miniature camera. As Margery breathed heavily in the dark, he took out the camera and turned on the black light. To his dismay, the artificial flowers on the mantelpiece and other objects in the room glowed brilliantly. Chemicals used to dye these objects were reacting to the ultraviolet rays. He quickly switched off the lamp and thrust the camera back into its hiding place.

Crandon realized Wood had been up to something, but he had not seen the camera. In a letter to McComas, dated April 30, 1926, the surgeon wrote: "Dr. Wood's trickery is discouraging. You will remember that when he turned on his harmless-looking red lamp Walter immediately said 'The room is flooded with light.' This shows that Walter has a kind of eye that we have not, since we could see no light but the red."

In the Seabrook biography, *Doctor Wood: Modern Wizard of the Laboratory*, published in 1941, the investigator gives a side-light on this incident. After the séance, Margery asked him what sort of lamp had made the flowers and other objects so bright. "How did you know about *that?*" Wood questioned. The medium chuckled and strode off.

Crandon, who night after night sat in the room with other men while his wife during some manifestations allowed her kimono to fall open and posed in the nude for the séance photographer, expressed indignation in a letter dated January 31, 1926, to an ASPR official about a word uttered during the sitting the night before. Crandon complained that Wood, after touching the "teleplasmic" rod extending from the medium in the dark, had blurted out: "The whatcha-ma-call-it feels to me like a——."

Crandon could not bring himself to write whatever indelicate term Wood had used, but he made it clear no gentleman would have uttered such a word with a lady present, especially as there were a number of other terms a more considerate man could have used. "A true scientist," Crandon said, "would have described the terminal as to its length, breadth, thickness, temperature, degree of hardness and softness, to superficial feel and to firm grasp, and other specifications."

The sentence Crandon cited does not appear in the committee report for January 30. At 10:53 P.M. Wood said "My hand was on the table holding the luminous doughnut, teleplasmic rod fell in the palm of my hand, feeling like a rigid rod covered with soft leather. It was placed between my thumb and finger holding the doughnut, I squeezed it very hard, which produced no ill effect." Eleven minutes later, he added: "My hand was put over [the psychic extension] and between my fingers I felt of 'it.' It is cold, soft, with rigid ruler-like core. I cannot say whether it is a single or multiple core!" At 11:16 Wood commented: "I have the rod in my hand. Psyche [a name Dr. Crandon often used for his wife] put my hand over and put the rod between my fingers, pushing my hand along so that the rod pushed through my fingers several inches. It was cold."

It should be noted that when the first extrusion appeared during a Dingwall session, it was limp. With the core to give it rigidity, the more recent rod could move objects. At the séance noted above, the medium's husband sat in the séance circle while Dunlap held her right hand and Wood her left. At one point Wood changed places with McComas. Her left hand was free as they traded seats. Walter expressed an opinion of the investigators: "I never saw such a bunch of stiffs in my life. Talk about dead people, my God!"

Soon after that things livened up. As a cold moist object struck McComas's hand, something touched Dunlap's hand, too; Dunlap reported the medium's feet were in his lap. She twisted, groaned, and threw her feet across into McComas's lap.

Several minutes later, as Margery continued to writhe, Dunlap said she put his hand "into contact with a smooth cylindrical something"; then McComas reported she "reached over" and put the back of his hand upon "a cold moist substance."

Before the first manifestation of the evening, Margery had complained, "I am in awful pain, don't feel good anyhow," and Walter's voice commented, "Nobody gives a damn if you are."

This interchange is important, since Crandon later charged that Margery was sick for days afterward because Wood had "pinched" the psychic rod. McComas, on the other hand, said the medium had seemed as active as usual and blithely climbed the stairs when he visited the house the next day.

There was another point of contention in later discussions of this the last séance Crandon permitted this committee to attend. The report signed at the doctor's insistence after the sitting by the members of the committee, says Margery had nausea and vomited. Later the three men affirmed that though she had gone through the pantomime of retching, there was no evidence on the floor that she actually had done so.

The final report of the McComas committee, dated April 18, 1927, appeared six years later in "The Margery Mediumship," Volume 2, published as Volumes XX–XXI of the American Society for Psychical Research's *Proceedings*. The report stressed that Crandon had permitted the group to attend *only* as observers; no scientific controls had been put into effect, or conclusive experiments made. At the initial informal sitting, attended by Crandon's friends as well as the investigators, Walter had caused the "doughnut," which had lost its glow, to become brightly luminescent in the dark.

Margery's fans had enthused about this new wonder, but Professor Wood later duplicated it with an ultraviolet filter on a small flashlight. The committee noted Crandon had a flashlight in the side pocket of his coat closest to the medium as he held her hand. She could easily have reached it.

Dunlap had observed a change in the tension of the spring on the bell box. He constructed a box with the spring inside, where it could not be manipulated; Crandon refused to let the Dunlap box take the place of the one regularly used.

Crandon had said the teleplasmic rods that came from the medium were so sensitive they could identify playing cards and wooden letters in the dark, yet when Wood squeezed one of them, neither the medium nor her spirit helper knew of this before Wood announced it.

Dunlap believed the rod to be an animal intestine filled with some soft material, possibly cotton, and made rigid by the insertion of several wires.

The McComas group also staged two séances at ASPR headquarters conducted by Grant H. Code, who had left Harvard to become a professor at the University of Delaware. He replicated Margery's levitation feats, the bell box ringing, and the naming of cards in a dark room. Fifteen ASPR members admitted they could not imagine how normal means could account for the manifestations he had shown on various other occasions.

The McComas committee's report to the American Society for Psychical Research concluded: "The Margery Mediumship is a clever and entertaining performance but is unworthy of serious consideration," a view shared by Joseph Banks Rhine and his wife, Louisa, after a single sitting on July 1, 1926.

The Rhines, who were later to make ESP and parapsychology household words in the United States, were shocked by what to them seemed "base and brazen trickery." In an article printed in the *Journal of Abnormal and Social Psychology* in February 1927, after it had been rejected by the pro-Crandon editor of the American Society for Psychical Research's *Journal,* the Rhines told of seeing Margery kick a megaphone across the floor toward her hand. This action was visible in the dark because her foot stood out against the glow of a luminous board.

When a luminous basket levitated in a glass-sided cabinet, where the medium sat with her wrists wired to the two wooden sections at the sides and her ankles wired to the bottom, it seemed reasonable for the Rhines to assume Margery had leaned forward and picked up the handle of the basket with her teeth.

The Rhines had not gone to the sitting to scoff. A moving lecture by Sir Arthur Conan Doyle had awakened their interest in mediums. They had spoken in favor of Margery at the University of West Virginia, and were searching for proof that the dead communicated with the living. After the séance at the Crandons', they had investigated the surgeon's background, and in their article they offered a possible explanation for his sponsorship of Margery as a medium. He had suffered "a decided loss of position and prestige" before he turned to the study of psychic phenomena. Knowing that he was a materialist and dreaded dying, his wife deceived him during the early table-tilting experiments with sleight of foot and hand. When he found she was cheating, he cooperated with her, enjoying his new prominence as a "martyr to the cause of science" and an authority on modern mediumship.

Robert J. Tillyard, an eminent entomologist, saw nothing to make him suspicious of the medium during two sittings with Margery in 1926. On the contrary, the inexplicable phenomena he witnessed provided him with material for a lecture sponsored by the National Laboratory of Psychical Research in London, before he returned to his post as head of the biological department at the Cawthorn Institute in Nelson, New Zealand.

During Tillyard's stay in Boston, Margery had produced a "psychic glove"; Crandon presented it to him as a souvenir. Two containers—one filled with hot paraffin, the other with cold water—had been on the medium's table. Theoretically a spirit hand dipped into the wax, then into the water, and left behind a wax shell, or glove, before dematerializing. This was a comparatively new marvel for Margery, though Franek Kluski and other European mediums had produced spirit gloves in the past.

J. P. S. Jamieson, Tillyard's physician in New Zealand, while examining the psychic glove from Boston, noticed that the thumb seemed swollen. While other friends of Tillyard were sure a human hand could not have been involved—the opening was too narrow to allow the removal of one without splitting the wax—the swollen thumb suggested a solution to the physician. He experimented and produced three perfect psychic gloves in the time it had taken Margery to finish one, according to Tillyard's "The Normal Production of Psychic Hands," published in the January–February 1928 issue of the *British Journal of Psychic Research*.

The secret, Jamieson found, was that the volume of a hand can be increased by about 10 percent by applying a tourniquet to the arm. The hand of the volunteer who helped the doctor make his spirit gloves was relaxed and held toward the floor until as much blood as possible ran into it. The physician then placed a tourniquet around the upper part of the arm and applied pressure. The tourniquet was adjusted "to obstruct the venous return from the hand, but not tightly enough to compress the artery." The swollen hand was inserted, fingers down, into hot melted paraffin, withdrawn, then dipped again as the wax covering began to harden. This process was continued until a sufficiently thick coating accumulated. Then the hand was plunged into a container of cold water.

After the wax became firm in the water, the subject held his hand straight up, as high as he could reach as the tourniquet was removed. In a few minutes the glove loosened; there was a space between the wax and skin. The hand, still straight up, was lowered by bending the elbow while the man pressed the upper part of his arm against a book held between his arm and his body. The firm pressure closed the brachial artery, preventing the flow of blood into the hand.

Finally, with a firm grip on the knuckles of the glove, the wax shell was pulled off. While the wax was still pliable, the opening was reduced in size by the fingers and by dipping this part of the glove into hot paraffin again.

If the fingers were slightly curled at the outset, this natural position made the glove more realistic, Tillyard noted. The fingers were held apart during the early dippings in the wax and closed for the final ones.

A New Zealand dentist, who had seen one of the gloves, succeeded in making a similar one without using a tourniquet; his wrists were larger than those of most people. He also made wax casts of his feet.

Tillyard returned to Boston in May 1928. Far from being disillusioned, after four more séances with Margery he reaffirmed his initial belief. His "Evidence of Survival of a Human Personality," appeared in the August 18, 1928, issue of *Nature*, one of the most respected scientific publications in Britain, prefaced by a quotation from Crandon.

> We are sitting in front of one of Nature's shows as a respectful audience. We are not to blame for the phenomena. We don't manufacture them. Here they are for any honest man to behold.

On the evening of June first of that year, Tillyard said, he arrived at the house of Dr. Mark Richardson, an old friend of the Crandons, who lived eight miles from Lime Street, with J. W. Evans, another entomologist. A box of Kerr dental wax was in his pocket. Each of the eight pieces of the dark red wax had been numbered and marked earlier; small bits had been broken from a corner of each.

Margery sat behind a table on which two dishes had been placed: one contained hot water, the other cold. During the séance, with the aid of a cloth, Walter submerged the pieces of Kerr wax under the hot water, withdrew them, and dropped them in the cold water to cool. While doing so, he caused seven clear thumbprints to appear—one, a reverse or mirror image of a normal print! These prints, Crandon assured Tillyard, were Walter's. His mother still had the razor Walter had used on the morning of the tragic railway accident many years before. When Tillyard compared a photograph of the thumbprint on Walter's razor with the impressions made that evening, they matched. As a good scientist, Tillyard also had thumbprints made of everyone in the séance room that night. None even vaguely resembled the Walter prints. Then Tillyard pressed his own thumb into the dental wax, softened by hot water, as it had been when Walter handled it.

He had some difficulty; the wax stuck to his thumb "until the water was quite cool." This could have given him a clue to the mystery, but he overlooked it.

Summing up his case in *Nature*, Tillyard said Walter's personality was quite unlike Margery's. Walter had a rough, masculine voice; he spoke with a Canadian accent, swore, and whistled. He could see what happened in the dark, find and describe articles that were unknown to any living person, transmit his impressions to the medium, and make prints of his thumb in a dark room far faster than Tillyard could in the light. "Walter Stinson," Tillyard declared, "has fully proven *in a scientific manner* his claim that his personality has survived physical death."

Sir Richard Gregory, the editor of *Nature*, ended his editorial comment on this contribution with these words: "We believe that Dr. Tillyard will have to bring much more convincing evidence of the actual existence of Walter's spiritual personality than presented by him in his article before it can pass the critical bar of science."

In the pages of the ASPR *Journal* and during his lecture tours, J. Malcolm Bird told of this marvelous new phase of Margery's mediumship—fingerprinting of the dead. Though he made fewer trips to Boston, he continued to endorse her mediumship until a rift developed. Thomas Tietze in his biography *Margery*, published by Harper & Row in 1973, says that an allegedly true account of how this came about is in the files of the society. Bird, who had been drinking heavily, arrived at the Crandon house with a woman, whose presence the surgeon and his wife would not tolerate. Bird, infuriated, retaliated with a few barbed comments charging Crandon and Margery with bizarre sexual interests.

Soon after this encounter the man who had given the medium the name she was known by and had done more than anyone else to publicize her, lost his position as chief research
officer of the pro-Crandon ASPR.

Why? Tietze quotes from the confidential report Bird made
to the trustees in May 1930. Bird confessed that Margery had
asked him to produce spurious phenomena—if her powers
failed—in the summer of 1924. He admitted he had seen her use
her feet and her elbow to cheat. He discovered one of her friends
had employed his foot to fake a manifestation on July 26, 1925.
He was aware that the medium's arm or leg played the part of a
"teleplasmic terminal" at a later séance.

As this report had not been printed, few people were aware
of its existence. After it had been submitted, Dr. Crandon and his
friends withdrew their support of Bird, and he gradually faded
from the psychic scene.

Crandon was instrumental in the appointment of Frederick
Bligh Bond as the new editor of the *Journal of the American Society for Psychical Research* in 1930. Bligh had edited the British
journal *Psychic Science* until 1926.

Meanwhile the production of spirit fingerprints on wax became an ever more important part of Margery's séances.
E. E. Dudley was engaged by the medium's husband to sort and
classify the hundred or so impressions. As early as 1925 Dudley
had written articles praising Margery as a medium. As time
passed, he was more and more often in the house on Lime Street.
He repaired séance-room equipment and aided Dr. Crandon in
preparing the official reports of the sittings.

Skeptics had charged that Margery used a metal die to put
the mysterious thumbprints on hot wax. To disprove this slander,
Dudley read books on fingerprinting, talked with police experts,
and began collecting the prints of every person who had attended a Margery séance.

Eventually he got around to a man who had been a frequent
guest at the start of the mediumship—Margery's dentist. When, as
he always did with the others, Dudley compared Dr. Frederick
Caldwell's prints with Walter's, he made a sensational discovery.
They were identical!

Dudley had been working on the material for the second volume of "The Margery Mediumship" for the American Society for

Psychical Research. On March 11, 1932, he wrote William H. Button, a New York corporation lawyer who was then president of the society, saying he had "additional evidence" which would necessitate the rewriting of the section covering psychic fingerprints.

Seven days later, Dudley sent another letter to Button. The first letter may not have excited Button's curiosity, but the second had the impact of a depth charge. Dudley stated bluntly that "three-dimensional prints" could be duplicated and that the thumbprints of Walter were those of "a living person."

Button went to Boston and, during a séance with Margery, asked Walter if the charge was true. When Walter denied it, Button wrote Dudley that the new report he had prepared would not be printed. The story broke in the October 1932 Bulletin XVIII of the Boston Society for Psychic Research—"Finger Print Demonstrations." It was not, however, until March twenty-first of the following year that the public learned about the most damaging accusation of Margery's career.

Under the headline "FIND 'GHOST' PRINTS ON LIVING HANDS," an article in *The New York Times* said that the fingerprints attributed to Walter and those of a man who wished to be known as "Dr. Kerwin" had been declared to be identical by New York and Boston police experts. When a reporter reached the house on Lime Street by telephone to get the medium's side of the story, Dr. Crandon spoke for her: "No comment."

The American Society for Psychical Research rushed the third and last volume of "The Margery Mediumship" into print later that year. Dudley's section on psychic fingerprints had been deleted from the second volume, *Proceedings* XX–XXI, issued several months earlier. All 228 pages of *Proceedings* XXII were devoted to an attempt to prove that the prints of the Boston dentist and Walter were not one and the same.

Charges and countercharges heightened the dissension between the Boston and New York societies. Then on May 12, 1935, *The New York Times* reported: "The American Society for Psychical Research of this city has come out in support of its rival, the Boston Society for Psychic Research." The change of opinion, the story continued, was expressed in the current ASPR *Journal*. The New York organization had accepted as final the

findings of Professor Harold Cummins, a Tulane University der-
matologist, which he had published in the *Proceedings* of the
British Society for Psychical Research. The Walter thumbprints
were those of a living Boston dentist; E. E. Dudley "stands vin-
dicated." The New York group acknowledged "the unfortunate
error" that led the authors of the American *Proceedings* to charge
Dudley with "responsibility for certain substitutions, confu-
sions, or falsifications of evidence."

All this was news to Button; as soon as he read this article, he stormed into the ASPR headquarters and made some
news himself. The next day *The Times* reported that Frederick
Bond Bligh, the editor of the *Journal,* had been fired. The views
he had expressed in print, Button said, were not those of the society.

Time and truth were on the side of Dudley and Bond. All except the most rabid Crandon supporters eventually admitted that
Dudley was right and that Margery had stamped with a die the
dentist's prints on hot wax. The dentist had shown the medium
how to make the impressions, Dudley said, and the block of wax
he had given her carried the imprints of his thumbs.

In 1939, Dr. Crandon slipped and fell down the stairs that
led to the séance room; he died several weeks later on December
27. By then the medium, whose sensuous appeal once excited
the men who sat with her in the dark, was drinking excessively.
The voice of Walter was still heard when she became entranced,
but his words, like her own, were often slurred and hard to understand.

In his article, "The Witch of Beacon Hill," published in the
January 1959 issue of *Horizon,* Francis Russell recalled the
séance he had attended in 1940. The "overdressed, dumpy little
woman" had "a faint elusive coarseness about her that one
sensed as soon as she spoke." That evening she tried unsuccessfully to produce a thumbprint of Dr. Crandon.

On November 1, 1941, the ravages of alcoholism took their
toll. Margery, the most versatile psychic in history, died as she
slept in the house on Lime Street, where eighteen years before,
to please her husband, she became a medium.

THE $100,000 PREDICTION

As a professional magician, I have studied the reactions of audiences for many years. Though I have made a live elephant disappear, caught bullets fired by marksmen between my teeth, and produced automobiles seemingly from nowhere, I have found that modern audiences are more intrigued by mentalism—feats in which the mind plays the most important part—than any other phase of conjuring.

Since my earliest shows I have known this to be true, but I didn't really appreciate how eager the public was to believe in the impossible until my visit to Cuba in May of 1957. For the first time I began to understand how unscrupulous psychics could take advantage of trusting believers.

Long before I flew to Havana, Cuban newspapers and magazines carried stories announcing that I would attempt to predict the winning number of the $100,000 national lottery. This feat was designed to publicize the first and only convention that the Society of American Magicians held beyond the continental limits of the United States.

As I passed through customs, newspaper men, photographers, and radio reporters and technicians surged around me. I answered their questions, and my voice was carried by radio throughout the island. I held up a sealed manila envelope for the cameramen. In it, I said, were two smaller envelopes; the innermost contained a folded piece of paper. On this was written the digits that would win the $100,000 prize.

Later at the Cubana Airlines office near the Nacional Hotel I gave the manila envelope to officials from the Chamber of Commerce. They signed it, front and back, then locked it in a safe with a glass front, and twisted the dial. The safe and the envelope inside it could be seen day and night through the plate-glass window facing the street. From that moment until after the lottery was drawn, armed guards in uniform paced back and forth on the pavement outside.

I had told the press I was not a psychic, that I was a magician, that magicians perform seemingly impossible tricks. Most papers quoted me correctly. One sensational weekly, however, said I was the seventh son of a seventh son and had performed miraculous feats since birth.

To advertise the magic show at the huge Radio Centro Theatre, I announced I would ride a bicycle from the airlines office down the Malecón to the Presidential Palace while blindfolded. The chief of police looked on, and more than a thousand people gathered in the street, as two of his officers stuffed wads of cotton over my eyes, wound my head with surgical bandage, then pulled a thick black bag over my head, and tied it at the neck with a rope.

Mounting a borrowed bicycle, I pedaled down the street, then turned right on the picturesque road by the sea. Two policemen on motorcycles preceded me; I was followed by an open truck, filled with cameramen and reporters. It was a hot afternoon. Even without the bag and the bandages I would have been uncomfortable under the blazing sun. With them I could scarcely breathe. Along the Malecón I heard voices shouting in Spanish: "Tell us the winning number." As I neared the palace, sirens on the advance motorcycles cleared the way through heavy traffic. Still, I was told later, I nearly collided with two cars at an intersection.

Almost half an hour after I started, I reached my destination. The policemen who had blindfolded me had gone ahead. They untied the rope, stripped off the bag, unwound the now wet bandages, and removed the wadded cotton from my eyes. A man in a military uniform stepped up and introduced himself as one of

President Batista's aides. I gave him a note inviting the president to attend the theatre performance.

I met Batista the day before the lottery drawing. He was living then at an army camp outside the city. Castro and his forces were far from the capital, but the president of Cuba was playing it safe. A military car picked me up at the hotel and drove me past the barriers. Soldiers escorted me up the steps of a large building and into a reception area.

I recognized the short, stocky "strong man of the Caribbean" from pictures I had seen. He was standing with a group of officers at the far end of the hall. As I walked toward him, I produced a sudden blast of fire in the air; for years this has been one of my trademarks, and I did it without thinking. Two men reached for their revolvers. For a moment they thought this was an assassination attempt. I smiled; the tension eased; and I was introduced as the American magician who had bicycled blindfolded through the streets and knew the number that would win the lottery.

I showed Batista and his friends several impromptu tricks. A rubber ball disappeared from my hand and joined one he gripped in his. I changed a silver coin into a Cuban banknote. He thought of a number after I had jotted something on a piece of paper and put it facedown on a table. The number he had in mind was thirty-eight. I turned the paper over. That was the number I had written. The magic had been well received, but this evoked gasps. Batista drew me aside before I left. "Confidentially," he said, "what number will win tomorrow?" I winked and put a finger to my lips. He laughed and walked with me to the door.

Since my arrival in Havana, I had received so many telephone messages that I asked the hotel switchboard to put through only outgoing calls. A man had phoned offering me a large interest in an investment firm if I gave him advice on the stock market. The owner of a rum factory offered shares in his company if I would tell him how to increase his export trade. Time and again I explained that I was not a psychic, that I performed only for the entertainment of audiences.

Most of the stack of mail I received each morning came from people who had read about me in the newspapers. A man was sure I could cure his blind eye. A boy asked for money to visit Hollywood. A woman wanted me to find her missing daughter.

The strangest letter came from a city on the far side of the island. The writer said he had seen my picture. By looking at my eyes, he could tell I had great power. He had studied witchcraft for years and hoped I would share my secrets with him. He could not get away from his job in a clothing store; he hoped I would visit him astrally—project my spirit body. He suggested a date and a time. If he expected me that night, he must have been very disappointed.

A beautiful young woman stopped me in the lobby one afternoon. She said she must talk with me privately. I listened as she explained that the man she loved had left her for another woman. She wanted him back and would pay me if I would use my psychical influence and make him return. I admitted I was unable to help her.

Had I claimed to be a psychic, in a single week I could have made a small fortune. So many people were beset with vexing problems. Unfortunately they believed mystics could solve them.

Oh, yes, my bodyguards. The day after I arrived, a man in a dark blue suit showed me his credentials and informed me that the organization he represented was the equivalent of the FBI. There was a possibility, he said, that foreign gamblers might attempt to kidnap me and force me to tell them the winning lottery number. The Cuban government would see to it that I had protection.

I said I would prefer not to be protected. Despite my objection, two men followed me at a discreet distance whenever I left the hotel. One was in the corridor as I locked my door each night. Another tagged after me as I crossed the lobby each morning.

The day of the drawing a member of the Chamber of Commerce picked me up in a car with two soldiers in the front seat. A machine gun rested on the seat beside the driver.

We drove down the hill from the Nacional and across to the airline office. Thousands of people had gathered in the street. The winning lottery number had been announced on the radio a few minutes earlier. The soldiers opened a passageway through the crowd. Inside the office, as men, women, and children looked through the large glass window, the president of the Chamber of Commerce turned the dial of the safe, swung open the glass door, and removed the manila envelope. Those who had signed it verified their signatures. As movie cameras recorded the scene, the brown manila envelope was opened. The white envelope inside it was withdrawn and opened. At this point the chief of police whispered to a friend, "If the magician tries trickery, I personally will expose him." I didn't hear this myself; one of the other officials told me about it later.

The third envelope was opened and the folded sheet of paper withdrawn. The president of the Chamber of Commerce smiled and displayed it. Written across it in large black numerals was 20050—the winning number. The officials around me applauded; the crowd in the street outside cheered. The police chief came over to me, patted me on the back, and said, "I will name my next son Christopher."

The lottery prediction was planned carefully but occasionally magicians—and psychics—will make lucky hits. For example, in an interview severals days before the drawing, when pressed by a writer from *Bohemia,* a popular magazine, to reveal just the last two digits of the lottery number, I narrowed down the field greatly by predicting they would be between 41 and 52. And they were!

Another strange incident occurred during a tour of British theatres with my illusion show in 1961. In most cities the theatre's press agents arranged for leading coal dealers to challenge me. They would write a name and an address on a piece of paper, fold it, and seal this in an opaque unmarked envelope, then give it to me when I arrived with cameramen and reporters. If I delivered it to the proper person, five old-age pensioners would get a free supply of coal. I did not open the envelopes, but I successfully delivered them in Glasgow, Bristol, and other cities on my route. In Liverpool, Mrs. Bessie Braddock, a member of Parliament, was the challenger. She went with me in a cab as street by street I instructed the driver to go ahead, to turn right, or to turn left. As we approached the Liverpool railway station, I asked the driver to stop there. I started to get out, then changed my mind. We drove on to the stadium. At the box office I concentrated and spelled out the name of the boxing promoter. Mrs. Braddock nodded and said that was correct. The man at the ticket window said the promoter had stepped out; he would be back in a few minutes. When he returned, Mrs. Braddock asked him where he had been. He said he had walked over to the railway station to buy a newspaper.

Although I know exactly how I delivered the unmarked letter to the right address, I still don't know why I asked the cab to stop at the railway station. But I don't think I have any superhuman powers.

Any magician who performs mental magic has had similar experiences. Is there something to what parapsychologists call spontaneous telepathy? I don't know. I do know that entertainers do not rely on this for their programs.

It distresses me that so many spectators are so eager to assert that simulated telepathy is the real thing. Some performers make ridiculous claims, and onlookers who accept extrasensory perception as a fact of life believe them unquestioningly.

A sleight-of-hand artist doesn't actually convert an ace of hearts into a three of spades; only the most gullible watcher believes so. I don't really cut an assistant in three pieces; I create this illusion. I have lectured before university audiences on parapsychology and demonstrated feats of precognition, thought transference, and clairvoyance, prefacing this exhibition with a disclaimer. After almost every performance of this sort, some of the audience afterward will say to me, "Mr. Christopher, you say you don't have extrasensory perception, but you do!"

When the Mike Douglas television show originated in Cleveland, the producer called me and asked if I would do him a favor. A film star, Diana Dors, had been booked as co-host; she expressed a strong interest in the occult. Would I play the part of a psychic, then explain how I had gathered the "psychic" information about her.

So that regular viewers wouldn't recognize me (I had been a co-host and appeared on the program frequently), he suggested that I disguise my appearance.

Changing my hair style, wearing dark makeup and a pair of sunglasses I had borrowed from actor Pat O'Brien, I sat across a table from Miss Dors, and gave her a reading. She shuffled a deck of cards, cut them three times, and passed them to me. I turned

Prior to the séance with Margery, the Boston medium, Houdini wore an elastic bandage around his right leg. It left his skin so tender he could feel the tiny movements she made to reach the bell box under his chair.

Partially freed when her "spirit" asked the sitter on her right to fetch an article for the séance, Margery quickly tipped the screen onto her toe, and put the megaphone on her head, while Houdini held her left hand.

Her hand still in Houdini's, she toppled the screen, put the guilty foot beside his, and then, seemingly immobilized, caused the megaphone to fly by jerking her head. He called it the *"slickest"* ruse he ever saw.

Houdini also told in his booklet on Margery how she levitated tables in the dark. Her "spirit" guide asked sitters to move back from the table so he might gather force—thus giving her room to lift it with her head.

Remarkable Case of Compound Spiritistic Paranoia

By Dr. John H. Quackinbos

In Spiritistic Paranoia, Mr. Bird outfunks Funk and overslops Hyslop, and it takes some Mollycoddle to do that. To make matters worse, Mr. Bird calls to his aid Hereward Carrington, a chronic sufferer from ectogenic hallucinations who is much given to talking through his hat. But there is hope for Bird because his position as a writer on scientific subjects will compel him to discontinue his psychical sprees. Outside of that he is quite normal. Carrington, however, will probably keep his imagination keyed up to the highest pitch, and will continue to sell his spiritistic "hot air" to the newspapers, as long as the newspapers will purchase it. Carrington, you know, is the "expert" who undertook to barnstorm this country with a European Shysteress called "The Despair of Science," and all of her tricks were promptly exposed by others before Hereward had time to rake off much dough. He is also the "expert" who wrote a hair-raising story about a lady who could press photographic negative plates against her forehead and get apparitions upon them after development. An investigation by others, however, revealed the fact that the lady was the dupe of a much exposed professional spirit photographer. A list of Carrington's vagaries would block traffic.

In the present Bird-Carrington case, we find that spirits without vocal organs talk, spirits without lips whistle, spirits without flesh or muscle bang things around, and a pigeon passes through a solid wall. There can be no doubt about the genuineness of all this because everything is done in total darkness, and nothing facilitates "scientific observation" so much as turning out the light. O Gosh! O Bosh! O Hell!

A satirical handbill found among Houdini's papers after his death in 1926. It may have been written either by the magician or by his secretary, Oscar Teale.

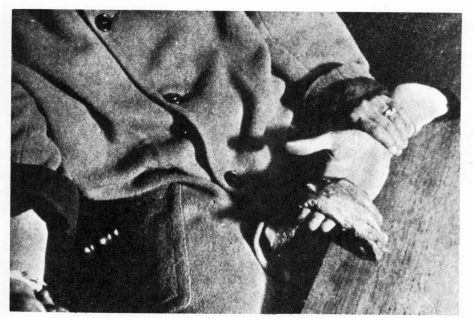

Close-up of "psychic hand" that extruded from Margery's body during séances. Sitters said it was about fifteen inches long and that it felt cold and clammy.

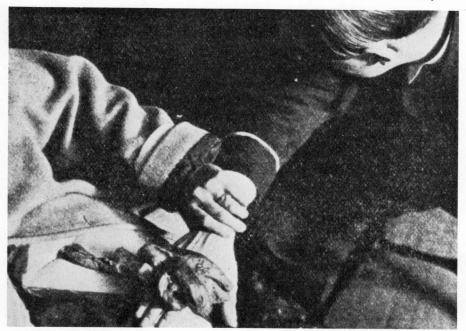

"Teleplasmic hand," apparently issuing from Margery's navel, is observed by Eric J. Dingwall, investigator from the British Society for Psychical Research.

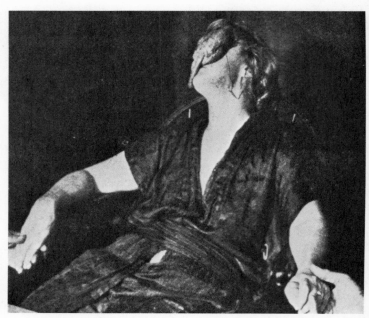

This mass of alleged ectoplasm, thrust into Margery's nose and attached by a fine cord to her left ear, was said by Walter, her dead brother and spirit guide, to be his speaking mechanism.

More of the mysterious ectoplasm produced by Margery in séances at her house on Lime Street in Boston. The séances in the dark were interrupted to take these photographs. Once the lights went out again, the strange material disappeared.

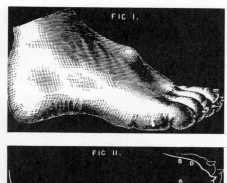

FIC I.

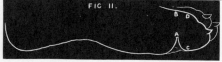

FIC II.

B D

A

C

FIC III.

The first "spirit" gloves produced in the dark by Margery were crude; later ones were considerably more realistic.

Such productions previously had been a European specialty. A British psychic even made a cast of a "spirit" foot.

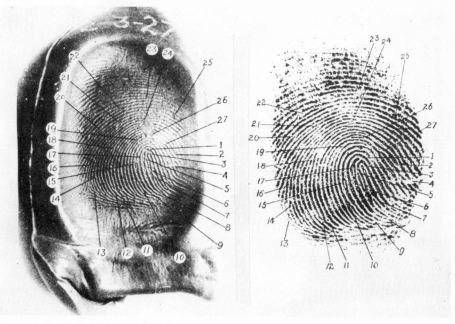

Damning evidence: The thumbprints in wax, supposedly made by Margery's dead brother, Walter, proved identical to ink prints of a living man—her dentist!

Uri Geller professes to bend metal with his mind. *Der Spiegel*, the German news magazine, investigated his claims, then told how some of his tricks were done.

Uri Geller scores a trillion to one by locating hidden objects, affects weight, influences laboratory equipment and demonstrates telepathy & telekinesis in scientifically controlled experiments at Stanford Research Institute.

Uri Geller's New Age *Inergy* is being witnessed by millions of TV viewers and live audiences. Join Uri now and experience the expanding frontiers of man and science.

AN ISIS CENTER PRESENTATION

Wednesday, 8 p.m., Nov. 7
LISNER AUDITORIUM
21st & H Sts., N.W.

RESERVED TICKETS: $6, 5, $4 Available at: Discount Book & Record Stores; YES Bookstore, WHFS Ticket Center. MAIL ORDERS TO: ISIS CENTER, P.O. 348, Silver Spring, Md. 20907 (Make checks payable to ISIS Center.) Sponsored by G.W.U.

An advertisement for a Geller performance. He is at his best, amazing those scientists who are predisposed to believe in paranormal phenomena.

Geller and his American sponsor, Dr. Andrija Puharich. Puharich says in his book, *Uri*, that Geller's "power" comes from a planet outside the solar system.

them up one at a time, and with each card, I told her something she had done in the past. An accident she had suffered as a girl, an experience that changed her life, her favorite foods, and so on. She was absolutely amazed. I also told her, her real name. This was the only thing she denied. She explained backstage after the show that she didn't want people to know it.

How did I know so much about her? I simply asked the Douglas staff to gather the data. They did a remarkable job. (Unscrupulous psychics have employed private detectives to assemble facts about wealthy clients who would pay exorbitant sums for the privilege of listening to information about themselves.)

I read the Dors data sheet an hour before the show. I have a good memory. No matter which card turned up, I tied it in with something I had learned about her. A jack cued me to mention an old friend of hers named Jack. A three inspired me to say there were three outstanding things she remembered from schooldays.

Sometimes it is not even necessary to do research or use a magician's technique to perform a startling "psychic" feat. While I was lunching at the Nacional restaurant, an American asked if he might talk with me about the show I had given at the Radio Centro Theatre. He said he didn't believe I could read thoughts. I said I agreed with him; I said I created the illusion that I did.

"If you're so good," he continued, becoming belligerent, "tell me my name." I said I wasn't about to give a performance at that moment. "I'll give you a thousand dollars if you can tell me my name," he went on.

I put down my fork and said, "I wouldn't take your money, Mr. ———." When I called him by his name, he almost fell off his chair.

Many of the feats I feature were developed after years of practice and are based on little-known psychological principles. This was not one of them.

Late the night before I had been watching Dai Vernon, one of the sleight-of-hand experts at the magic convention, perform with playing cards in the hotel bar. Two men were talking in distractingly loud voices several tables away. A third man approached the pair and was introduced by one man to the other. I heard his name and saw him as he shook hands with the man with the loudest voice. This name stayed in my mind, as odd bits of information sometimes do. The stranger who challenged me at lunch the next day was the third man of the night before.

It could have been the easiest thousand I ever earned!

SEARCH FOR A SOUL

Late in December 1972 more than a quarter of a million dollars—the entire estate of James Kidd, a missing miner who had been declared legally dead ten years earlier—was awarded by the Superior Court of Maricopa County, Arizona, to the American Society for Psychical Research in New York. This money, as specified in the Kidd will, is being used to search for scientific proof that the soul leaves the body at death. If possible, photographs are to be made of a soul in flight.

Efforts have been made in the past to weigh and photograph souls, but the current research is centered on the study of alleged out-of-body experiences of living psychics and reports from physicians and nurses of the visions described by patients on their deathbeds.

Since no one knows for sure that the soul has a physical dimension, or what form it might take after death, or even where the soul is lodged in the body, experiments to prove its existence are difficult to design.

Many mystics have claimed to see the soul-from-body separation. As long ago as 1865 Andrew Jackson Davis gave a particularly vivid description of the process in his book *Death and the After Life*. "The Poughkeepsie Seer," a pioneer American trance medium, said that a golden halo arose from the head of a dying man as his feet became cold. After the body chilled, this magnetic aura expanded and gradually took the shape of the man's physical body. The golden form, extending upward, was fastened to the brain "by a very fine life-thread." When the slender mooring line broke, the spiritual force, or soul, was set free.

The earliest-known scientific attempts to weigh souls were reported by Dr. Duncan MacDougall in his "Hypothesis Concerning Soul Substance, Together with Experimental Evidence of the Existence of Such Substance" in the May 1907 issue of the *Journal of the American Society for Psychical Research.* Six terminal patients agreed to participate in the tests. The first, a man with advanced tuberculosis, was moved to a light bed supported by "very delicately balanced platform beam scales" three hours and forty minutes prior to his death. His weight dropped an ounce each hour. This loss, the physician-experimenter said, was caused by the evaporation of moisture produced by respiration and perspiration. At the moment of death a sudden inexplicable loss of three quarters of a ounce of weight occurred.

The second subject, also a sufferer from consumption, breathed at a slower pace; since this meant less moisture loss, his weight dropped just three quarters of an ounce each hour. MacDougall could not ascertain the exact time of death, but during the eighteen-minute span between the man's last gasp and the absolute certainty of his death "one ounce and a half and fifty grains" of weight mysteriously disappeared.

Another tubercular patient's weight dropped half an ounce at death, and an additional ounce shortly afterward. When the fourth volunteer, who was a woman, expired in a diabetic coma, MacDougall noted the scales were not functioning properly, and "there was a great deal of interference by people opposed to our work." A weight loss between three eighths and one half of an ounce was observed, but because of the circumstances, the investigator decided this experiment should be ignored.

A loss of three eighths of an ounce occurred at the time of the fifth patient's death; he, like the two first subjects, had been a victim of tuberculosis. The sixth volunteer, a man with an unnamed illness, died less than five minutes after he had been placed in the special bed while MacDougall was trying to balance the scales. There was a loss of an ounce and a half of weight, possibly "due to accidental shifting of the sliding weight on the beam," the physician admitted.

MacDougall also carried out fifteen experiments with dying dogs. They had been drugged to keep them motionless on the scales. No weight variance was observed at the moment of their deaths. He thought this might indicate that canines and perhaps other animals, unlike humans, had no "soul substance."

Hyppolite Baraduc, a French physician and avid psychical researcher, whose treatise on the human soul was published in Paris in 1913, sought to document the soul-separation process photographically. Focusing a camera for three hours on his dying son, he took pictures at fifteen-minute intervals. Some of these revealed a hazy blob of light above the body.

Hereward Carrington, prolific writer of more than a hundred books mostly on psychical research but some on such subjects as conjuring, nutrition, dreams, sideshow tricks, the Great Pyramid, and yoga, had been critical of the MacDougall and Baraduc experiments; he said attempts to duplicate them by other researchers had failed. In "Physical and Psycho-Physiological Researches in Mediumship," the paper Carrington read at the First International Psychical Congress in Copenhagen in 1921, he suggested another experiment that might be made with an animal on the assumption that it, like a human, might have an "astral body."

A cat, monkey, or dog was to be sealed in a small aluminum box with a transparent window. Suspended by chains inside a larger air-tight glass container, this box was to be in "an atmosphere of perfectly dust-free air or water vapor." When gas was piped into the smaller box, the animal would die, and according to Carrington's theory, its spiritual emanation would "occupy a position between the two boxes" and "cause ionization." After the removal of a portion of the air, by a pump fastened to the outer container, the air left behind would immediately expand, and there would be a sudden drop in temperature. The vapor would "condense upon the ions," causing the shape of the astral body to appear in outline form.

Though Carrington himself did not try this experiment, ten years later he began corresponding with a physicist and X-ray technician who did. In his book *The Invisible World*, published in 1946, Carrington said Dr. R. A. Watters had killed mice, frogs, chicks, and grasshoppers with electric shocks or ether but was unable to ascertain the exact moment of death. Only after installing a small guillotine in his hermetically sealed enclosure, could he make precise calculations. His first fifty photographs included fourteen with a nebulous mass in the misty test chamber. Watters asserted that this cloudy material did not appear until the animal died.

Later B. J. Hopper conducted a similar investigation at the International Institute for Psychical Research in London. No cloudy forms materialized. Then Watters continued his tests, employing increasingly ingenious and more reliable apparatus— and discovered to his chagrin that the cloudy masses, which resembled the outlines of the animals he had killed in the course of the earlier tests, no longer appeared. There had been flaws in his initial procedures. Afterdeath chemical reactions in the corpses had produced the fogged areas in the photographs which he had mistaken for the creatures' astral doubles.

Carrington wrote: "If all this has proved nothing else, it has at least proved the vast amount of painstaking investigation necessary in order to settle a problem in psychical research, and the utter futility of trying to solve such problems in the absence of proper laboratory equipment." Far from being disillusioned or discouraged, he went on to propose a larger experimental chamber that would hold a human body. If anyone would put up the money for extensive moment-of-death research, he offered to volunteer as a human guinea pig. No one invested in the project, nor when Carrington's death approached in 1959, was a soul experiment made.

Unknown to Carrington, several months before *The Invisible World* was published, James Kidd, the Arizona miner, wrote the will that was to open the way for a new era in experimentation in afterdeath phenomena. Unwitnessed, written on a scrap of white paper, with blue-ruled lines, probably torn from an old ledger, the scrawled words read:

> This is my first and only will and is dated the 2nd day in January, 1946. I have no heirs, have not been married in my life, and after all my funeral expenses have been paid and $100 to some preacher of the gospitel [sic] to say fare well at my grave, sell all my property

which is all in cash and stock with E. F. Hutton Co., Phoenix, some
in safety box, and have this balance money to go in a research [f]or
some scientific proof of a soul of the human body which leaves at
death. I think in time there can be a photograph of the soul leaving
the human at death.

Kidd, born in Ogdensburg, New York, on July 18, 1879, had
traveled as far west as California, but most of his later years were
spent in the mining towns of Arizona. He had worked for the
Miami Copper Company for twenty-eight years before he cashed
his last pay check in 1948 and moved from Miami to Phoenix. He
lived there as he had in the copper camps where he had been a
pumpman, eating at inexpensive restaurants and smoking cheap
cigars. He left the single room on North Ninth Avenue, for which
he paid four dollars a week, one day in November 1949 carrying
a borrowed miner's pick. The friend who lent him the tool never
saw it or him again.

Weeks went by. Finally, on December ninth Kidd's landlord
informed the police his tenant was missing. The few men who
knew Kidd more than casually noted he often prospected alone.
They thought he might be searching for one of the rich lodes said
to be near the sites of abandoned mines. Intensive efforts by the
Arizona state police and the FBI turned up no clues to the mysterious disappearance. Investigators did learn, however, that the
prospector, who lived so frugally, had acquired over the years a
sizeable income from mining stocks and kept accounts in several
banks.

Fourteen years and two months after the miner was last
seen, the scrap of paper on which he had written his will came to
light. Arizona Estate Tax Commissioner Geraldine C. Swift discovered it by chance in the vault of the First National Bank in
Phoenix, while thumbing through a sheaf of Kidd's stock-
purchase slips, which had been stored in a box along with other
documents, during her January 1964 audit of his property.

The Superior Court of Maricopa County accepted the will
for probate. News quickly spread that a sum—eventually to ex-
ceed a quarter of a million dollars—would be awarded to the person or organization best qualified to conduct Kidd's requested
search.

Even before the court convened to award the money for

research, the University of Life Church, Inc., filed a petition for the assignment. Richard T. Ireland, the president and pastor of this Phoenix congregation, had performed as a blindfolded psychic in nightclubs as well as in church.

In his book, *The Phoenix Oracle*, published in 1970, he recalled discovering his talent at the age of five. Recovering from eye surgery at the Columbus, Ohio, Children's Hospital, he lay blindfolded in bed, playing with a ball. When it fell to the floor, he crawled over the protective rail and retrieved the toy. A few years later, Ireland's psychic powers so startled his brothers that they gave him the name, "Crazy Dick."

Once, Ireland claimed, he projected himself astrally in space—somewhere between the earth and the moon.

During a trance session at the University of Life Church in 1969, he answered questions with the aid of his spirit guide, Dr. Ellington, and predicted events that were to occur in the year 1970. Among the misses are the following:

> He said Lyndon Johnson would serve another four years as President.
> He reiterated a previous prophesy—the death of Fidel Castro.
> He said the Pope's authority would be "threatened," and the pontiff might be forced to relinquish some of his powers.
> He predicted a king would replace Generalissimo Franco in Spain.
> He prophesied that Prince Charles of Great Britain might lose his life in an automobile accident.

Whether Ireland's spirit guide informed him that the University of Life Church would receive the Kidd estate is not indicated in the church's petition to the Arizona court, nor is this formal request mentioned in Ireland's book.

The worldwide publicity accorded the soul case produced more than four thousand letters, addressed to the court, some from as far away as India, Brazil, and Germany. Lieutenant Colonel Virat Ambudha, an officer in the Thai army, came from Bangkok, hoping the Kidd money would enable him to publish and promulgate his views on the afterlife in a text, *Increasing Brain Power*, which he intended to circulate on a global scale.

Nora Higgins journeyed to Phoenix from Branscomb, California, to present her claim. She said she had often met James Kidd in the spirit, if never in the flesh; he first appeared in her bedroom in 1964, and frequently chatted with her. Subsequently, Mrs. Higgins was the only petitioner who claimed to see the spirit of her hoped-for benefactor in the courtroom.

A South Bend, Indiana, medium offered photographic "proof" of his encounter with the missing miner. The Reverend Russell Dilts assured the judge that the shadowy figure on some of his prints was James Kidd. The Right Reverend Robert Raleigh, bishop of the Thousand Oaks, California, Antioch Church, had not seen or conversed with the specter of Kidd, but he testified he had been in Malabra, California, when a spacecraft landed there in 1949. The navigator told him that travelers from outer space had flown to the earth two millions years before.

Though Kidd said he had no heirs, two Canadians in their eighties, Herman Silas Kidd and John Herbert Kidd, claimed he was their long-lost brother. They and other members of the Ontario Kidd family tried without success to have the will disallowed.

A total of 134 claimants applied for the legacy. During the preliminary procedures some applications were denied; others were withdrawn. Still, because of the many petitioners, Judge Robert L. Myers thought the hearing would extend for six weeks.

On the morning of June 6, 1967, Dr. Gardner Murphy, president of the American Society for Psychical Research, took the stand as the first witness. Tall, lean, wrinkled, with sparse white hair and clear plastic-rimmed glasses, he spoke with authority. He had studied unexplained mental phenomena since he was sixteen. He had conducted telepathy experiments under a grant from the Richard Hodgson Fellowship at Harvard, after receiving a doctorate at Columbia. In more recent years he had been chairman of the psychology department of the City College of New York and director of research for the Menninger Foundation in Topeka, Kansas. A former president of the British Society for Psychical Research, he had headed the American organization since 1962.

Answering questions put to him by George Balataze, one of the two attorneys representing the American Society for Psychical Research, Murphy defined several terms which were to be heard frequently in the courtroom:

PSYCHICAL RESEARCH: The study of psychological processes for which we have no physical explanation as physics now exist.

TELEPATHY: The exchange of information from one person to another by means other than sensory.

SECOND SIGHT or CLAIRVOYANCE: In which a person might get an impression of a purely physical source not necessarily involving telepathy.

A MEDIUM: An intermediary between the living and the deceased without prejudice as to whether or not, in fact, the communications do come.

PARAPSYCHOLOGY: An aspect of psychical research which uses experimental methods.

The judge listened to Murphy with keen attention. Before he began the case, Myers had not the slightest interest in the occult. Once the hearings got under way, he was exposed to Jean Bright, a widow from Encino, California, who said a dead dentist caused the muscles of her head and limbs to twitch, and Professor Richard Carl Spurney of Mount San Antonio College, California, who enlivened his discourse on the difference between the brain and the mind by comparing the former to a can of spaghetti and using apples, grapefruit, and a television receiver to illustrate the functions of the latter. Meanwhile, the Reverend Franklin Loehr, chief investigation officer of the Religious Research Foundation of America at Princeton, New Jersey, testified that he had proven, at least to his own satisfaction, that General Charles de Gaulle, was a reincarnation of Napoleon Buonaparte.

Gardner Murphy, by contrast, bolstered his petition on behalf of the American Society for Psychical Research by naming some of the distinguished men who had been active or honorary members: former British Prime Minister Arthur J. Balfour; philosopher William James; educator John Dewey; psychoanalyst Sigmund Freud; physicist Sir Oliver Lodge; and parapsychologist J. B. Rhine. Chester F. Carlson, the inventor of xerography, was currently a trustee.

Murphy emphasized that his society had two well-equipped

scientific laboratories and rooms, which were used for other investigations, at its headquarters on West 73 Street in New York City. The director of research, Dr. Karlis Osis, had received his Ph.D. in Munich in 1950. He had worked with Rhine at Duke University in Durham, North Carolina, and with the Parapsychology Foundation in New York, before taking his present position. Osis studied deathbed phenomena as well as other relevant phases of psychical research.

Murphy said he himself had investigated a moment-of-death case. The son of a Mrs. Hale in Montreal promised to communicate with her should he be killed after he went overseas with the Canadian air force during World War II. He was reported missing in action, but his mother told his father that as long as their electric clock kept ticking, she knew their son was alive. A moment later, there was "a whirring noise," and the clock stopped. Murphy admitted he did not know why this had happened at the time the airman died, but he said he thought such incidents should be verified.

The ASPR lawyer turned Murphy's attention to the Kidd will and asked what the society could do to carry out its terms. Murphy replied that more in-depth studies would be made of deathbed visions and crisis apparitions.

He then proceeded to describe an example of the latter phenomena. A Mr. Hayworth sat on the edge of his bed late one night in Dallas before going to sleep. He knew his father was in California, but he saw him in the room, dressed in "heavy work clothes," with a ruler extending from one of his pockets. Hayworth reached out and shook hands with him; then the older man vanished.

A messenger delivered a telegram to Hayworth minutes later. It was from his mother saying his father had died. Hayworth learned several days afterward that the ruler and the work clothes had been on a chair by his father's deathbed.

At the lawyer's suggestion, Murphy talked about possible moment-of-death experiments. Among them, taking infrared photographs as the end neared; using sensitive measuring instruments to detect if there was a temperature drop in the room; employing a photoelectric beam to ascertain if something left the body and moved on its own. The basic problem, he said, was to determine "whether the soul has a material aspect or is purely psychological."

If a large sum of money were available for this research, the lawyer asked, could Murphy "prove" that a soul existed? "No," the president of the American Society for Psychical Research answered. "Proof is much too strong a word."

Some contenders for the Kidd legacy tried to avoid the word *soul*. Witnesses for the Barrow Neurological Institute at St. Joseph's Hospital in Phoenix and the Neurological Sciences Foundation, which raised funds for the institute, preferred to discuss their internationally acclaimed achievements relating to the nervous system. Soul was not a scientifically acceptable term to them. They had never studied the possible survival of the human personality in the past; it seemed obvious that the course of their research would not change in the future.

The Arizona Board of Regents applied for the legacy to endow a Northern Arizona University Chair of Philosophy. They had no intention of sponsoring soul-separation experiments, but were willing to endorse a program that included discussion of various concepts of what a soul might be.

From the start there had been a clash between those who were convinced parapsychology was a worthy subject for scientific scrutiny and those who were not. The Barrow Neurological Institute sought to learn more about life processes. The Psychical Research Foundation of Durham, North Carolina, had been established to study the possibility that the human personality survived and manifested in some way after death.

Founded in 1961, the latter organization, unlike the American Society for Psychical Research, the Parapsychology Foundation, and other similar groups that were vying for the legacy, did not probe the entire psychic spectrum. Project Director William G. Roll limited investigations to areas that seemed to have some relation to the survival issue—poltergeist phenomena, for example. He thought the disruptive invisible forces that wrought havoc in houses might be disembodied personalities, not rebellious youngsters or disgruntled employees as skeptics had suggested.

Dr. Joseph Gaither Pratt, president of the board of directors of the Psychical Research Foundation, had worked at J. B.

Rhine's Duke University Parapsychology Laboratory. Now a staff researcher with the parapsychology unit at the University of Virginia School of Medicine, Pratt believed that the Psychical Research Foundation, because of its specialized interests, could carry out the intent of the Kidd will effectively.

Dr. Ian Stevenson, another member of the Psychical Research Foundation board, also came to Phoenix to endorse its application. A year earlier Chester F. Carlson, the Xerox magnate who contributed heavily to projects of the American Society for Psychical Research, had endowed a research professorship in psychiatry at the University of Virginia. Stevenson, chairman of the department of neuropsychiatry at the University's medical school, occupied this post. He assured the court he would be spending most of his time investigating in the field of parapsychology himself, but would continue to be a board member of the Psychical Research Foundation in Durham.

The lengthy June-to-September soul case ended with no hint as to its outcome. On October 20, 1967, Judge Myers delivered his verdict. James Kidd had intended that "his estate be used for the purpose of research which may lead to some scientific proof of a soul of the individual human which leaves the body at death. . . . Such research," Myers said, "can best be done in the combined fields of medical science, psychiatry and psychology, and can best be performed and carried on by the Barrow Neurological Institute, Phoenix, Arizona."

John G. Fuller, who covered the events up to this point in *The Great Soul Trial*, published by Macmillan Company in 1969, noted that "several of the parapsychology groups" were planning to contest Judge Myers's decision. Fuller visited Douglas Johnson, a British medium then living in Manhattan, and was stunned by Johnson's performance. The medium sensed the spirit of an elderly woman in the room. He had the impression she was a grandmother; her first name began with an E. The writer said the name of one of his grandmothers was Emma. Johnson identified another spirit as this woman's middle-aged son, Robert.

Fuller was amazed; he had fond recollections of his Uncle Robert. Then the psychic mentioned the letter *K* and went on,

"Kinn, Kidd, or—" Fuller stopped him to say the name was Kidd. Johnson continued to give Fuller other bits and pieces of psychic information, but the writer neglected to ask the medium an important question: "Who will eventually receive the Kidd legacy?"

Two men and two organizations appealed Judge Myers's decision. The men—the Reverend Russell Dilts, who allegedly had captured the spirit of the missing miner on film, and Joseph W. Still, an El Monte, California, physician, who had been studying aging and dying processes—and the organizations—the American Society for Psychical Research and the Psychical Research Foundation—contended that the Barrow Neurological Institute had no intention of using the Kidd money for the purpose the miner had specified.

In February 1971 Fred Stuckmeyer, chief justice of the Arizona Supreme Court, reversed the finding of the lower court and ruled that the legacy should be awarded by the Superior Court of Maricopa County to one or several of the claimants who had contested the decision.

The two parapsychology groups joined forces. The American Society for Psychical Research outlined how the money would be spent if the court found in its favor; two thirds of the sum would be allotted to ASPR investigations, the remaining third would go to the Psychical Research Foundation.

This proved to be a sound strategy. On December 29, 1972, the Kidd estate—by then amounting to $270,000—was awarded to the American Society for Psychical Research. Since that date, the two organizations have been trying to track down that elusive intangible something that James Kidd referred to as soul.

A progress report in the Summer 1974 *ASPR Newsletter* told of the "fly-in" experiments Research Director Karlis Osis had supervised. People who thought they could project themselves astrally from their homes to Osis's office on West 73 Street in New York were invited to "fly in" and see the target objects on a table near his fireplace. They were instructed precisely when to come and where "to stand"—in front of the fireplace—for an unobstructed viewing.

More than a hundred volunteers participated. They filled in

after-visit questionnaires and explained as best they could how they had left their bodies and what they had observed on the table.

No scores were given in this report; Osis said the over-all results had not been significant. An unspecified number of these astral voyagers, however, were tested further under laboratory conditions.

The best "fly-ins," Osis continued, occurred when a volunteer was not consciously aware he had left his body. Those who prolonged the separation or were aware of a struggle to get free of their physical bonds sometimes drifted far away from their goal.

Two specially constructed testing machines were installed at ASPR headquarters for out-of-body vision experiments. The first, an "Optical Image Device," was housed in a two- by two- by three-foot structure. Unless a disembodied personality peered through a small window at the front, the target image could not be seen. When an experimenter activated a mechanism, a disk, divided in four equal parts like a pie, revolved. Each section of this circle bore a different color. One of five symbols, selected at random by the machine, appeared on a colored quadrant, also chosen by chance. The operator of the machine did not learn until later which symbols, colors, or quadrants were involved in a specific experiment until data from an automatic recording instrument was decoded.

The second machine featured a "Color Wheel," similar to those at roulette tables. When this fourteen-inch spinning circle was stopped by chance, a target symbol in color stood out against a black surface. Only by peeking through an opening at the top of the box could the image be perceived.

This device, like the first, was designed to preclude the passage of telepathic clues from the experimenter to the volunteer. According to Osis, one volunteer, Alex Tanous, learned to evaluate his out-of-body vision scores before they were announced. After much effort, Tanous visualized his consciousness as a hazy luminous cloud. When the light focused in a single, dime-sized spot, Tanous was sure he was on target.

The preliminary out-of-body vision tests indicated that the

best scorers were somehow able to glance through the windows of the testing machines while their physical bodies were in another room.

Another experiment, which Osis calls a "Diving Pool," centered on an object suspended by a string in "an enclosed, electrically isolated space." Volunteers, in a soundproof chamber forty feet distant, attempted to move the pendulum by projecting their inner selves into the enclosure. Jim Merewether, the physicist who monitored the sessions, reported minimal action during early tests on the polygraph chart used to record pendulum movements. Then Pat Price, a retired California police official, caused the electronic instrument to fluctuate wildly during his first visit. In subsequent trials only an eighth of this variance was noted, but Osis said it appeared "a real breakthrough" might be made in this area.

As part of the ASPR research program, Osis and Erlendur Haraldsson traveled to India in the winter of 1972 to collect accounts of deathbed visions. They met two avatars, or living incarnate gods who, unlike many others, impressed them greatly. They talked to men who were positive they had been with one of these avatars in one particular place and to other men, on the opposite side of the country, who swore they had seen at that precise time the avatar's astral double. After twenty years as a researcher, Osis admitted, he had to revise his views on alleged Indian marvels. He said the testimony he had heard in India when thoroughly studied and documented might be the strongest evidence in favor of the soul-separation-at-death concept that James Kidd, the missing miner, wished to have proved.

Attempts were made to photograph or tape the arrival of out-of-body visitors in front of the fireplace in Osis's office. Though he tried to keep a watchful eye on the area while volunteers were striving to project themselves there, Osis never saw anything to indicate the presence of an astral guest.

One of his aides, Boneita Perskari, reported seeing a fireball and a misty blue haze on one occasion; a medium who was in the office with her also attested to these phenomena. Another time, as preparations were being made to photograph and videotape the scene previous to an expected "fly-in," Osis observed his assistant suddenly pick up a camera and take several pictures. Minutes later, the woman who had been scheduled to "fly-in" telephoned to complain that a flashbulb had been fired under her astral nose.

Did the woman's psychic image appear on the film? Osis says the camera was stolen before the film could be removed and developed.

Osis, who is not usually overly optimistic, concluded his 1974 report in the *ASPR Newsletter* with high hopes that, after further investigations, evidence of the existence of the human personality outside the body would be found.

The authentic photograph of a soul in flight that James Kidd, whose money is paying for most of the current out-of-body experiments, thought might eventually be taken has yet to be made. His legacy, however, is being spent as he wished it to be.

So far we have not learned anything about souls, but we have learned the strange avenues men take when they search for them.

Scientists who are convinced that human beings have extrasensory powers rarely take the proper precautions to rule out the possibility of trickery. Indeed, unless they are experts in the subtle techniques used by magicians and mentalists, or have someone who is to assist them during their experiments, it is almost impossible for them to detect ingenious deceptions. As a result, the important issues that intrigued Sir William Crookes and other distinguished investigators of psychic phenomena are still unresolved.

BIBLIOGRAPHY

ABBOTT, DAVID P., *Behind the Scenes with the Mediums,* Chicago, The Open Court Publishing Company, 1907.

ANNEMANN, THEODORE, *Annemann's Practical Mental Effects,* New York, Max Holden's Magic Shops, 1944.

BALDWIN, SAMRI S., *The Secrets of Mahatma Land Explained,* Brooklyn, author's publication, 1895.

BARNUM, P. T., *Humbugs of the World,* London, John Camden Hotten, 1866.

BIRD, J. MALCOLM, *"Margery" the Medium,* Boston, Small, Maynard & Company, 1925.

BISHOP, GEORGE, *Faith Healing: God or Fraud,* Los Angeles, Sherbourne Press, 1967.

BRITTEN, EMMA HARDINGE, *Nineteenth-Century Miracles,* Manchester, England, William Britten, 1883.

BROWN, SLATER, *The Heyday of Spiritualism,* New York, Hawthorn Books, 1970.

BROWNING, NORMA LEE, *The Psychic World of Peter Hurkos,* Garden City, N.Y., Doubleday & Company, 1970.

BRUNTON, PAUL, *A Search in Secret India,* New York, E. P. Dutton & Company, 1935.

CAPRON, ELIAS W., and BARRON, HENRY D., *Explanation and History of the Mysterious Communication with Spirits,* Auburn, N.Y., Capron and Barron, 1850.

CARRINGTON, HEREWARD, *The Physical Phenomena of Spiritualism,* Boston, Small, Maynard & Company, 1908.

——, *The Coming Science,* Boston, Small, Maynard & Company, 1908.

——, *Modern Psychical Phenomena,* New York, Dodd, Mead & Company, 1919.

——, *The Story of Psychic Science,* London, Rider & Company, 1930.

——, *The Psychic World,* New York, G. P. Putnam's Sons, 1937.

——, *The Invisible World,* New York, Beechhurst Press, Bernard Ackerman, Inc., 1946.

——, *Psychic Science and Survival,* New York, Beechhurst Press, Bernard Ackerman, Inc., 1947.

——, *Psychic Oddities,* London, Rider & Company, 1952.

CHRISTOPHER, MILBOURNE, *Panorama of Magic,* New York, Dover Publications, 1962.

——, *Houdini: The Untold Story,* New York, Thomas Y. Crowell Company, 1969.

——, *ESP, Seers & Psychics,* New York, Thomas Y. Crowell Company, 1970.

——, *The Illustrated History of Magic,* New York, Thomas Y. Crowell Company, 1973.

CRAWFORD, WILLIAM JACKSON, *The Psychic Structures at the Goligher Circle,* London, John M. Watkins, 1921.

CROOKES, WILLIAM, *Researches in the Phenomena of Spiritualism,* London, J. Burns, 1874.

COLLINS, PETE, *No People like Show People,* London, Fredrick Muller, Ltd., 1957.

DAVENPORT, REUBEN BRIGGS, *The Death-Blow to Spiritualism; being The True Story of the Fox Sisters, as Revealed by Authority of Margaret Fox Kane and Catherine Fox Jencken,* New York, G. W. Dillingham, 1888.

DEXTER, WILL, *Sealed Vision,* London, George Armstrong, 1956

DINGWALL, ERIC JOHN, and PRICE, HARRY, eds., *Revelations of a Spirit Medium,* London, Kegan Paul, 1925.

DOYLE, ARTHUR CONAN, *The Case for Spirit Photography,* New York, George H. Doran Company, 1923.

DUNNINGER, JOSEPH, *Inside the Medium's Cabinet,* New York, David Kemp and Company, 1935.

EISENBUD, JULE, *The World of Ted Serios: "Thoughtographic" Studies of an Extraordinary Mind,* New York, William Morrow and Comapny, 1967.

EVANS, HENRY RIDGELY, *Hours with the Ghosts,* Chicago, Laird & Lee, 1897.

FAST, FRANCIS R., *The Houdini Messages: The Facts Concerning the Messages Received Through the Mediumship of Arthur Ford,* New York, author's publication, 1929.

FORD, ARTHUR, in collaboration with MARGUERITTE HARMON BRO, *Nothing So Strange,* New York, Harper & Brothers, 1958.

———, *Unknown but Known,* New York, Harper & Row, 1968.

———, as told to Jerome Ellison, *The Life Beyond Death,* G. P. Putnam Sons, 1971.

FORNELL, EARL WESLEY, *The Unhappy Medium: Spiritualism and the Life of Margaret Fox,* Austin, University of Texas Press, 1964.

FLOURNOY, THEODORE, *Spiritism and Psychology,* translated, abridged, and with an introduction by Hereward Carrington, New York and London, Harper & Brothers, 1911.

———, *From India to the Planet Mars,* with an introduction by C. T. K. Charis, New Hyde Park, N.Y., University Books, 1963.

FODOR, NANDOR, *Encyclopaedia of Psychic Science,* New Hyde Park, N.Y., University Books, 1966.

FRANK, GEROLD, *The Boston Strangler,* New York, New American Library, 1966.

FRIKELL, SAMRI, *Spirit Mediums Exposed,* New York, New Metropolitan Fiction, 1930.

FULLER, JOHN G., *The Great Soul Trial,* New York, Macmillan Company, 1969.

———, *Arigo: Surgeon of the Rusty Knife,* New York, Thomas Y. Crowell Company, 1974.

GAULD, ALAN, *The Founders of Psychical Research,* New York, Schocken Books, 1968.

HALL, TREVOR, *The Spiritualists,* New York, Helix Press, Garrett Publications, 1963.

HARDINGE, EMMA, *Modern American Spiritualism*, New York, author's publication, 1870.

HEUZÉ, PAUL, Fakirs, Fumistes & Cie, Paris, Les Editions de France, 1926.

HOUDINI, HARRY, *Houdini Exposes the Tricks used by the Boston Medium "Margery"* . . . . *Also a Complete Exposure of Argamasilla*, New York, Adams Press Publishers, 1924.

———, *A Magician Among the Spirits*, New York, Harper & Brothers, 1924.

HULL, BURLING, *Fifty Sealed Message Reading Methods*, Woodside, Long Island, New York, author's publication, 1944.

HURKOS, PETER, *Psychic: The Story of Peter Hurkos*, Indianapolis, Bobbs-Merrill, 1961.

IRELAND, RICHARD T., *The Phoenix Oracle*, New York, Tower Publications, Inc., 1970.

JACKSON, JR., HERBERT G., *The Spirit Rappers*, Garden City, N.Y., Doubleday & Company, 1972.

KIRBY, R. S., *Kirby's Wonderful and Eccentric Museum: or Magazine*, Volume VI, London, R. S. Kirby, 1820.

LAWTON, GEORGE S., *The Drama of Life After Death*, New York, Henry Holt and Co., 1932.

MCGREGOR, PEDRO, with T. STRATTON SMITH, *The Moon and Two Mountains*, London, Souvenir Press, 1966.

MASKELYNE, JOHN NEVIL, *Modern Spiritualism*, London, Frederick Warne & Company, 1876.

MEDHURST, R. G., *Crookes and the Spirit World*, in association with K. M. Goldney and M. R. Barrington, New York, Taplinger Publishing Company, 1972.

MULHOLLAND, JOHN, *Beware Familiar Spirits*, New York, Charles Scribner's Sons, 1938.

MURCHISON, CARL, editor, *The Case For and Against Psychical Belief*, Worcester, Clark University, 1927.

OSTRANDER, SHEILA, and SCHROEDER, LYNN, *Psychic Discoveries Behind the Iron Curtain*, New York, Prentice-Hall, 1970.

PIKE, JAMES A., with DIANE KENNEDY, *The Other Side*, Garden City, N.Y., Doubleday and Company, 1968.

PINKERTON, ALLAN, *Spiritualists and the Detectives*, New York, G. W. Carleton & Co., 1877.

PODMORE, FRANK, *Modern Spiritualism*, 2 vols., London, Methuen & Co., 1902.

——, *The Naturalization of the Supernormal*, New York and London, G. P. Putnam's Sons, 1908.

——, *The Newer Spiritualism*, London and Leipzig, T. Fisher Unwin, 1910.

POYEN, CHARLES, *Letter to Col. Wm. L. Stone*, Boston, Weeks, Jordan and Company, 1837.

Preliminary Report of the Commission appointed by the University of Pennsylvania to investigate Modern Spiritualism in accordance with the request of the late Henry Seybert, Philadelphia, J. B. Lippincott Company, 1887.

PRICE, HARRY, *Leaves from a Psychist's Case-Book*, London, Putnam & Company, 1933.

——, *Confessions of a Ghost-Hunter*, London, Putnam & Company, 1936.

——, *Fifty Years of Psychical Research*, London, Longmans, Green, 1939.

PROSKAUER, JULIEN J., *Spook Crooks*, New York and Chicago, A. L. Burt Company, 1946.

PUHARICH, ANDRIJA, *The Sacred Mushroom: Key to the Door of Eternity*, Garden City, N.Y., Doubleday & Company, 1959.

——, *Beyond Telepathy*, Garden City, N. Y., Doubleday & Company, 1962.

——, *Uri: A Journal of the Mystery of Uri Geller*, Garden City, N. Y., Anchor Press, Doubleday & Company, 1974.

RAUDIVE, KONSTANTIN, *Breakthrough: An Amazing Experiment in Electronic Communication with the Dead*, New York, Taplinger Publishing Co., 1971.

RINN, JOSEPH F., *Sixty Years of Psychical Research*, New York, The Truth Seeker Company, 1950.

ROSS, ISHBEL, *Charmers & Cranks*, New York, Harper & Row, 1965.

SCHULMAN, ARNOLD, *Baba*, New York, Viking Press, 1971.

SEABROOK, WILLIAM, *Doctor Wood: Modern Wizard of the Laboratory*, New York, Harcourt, Brace and Company, 1941.

SHERMAN, HAROLD, *'Wonder' Healers of the Philippines*, Los Angeles, Devorss & Co., 1967.

SPRAGGETT, ALLEN, *The Unexplained,* foreword by Bishop James A. Pike, New York, New American Library, 1967.

———, *The Bishop Pike Story,* New York, New American Library, 1970.

———, with WILLIAM V. RAUSCHER, *Arthur Ford: The Man Who Talked with the Dead,* New York, New American Library, 1973.

STEARN, JESS, *The Door to the Future,* New York, Doubleday & Company, 1963.

TIETZE, THOMAS, *Margery,* New York, Harper & Row, 1973.

TONDRIAU, JULIEN, *Du Yoga au Fakirism,* Bruxelles, Presses Académiques Européennes, 1960.

TRUESDELL, JOHN W., *The Bottom Facts Concerning the Science of Spiritualism,* New York, G. W. Carleton & Co., 1883.

UNDERHILL, A. LEAH, *The Missing Link in Modern Spiritualism,* New York, Thomas R. Knox & Co., 1885.

YOGANANDA, PARAMAHANSA, *Autobiography of a Yogi,* Los Angeles, Self-Realization Foundation, 1973.

ZÖLLNER, JOHANN CARL FREDRICK, *Transcendental Physics,* translated by Charles Carleton Massey, Boston, Colby & Rich, 1881.

In addition to the volumes cited above and the periodicals cited in the text, unpublished manuscripts and documents in the Christopher Collection relating to the Fox sisters, the Davenport Brothers, Harry Kellar, Houdini, Anna Eva Fay, Margery, and others were used.

I am indebted to Clifford Davis, Dr. Eric J. Dingwall and Mostyn Gilbert of England, Ronald A. Hecker of Israel, Klingsor of Belgium, the late P. C. Sorcar of India, Bjørn Sørum and Finn Jon of Norway, and Charles Reynolds, Martin Gardner, James Randi, Milton Schwartz, Persi Diaconis, Allen Berlinski, and John Booth in the United States for aiding in various phases of the research.

INDEX

Welch, Paul, 119
White, Daisy, 132
Whittlesey, Frederick, 2
Winchell, Walter, 132
Windsor, H. H., 186
Wolbach, Simeon B., 216
Wood, Mrs. Katherine Thompson, 75
Wood, Prof. Robert W., 216, 217-219, 220
World Beyond, A (Montgomery), 143

World of Ted Serios, The (Eisenbud), 116, 117

Yogananda, Swami, 147-148, 154
Young, Jimmy, 39
Youtz, Richard P., 87-88

Zöllner, Johann K. F., 5
Zubin, Joseph, 89, 99

This book may be kept